Software for Parallel Computers

UNICOM Applied Information Technology

Each book in the series is based upon papers given at a seminar organized by UNICOM Seminars Ltd. The reports cover subjects at the forefront of information technology, and the contributors are all authorities in the subject on which they are invited to write, either as researchers or as practitioners.

Software for Parallel Computers

UNICOM
APPLIED INFORMATION TECHNOLOGY 9

Edited by **R. H. Perrott**

Professor of Software Engineering, The Queen's University of Belfast

CHAPMAN & HALL
London · New York · Tokyo · Melbourne · Madras

Published by Chapman & Hall, 2–6 Boundary Row, London SE1 8HN

Chapman & Hall, 2–6 Boundary Row, London SE1 8HN, UK
Van Nostrand Reinhold, 115 5th Avenue, New York NY10003, USA
Chapman & Hall Japan, Thomson Publishing Japan, Hirakawacho Nemoto Building, 7F,
1-7-11 Hirakawa-cho, Chiyoda-ku, Tokyo 102, Japan
Chapman & Hall Australia, Thomas Nelson Australia, 102 Dodds Street, South Melbourne,
Victoria 3205, Australia
Chapman & Hall India, R. Seshadri, 32 Second Main Road, CIT East, Madras 600 035,
India

First edition 1992

© 1992 UNICOM and contributors

Printed in Great Britain by T.J. Press, Padstow, Cornwall

ISBN 0 412 39960 1   0 442 31410 8 (USA)

A catalogue record for this book is available from the British Library

Library of Congress Cataloging-in-Publication Data available

CONTENTS

CONTRIBUTORS

P. Amestoy, M. Dayde and I. Duff
CERFACS
Toulouse
France

J. Barr
Omnisoft
Reading
UK

G. Bell
California
USA

C. Cheetham
Information Engineering Directorate
DTI
London
UK

M. Cole
Computing Science Dept
The University
Glasgow
UK

L. Delves
Dept Statistics and Computational
Mathematics
Liverpool University
UK

**J. Dongarra, D. Sorensen and
O. Brewer**
Dept Computer Science
University of Tennessee
USA

M. Furtney
Cray Research
Minneapolis
USA

M. Gittins
Artificial Intelligence
Herts
UK

**P. Kacsuk, I. Futo and
K. Wiederanders**
Densitron/Multilogic Computing
Budapest
Hungary

T. Lake
GLOSSA
Reading
UK

H. Liddell
Centre for Parallel Computing
Queen Mary College
University of London
UK

D. Moody
Intel Scientific Computers
Swindon
UK

D. Parkinson
AMT
Reading
UK

R. Perrott
Dept Computer Science
Queen's University of Belfast
Belfast
UK

P. van Santen and S. Robinson
Dept Computer Science
Brunel University
Uxbridge
UK

A. van der Steen
Academisch Computercentrum
Utrecht
The Netherlands

M. van Steen and H. Sips
TNO Institute of Applied
Computer Science
Delft
The Netherlands

C. Wadsworth
Rutherford Appleton Laboratory
SERC/DTI Transputer Initiative
Oxon
UK

M. Wolfe
Dept Computer Science and
Engineering
Oregon Graduate Institute of Science
and Technology
USA

S. Zenios
Wharton School
University of Pennsylvania
PA
USA

S. Zenith
Centre d'Automatique et
Informatique
Ecole National Superieur des Mines
d'Paris
France

H. Zima
Institut fur Statistik und Informatik
University of Vienne
Austria

PREFACE

The mid 1950s can be regarded as the period when computers became more widely available and recognized for their contribution and potential in many fields of science, engineering and commerce. The decades which followed saw vast improvements in their technology and their application. Today sequential machines are increasingly being regarded as a technology, both in the hardware and software sense, which is well understood but limited in application. They are not therefore offering the same intellectual challenge to hardware designers, software designers and applications programmers.

The limitations of these machines were first recognized by the scientific and engineering communities who demanded computational power which could only be satisfied by some form of parallel processor; these were mainly array and vector processors which enable economical and/or time constrained applications to be executed. However the software that was provided was limited in that usually existing applications were required to be used. This in turn compelled manufacturers to provide compilers which could take existing programs and determine as far as possible which parts of the program could be executed in parallel. The next major innovation in this field was machines which incorporated more than one processor. Such machines can usually be classified either as machines which share the same global memory or machines in which the memory is distributed among the processors. Experience is now being accumulated in the use of both types of machines and preliminary results suggest that shared memory machines are easier to program but more difficult to debug. As a result of rapid developments parallel processors are no longer the novelty they were in the 1970s or early 1980s; parallel processing rather than sequential processing is rapidly becoming the norm among the programming community. If the 1980s is regarded as the dawn of parallel processing how long will it be before this technology is fully understood and the application of parallel processing is easily performed?

In order to answer some of the major questions concerning parallel processors a series of seminars was organized by Unicom. The first seminar, 'Major Advances in Parallel Processing' (1986), concentrated on the advances in technology which have moved parallel processing into the general computing arena. This was followed by 'Evaluating Supercomputers' (1988) which dealt with how to measure the performance of complex high speed computers. The seminar reported in these proceedings was 'Software for Parallel Computers' and considered how to exploit parallelism through software environments, tools, algorithms and application libraries. It represents a natural progression in the examination of major issues affecting the promotion and spread of parallel processing among the programming community.

The seminar was fortunate because of the relevance of its technical area to enlist the support and collaboration of the Department for Trade and Industry

(DTI). Parallelogram, BCS Parallel Processing Specialist Group and the Belgian Institute of Automatic Control. The range of speakers was carefully chosen to represent designers, users, researchers and manufacturers of parallel computers so that all aspects of parallel processing would be considered. The purpose of the seminar was therefore to present the leading developments in software systems for parallel processors.

The proceedings cover research results and *de facto* development tools which provide insight into major problem areas such as portability, performance and reorganization of data and algorithms. In short all aspects of software for parallel processors ranging from conceptual frameworks to implementation vehicles.

More specifically, the contents of this volume are structured around six sections which can be briefly summarized as follows:

Part One. Strategies and future trends, considers both technical issues as well as research priorities which are required and will be required in the future to promote the wide acceptance and advancement of parallel machines.

Part Two. Algorithms, considers how to design algorithms for a parallel architecture with particular examples for the DAP and the Connection Machine.

Part Three. Autoparallelization, considers the topic of how to take a sequential program and determine which parts can be executed in parallel; this is considered for both vector machines and also multiprocessor configurations.

Part Four. Tools, considers what tools are required for vector and parallel processing and examines several existing tools which have proved of benefit in helping users understand the concepts of parallel processing.

Part Five. Libraries, considers the provision of libraries for parallel machines, a necessary facility for many users who wish to move a parallel machine.

Part Six. Languages, considers languages other than scientific languages for parallel machines.

The speakers for these topics included representatives of computer manufacturers as well as researchers from universities and government laboratories providing a useful insight into what is currently available and what may be available in the future.

The success of parallel processors has now percolated through mini supercomputers down to engineering, scientific and even personal workstations. Parallel processing has been shown to enhance the performance of many application systems in such diverse fields as image processing, animation, fluid dynamics, linear and nonlinear optimizations, simulation and expert systems applications. To exploit the parallel systems which are available it is essential that suitable software support systems must be fully understood and utilized.

These proceedings detail how to create new applications for this new generation of computer.

R.H. Perrott
Dept of Computer Science
Queen's University
Belfast

Part One

Strategies and Future Trends

1 Strategy and workplans for parallel and novel architectures

C. Cheetham

Department of Trade and Industry

1.1 STRATEGY

1.1.1 Devices

R&D in the materials of highly parallel systems needs to be, and already is, an activity on the European and international scale. None of the basic material components, including now the transputer, is in UK sole or main ownership. There is a need under the existing IEATP collaborative programme for work on the overall design of complex systems, on correctness of design and on processes for easy creation of chips, to support experimentation by systems architects.

1.1.2 Parallel systems technology

The UK has considerable strength in parallel systems, but future development of the main parallel systems technologies needs to be on a European scale. There is specific need for a European collaborative R&D programme in architecture definition, which can bring together the many different threads of development into a systematic whole. This should not constrain innovation, but should make it easier to understand which types of systems are best for which applications. There should also be large-scale European collaborative R&D programmes to develop technology.

1.1.3 Exploitation of UK technology and skills

The priorities for the UK should be to improve productivity by technology exploitation, and to strongly develop existing skills. The priority for the UK collaborative programmes is to improve productivity by exploitation of the technologies: projects should use best available technology; programmes should not explicitly support UK suppliers' competitive edge. The current Information Engineering Advanced Technology programme should continue with the same workplan, and be supplemented with additional, more use-oriented programmes.

- The emphasis of the IEATP programme continues to be heavily on understanding how best to exploit parallel systems:

    ○ the underlying theory and understanding of emerging systems requirements and of related viable solutions;

    ○ the investigation and evaluation of novel architecture concepts, initially by simulation and analysis;

    ○ the methodologies, techniques and aids required to implement and exploit new ideas in a cost effective, timely and competitive manner.

- Exploitation of parallel and novel architectures: this is a proposed new programme to fund R&D into the applicability of parallel architectures across a wide variety of areas of use. The need is well covered by the applications received at the first IEATP call: these were ineligible for funding, because the IEATP is specifically addressing the generic methods of exploitation (see above). This proposed programme might well be implemented as an Exploitation Club, based round existing Centres of Expertise.

- Algorithm libraries for vision and parallel systems; this is a proposed new programme to make algorithms being developed available in standard libraries. A major contribution will be to productivity: in the absence of this programme the work will be done less well and more expensively through individual research programmes. It will also maintain the UK as one of only two global competitors in this field.

1.1.4   Science base

While focusing on exploitation, it is also an important objective to have a very broad programme of academic research in PNA. Consolidation of existing work into standards and unifying architecture should go hand in hand with innovative research into a wide range of novel architectures. Selected work should also be carried on to the next stage to prepare for potential European scale activities. The PNA strategy identifies particularly intelligent file stores as such an area. There are two major priorities for the science base, both of which result from the Alvey focus on collaborative R&D within the industry.

- It is important to have a very broad programme of academic research in PNA: historically, there has been no previous spending in the years up to 1988/9.

- It is important that medical, science and other engineering disciplines can exploit the technology, and that future research reflects their needs. UK should put more resources into existing centres of expertise in the UK. This should meet the needs expressed in connection with a previously proposed IRC in parallel computing.

1.1.5   Neural networks

A potential priority area is neural networks. Reasons to consider this as high priority include the following:

- applicability to specific problems, such as pattern recognition;

- potentially valuable characteristics such as fault tolerance;

- ability to exploit novel materials: opto-electronics enables completely optical, massively parallel neural computers; future bio-molecular electronics enables massively parallel application specific systems;

- current interest worldwide: DARPA has just announced a major R&D programme; Japan has much longer term and broader R&D programme; Italy has raised the need for a major European programme in the margins of the European Research Council.

The previous point show considerable disparity in timescale, resource level, objective and means, which suggest the primary aim at this stage should be a wider research base.

The strategy for neural networks has not been thoroughly examined yet. Meanwhile, it is proposed to continue selective R&D under the collaborative programme. It is also proposed to extend an existing programme (RIPR): this is an existing NERI (National Electronic Research Initiative), in exploitation of neural techniques for pattern recognition.

1.2   IEATP STRATEGY AND WORKPLAN

1.2.1   Outcome of 1988 call

On the whole, the workplan topic area was well covered by the 12 projects selected. Indeed, a large number of proposals was received for exploitation of parallelism. Many of these, however, were judged at outline stage to fully justify funding, but to be too application oriented to lie inside the published strategy: a new programme is being proposed for these. This left a wealth of good applications in that core area which blends development of theoretical understanding of architectures and computational models with exploitation in practicable applications through R&D in exploitation tools, languages, etc.

Two large, ambitious projects address the fundamental issues of building fault-tolerant systems and totally verified systems. One project involves SIMD architecture in 'A programming workbench for a massively-parallel computer.' Another is concerned with SIMD-MIMD Interconnect. The remainder involves MIMD architectures, mostly employing transputers. A number promote the exploitation of parallelism via languages and language extensions: parallel object-oriented languages for transputer-based systems; Fortran for scalably parallel computers. Declarative modes are supported in three projects: functional languages and program transformation; functional programming for arrays of transputers; and functional and logic programming on a graph reduction machine in graph reduction applications support. Knowledge manipulation is supported in parallel processing with intelligent knowledge bases. Two projects have been selected specifically against the workplan area for research into novel architectures: logical neural networks and GANNET, also a neural networks project.

1.2.2 Strategy Changes in 1989

There are no fundamental changes of strategy for 1989, but applicants are reminded that the IEATP workplans are specifically intended to be complementary to European initiatives. Large-scale initiatives, such as building major novel processor systems, are handled by European programmes such as ESPRIT. Other areas, such as declarative languages and intelligent file stores, are under-supported by ESPRIT, and are nurtured by the UK programme.

The emphasis therefore continues to be heavily on understanding how best to exploit parallel systems:

- the underlying theory and understanding of emerging systems requirements and of related viable solutions;

- the investigation and evaluation of novel architecture concepts, initially by simulation and analysis;

- the methodologies, techniques and aids required to implement and then exploit new ideas in a cost effective, timely and competitive manner.

Note, however, that projects which are specifically about exploiting a particular architecture, for a particular application, are explicitly excluded from this workplan.

1.2.3 Workplan for 1989

Projects are invited which address one or more of the following topics.

(a) Exploitation of parallelism

One of the industry's difficulties is that the focus of interest has been on the design and building of powerful parallel systems but insufficient work has been done on effective and economic exploitation of the latent power becoming available. This is a key theme.

Two main approaches to exploiting parallelism have emerged. The top-down approach starts with formalisms and/or languages and tries to design parallel systems to execute them efficiently. The bottom-up approach begins with known extensible hardware, and seeks to learn how to program it effectively. Both approaches include the possibility of defining new hardware functionality. Both approaches are valuable, and projects will be funded under either.

There are a number of research threads which could contribute to the solution of the problems of cost-effective utilization of parallel power. These include:

- computational models (e.g. graph re-write)

- computational strategies (e.g. processor farms);

- generic problem solving algorithms

- languages and language extensions

- compilation techniques

- knowledge representation formalisms

(b)   Declarative modes

There continues to be an emphasis on the declarative styles. The concern is not so much with well structured problems which map fairly naturally on to imperatively driven parallel processing arrays. The problem to be addressed is the vast area of general information processing which may not be so clearly structured, but which is of considerable commercial importance. In these areas, the declarative styles can assist both the expression of the method of solution and also the exploitation of the available parallelism.

Both functional and logic programming styles have advantages in given circumstances and, ideally, some controlled and efficient blend of functionality is desirable. Certainly the IEATP should encourage further research and experimentation on declarative language extensions, aimed at broadening the efficient application of such modes.

(c)   Intelligent file stores

High on the list of priorities is the requirement for fast, intelligent, knowledge representation and manipulation. The user communities are declaring an established need for 100 times the performance of existing large knowledge base systems, and this will grow in time. Certainly exploiting the latent power of parallel processing systems will be inhibited if access to data and knowledge are not greatly improved. Worldwide achievements in this field leave much to be desired, but the UK has a core of research and expertise on which to build.

(d) Simulation and analysis

Simulation and analysis are themes common to the development of most parallel architectures. They are also research themes in their own right. Designers have a fairly natural tendency to build experimental pre-prototypes to test out their concepts, but this is a time and resource consuming approach. Furthermore, as flaws in the design are encountered, progressive modification is expensive, technically difficult and sometimes not even possible. Pre-prototyping, analysis and refinement by simulation and support tools is more cost effective in terms of both people and money. It should be a requirement on projects wherever it is feasible and a centre of expertise could be fostered to support this activity. Projects which are built round, and strengthen, DTI Technology Transfer programmes are particularly sought. The same facilities can map user applications onto parallel systems and therefore can serve not only the R&D community, but also the user communities in terms of awareness, pull-through and training.

(e) Novel architectural concepts

It would be unrealistic, and even dangerous, for a collaborative programme on systems architecture to attempt to establish, in advance, all the technological opportunities which it would wish to explore. Some reasonable provision should be made for new ideas which are likely to emerge, and to justify examination, during the course of the planned programme. An immediate candidate which is recommended for investigation is neural computing. This concept has been around for some years, but recently has started to gain credence. The programme should seek to understand and assess its potential.

1.2.4 Relationship to other workplans

Projects are sought under the following headings, which relate also to other workplans (respectively to integrated I/O systems, and to devices).

(a) Sensor data processing

This topic has strong links into related programmes, such as vision, and is seen to be of increasing importance into the plannable future. At first sight it might be assumed to be purely a matter of hardware experts inventing the requisite range of devices and related analogue/digital conversion equipment, whilst the application programmers cope with processing the digitized data. However, the architectural implications of this mode of information capture, interpretation and processing cannot be ignored, particularly at the more demanding end of the applications spectrum.

(b)   Systems architecture on silicon

An area which has importance in the context of future UK production of cost/performance competitive systems is the error-free transformation of formal specification of system requirements into silicon components. The UK has created a forum in which systems architects and silicon architects come together to dicuss problems and solutions. This link between VLSI, CAD systems has generated commendable progress, but we need to build on these foundations. Furthermore we need other cross-boundary links, for example with the formal methods experts, and we need to foster selected research threads in such areas as transformation tools and techniques. These links will often be cross disciplinary with the other areas of the IEATP, namely systems engineering and devices.

2 An insider's views on the technology and evolution of parallel computing

*G. Bell**

Ardent Computer Corporation, USA

This paper is written from the viewpoint of one who is interested in building commercially viable parallel computers. In all, I have been involved in the building of ten machines that were multiproc essors, microprocessors or multicomputers of one kind or another. Some of these projects eventually led to commercial products, others where undertaken solely for research purposes.

In this paper I consider six separate but related issues:

1. The nature of the Fifth Generation.

2. The three styles of computers that I foresee emerging. This proposed taxonomy is based on what the machines will be used for, and also takes into account their commercial viability.

3. A review of the characteristcs of supercomputers taking into account what I learned from my own involvement in building a supercomputer.

4. The current plethora of parallel computers and the reasons why, in my view, many of these machines are doomed.

5. The needs of the parallel computing community, in terms of programming paradigms and standards.

6. Some other priorities for both high performance and parallel computers.

---

*   This paper has been compiled and written from a presentation given by G. Bell.

2.1   THE NATURE OF THE FIFTH GENERATION

The Fifth Generation is already with us. But it has turned out to be very different from the concept originally proposed by the Japanese - despite the fact that a number of us successfully sold that concept to the US Government and the funding agencies. What the reality, as it is now emerging, does have in common with the idea as originally formulated is that it is characterized by the beginning of the mastery of what we may, looking back in ten or twenty years' time, see as simple parallelism.

In retrospect, I think that the 1990s will be identified with the conquest of parallelism, just as previous decades are already associated with the introduction of other fundamental advances.

The assault on parallelism began in about 1985, and its progress has so far been due to advances in basic technologies. One of these advances is the arrival of C-MOS technology which is providing us with chips containing a million transistors. Another is the switch to the RISC architecture - although I would stress that I see the RISC architecture as something that just happens to have developed at this time rather than as something which is crucial to the Fifth Generation. What I do see as critical is the adoption, for scientific computing, of vector processing or the Cray-style architecture and, in the case of smaller machines, the handling of more than one instruction per clock tick.

This latter point brings us back to the POP - the plain old processor. If you look at POPs, or more specifically at their technology from which, I repeat, all progress derives, it becomes clear that a prophecy I made some years ago has turned out to have been correct. At the time I produced a graph plotting the log performance (vertical axis) of contemporary machines. This showed that the performance of mainframes was advancing at the rate of 14% per year − i.e. it was doubling every five years − and that minis were progressing at a similar rate but delayed in time. At that point the microprocessor was already coming up at a fairly fast clip, and today it has overtaken the mini − indeed Intel even argues that the 486 has crossed the mainframe's line.

Basically, the lines represent increases in clock speeds and it can be seen that the C-MOS line was already gaining 40% per year, or doubling its speed in two years. What I was predicting was that a new, parallel line would develop representing the RISC shift. As it turns out, this has not happened. Instead the performance of RISC machines showed a shift which has surprised a number of us. If this continues, then the RISC processor will overtake the mainframe in virtually every respect (except for vector processing) no matter what measures of performance are used - MIPS, scalar megaflops or Cobol terms. The fact that this technological progress has improved performance at the rate of 70% per year is making it very hard to build parallel machines.

Those of us who were involved in the early parallel computer projects forecasted these developments several years ago. Essentially we said that it did not much matter how far into the future one looked, at whatever point you chose to actually build a parallel machine you would be likely to get a performance that was at least one or two orders of magnitude better than that of traditional machines, and you would get it at a much lower price.

It is this latter point, the fact that parallel machines cost virtually nothing compared with the mainframe and the mini, which is driving us forward.

The technological developments which I have outlined are producing two styles of computer. The multiprocessor architecture is being used for transaction-processing, time-sharing machines and even data processing (e.g. Erte, Encore and Sequent) and has now been adopted by DEC for the silicon graphics and workstation area. This trend will continue with the multiprocessor becoming the mainline tool for one-dimensional programming and software engineering, for 2-D graphics and for 2 1/2-D work which is basically electrical CAD.

The area of 3-D, will, I believe, be dominated by the Cray architecture, with minisupers using the multiple vector processing structure.

In both cases, the technology will only advance if it is driven by a percieved market for its products and, conversely, there must be a market which is attracted by the technology. Unfortunately, the parallel processing community has sometimes failed to remember that their work will only continue to be attractive if it can be put to practical use.

In fact I see two principal roles for parallel machines - leaving aside ordinary transaction-processing work, which generally does not demand parallelism except, for example, in the relational database area.

The first role is, obviously, scientific computing. The second, which grows out of the first, is the realization of what Ken Olson has referred to as the 'Third Paradigm of Science' - the replacement of experimentation by simulation. When I visited CERN recently, I asked the physicists why they were building a 27-mile-long accelerator when they could simply simulate all the processes that interested them by filling the same amount of space with Transputers, or something similar. Unfortunately, they did not buy that idea.

More seriously, however, it is a fact that simulation is becoming a very valuable tool for scientists. Sometimes, indeed, it is the only one available. No one has the time to watch what happens when two galaxies collide, but it is perfectly possible to investigate what happens when 200 000 stars hit another 200 000 stars by simulating the event. For others, such as the weapons designers at Los Alamos and elsewhere who can never do enough experimentation, simulation is a good alternative.

In the engineering domain, it is now obvious that the workstation has already revolutionized the task of designing digital systems - i.e. computers. There is now no hardware, no computer or chip, which cannot be built by a very small team in one to two years; or at least I would argue that if it is going to take longer than that it should not be built at all since it will probably be too complicated.

With the advent of the 3-D machines, the supercomputers, I think the same kind of revolution is going to overtake mechanical engineering. We should be looking forward to the day when we will be able to design and simulate the operations of 3-D mechanisms such as a car, or even structures as large as an aircraft or spacecraft, in full confidence that when they are built they will work properly first time. I see the automotive industry of tomorrow working like the computer industry of today. The people who design computers no longer build prototypes, we design the machines in the expectation that they will function correctly as soon as the power is switched on.

The same principle will apply to chemistry, whether the people concerned are building molecular models or designing process plant, and to computational fluid dynamics as applied to the design of petro-chemical plant or to the modelling and management of large subterranean reservoirs. It is these sort of applications, plus the use of image processing for making movies and visualizing processes, which, it seems to me, will benefit from the arrival of the Fifth Generation.

2.2   A CLASSIFICATION BASED ON USE

My second theme is the emergence of three distinct styles of parallel computer, each of which will be characterized by the use to which it is put.

The first category covers machines which are designed with one application in mind and which capitalize on hardware and/or software which is very specific to that application. An excellent example of what computer scientists can do, using specialized (but not very specialized) silicon, in order to help people who have a specific problem is a device developed by a group at CalTech. The problem, in this case, was the cataloguing and sequencing of the human genome, a task which has been undertaken as an international project on a worldwide basis. The work may well have been speeded up by several orders of magnitude, not by the sort of supercomputer that will be familiar to readers, but by a texturing search chip that had been built by TRW for use in specialized text-searching applications and which had, I believe, already been on the market for several years.

Another example is what I believe to be the fastest machine in the world today. This is a computer built by AT&T for speech research which operates on the order of a quarter to an eighth of a Teraflop (and those are 32-bit flops) performing a particular kind of pattern matching and signal processing which is required for speech. Again, I understand that people have built fairly spectacular specialized machines for QCD calculations and some classes of CFD applications.

It should be added that these kinds of systems would be even better, and easier to build, if the computer science community would become more involved with them. They do not pose major problems for the computer scientist, indeed they could be seen simply as advanced class projects, but many people's time could better be spent helping to design them rather than building yet another RISC chip or whatever.

This first style of parallel computer should, typically, improve the price/performance ratio for a particular application by a factor of up to 100.

The second category is one that currently engages the attention of much of the parallel processing community. It consists of what I call mono-program machines and can be broken down into two sub- categories. The first embraces the SIMD computers, such as the Connection Machine, which can be used for a number of different purposes but can only run one program at a time. In other words, they are used in the way we used computers many years ago - you book the machine, write your program and then run it when your turn comes round. The other subcate gory consists of what I call - I hope everyone calls - multicomputers. To build one you take a number of your favourite processors, add some memory, and connect all the hardware together. How you do it is not too important; we have now passed beyond the stage of topomania when people believed there was some magic in the way that you connected one computer to its neighbours and how many of those neighbours it communicated with. The essential point is that a multicomputer (unlike a member of the first subcategory such as the Connection Machine, which has only one program counter) has many program counters and that each processor communicates with its neighbours using what is, fundamentally, a message- passing paradigm. I include these in the category of mono-progam machines because I think the trick is to get the machine to allocate the work to the processors and, so far, no one has found a way of dividing their resources between a number of users. Perhaps the problem (or the challenge) is that no one has been taught to program them that way.

The third style of parallel computer is the one that I have personally been most interested in, this is what I consider to be the category of mainline, general-purpose machines, and it embraces three classes of computer.

First comes the traditional multiprocessor, which is evolving from systems whose processors are numbered in the tens or twenties to ones with hundreds of processors, all sharing a single memory. Thus, because all the processors operate on fundamentally the same data- set, these machines have one copy of an operating system, lots of programs counters, lots of processors and lots of communication bandwidth. I see these kind of systems as being in the mainstream of traditional computer development.

The second subcategory is basically a specialized variant of the first, in that it is created by taking the kind of multiprocessor described above and adding a turbo unit which understands vectors to each processor. The result is what we call a supercomputer. I will come back to supercomputers in the next section, for the main problem with them is simply that there are not enough people trained to drive them.

Finally, there is a third form of parallelism that falls within this category and which has been too little exploited, and that is the workstation cluster. Already some interesting problems have begun to be solved by people who have realized that virtually every group of scientists or engineers has access to what is potentially, in terms of the available megaflops, their own Cray. In supercomputing terms, a

Sun workstation is not so fast, it will do about a megaflop; but if you put fifty or a hundred of them together then you have the equivalent of the processing power of a Cray - that is, they have the potential to process data at the same rate as a supercomputer.

The problems of programming such a cluster are inherently no different from those you would face if you built a network of a hundred Transputers or lashed togther a hundred-node hypercube. The difference is that the workstation cluster is already available off the shelf and, if it it turns out that your program does not after all lend itself to parallelism (which is highly likely), you will still end up with a hundred happy people getting the job done on the individual workstations. Thus I would recommend anyone working in multicomputers to start out with a workstation cluster because even if the group fails to conquer paralllism, and I think many will fail, they will still be left with a very nice computing configuration.

2.3 WHAT IS A SUPERCOMPUTER?

I see the supercomputer becoming a mainline tool in the next decade, and I would like to persuade more people to become involved in supercomputing. So, what is a supercomputer?

The generally accepted definition is that a supercomputer is one of a kind; it is quite simply the machine that goes the fastest - in terms of numerical processing - and has the mostest- in terms of memory and every other kind of facility you might need. In other words, a supercomputer is the ultimate computing weapon that can be brought to bear on a problem. But over the last ten years matters have got more complicated as different sub-species of supercomputers emerged and new terms were coined to descibe them.

The first development came in the early 1980s when two groups, one in Texas the other in Massachusetts, started building machines based on the Cray formula - that is, computers with one or more processors which used vector processing techniques - but more modest in scale. The resulting designs looked like supercomputers and programmed like super computers, so they were quickly christened minisupercomputers.

Next, a bunch of us in California put our heads together. We already had a good scalar processor, and it seemed to us that if we added a vector processor to that, and then put several of them together, we, too, would have a supercomputer. But what should we call it? We thought of several possible names, solo supercomputer, for example, and personal supercomputer. But the one we settled on was graphics supercomputer because it had supercomputing power plus graphics capability.

Today, it is generally accepted that these qualifying adjectives in front of the noun supercomputer also imply a price range. Thus if a machine is called a minisupercomputer it is going to cost less than a million dollars, and if it is descibed as a graphics super computer it not only has to have graphics capabuility, it is also going to be in the $100 000 price bracket. In the next year or two we are going to see a third kind of supercomputer, the personal supcomputer, which will sell for less than $50 000. This is the machine that should be on the desk of every scientist and engineer and it is the one that I am personally most interested in.

So now the word supercomputer is used in two ways: in the original sense of meaning the biggest and fastest machine available to anyone anywhere, and to describe a variety of other machines that are supercomputer-like. I think that it is important that we restrict the use of the term in this second sense by declaring that a machine is not a supercomputer of any kind unless it provides the user or users with the same amount of computing power that they would get from shared use of a traditional supercomputer. In other words if it cannot give you what you would get from a time-shared Cray or NEC, for example, then it is not a supercomputer.

This constraint is not as restrictive as it might seem. A few years ago, when I was running the five National Science Foundation supercomputers for the Computing Directorate of the NSF, I analysed the amount of computing power that each scientist was getting. It turned out that the average user at the the largest centre was getting one hour a week. That did not seem like a lot to me. A large user was getting one processor-hour a day; that is, roughly .01% of the machine's total resources. Even the third class of user, the very large user, was only getting three hours a day. As a result I concluded that if you can provide a user with the equivalent of three hours a day you will basically satisfy even the most demanding supercomputer user. The cost of that time, if you manage your own system under a tight NSF budget, is about $2-300 per hour; if you have to buy the time from someone else it will typically cost you about $2000 an hour. All the machines I have described above can deliver the equivalent of this kind of computing power, which means that for the regular user their price tags are by no means unreasonable.

Since we started building what we choose to call a graphics supercomputer - that is, a multiple vector-processor machine with wholly transparent parallelism provided by automatic vecorization - I have been trying to define the basic design rules required. The first issues to look at were Amdahl's Law and the vector/scalar problem. One thing we learned was that the First Law of Supercomputers not quite the same as Amdahl's Law; in fact, like other inventions I have been involved with such as Unibus, the general register stuff and the PDP-11, it is a generalization of Amdahl's Law.

The crucial point when building a high performance machine is that you cannot afford to simply concentrate on, say, the scalar/vector issue because, to put it crudely, everything matters. Your starting point must therefore be the clock speed, which pretty much sets a lower bound to your costs; you need the fastest clock you can afford for the price range you are aiming for. If, for example, you choose a nanosecond clock then you are committing yourself to a development budget of around $100 million a year. At the other end of the scale, the choice of a 20-30 MHz clock implies a project that could be handled by a couple of guys working in a garage! Somewhere in the middle, around 100-200MHz,we are talking in terms of a $30-50 million development budget.

Once you have set the clock speed and thus decided how much money you are putting into the development, the first design priority is to maximize the scalar speed. By now I think everyone who has built a supercomputer would accept this rule, which was learnt the hard way by the builders of the first supercomputer, the Star 100. The Star's scalar speed was only one-third that of the 7600 and consequently, although it computed 100 megaflops on long vectors, it was never widely used because people could not achieve a sufficiently high degree of vectorization to make use of its potential.

In a sense, the Star's failure was the fault of those who could have benefited from using it but did not know how to. Indeed, this seems to me to illustrate a general problem with supercomputing, which is that because there have not been up until now, many such machines available, very few people have been trained to make proper use of them. Apathy is probably too weak a term to describe the attitude of the computer science conmmunity towards supercomputers. Indeed, I have often encountered active hostility, especially when I controlled a budget that covered both computer science and supercomputing.

I regret that I did not make more progress in bringing the two communities together because I now feel that supercomputing is the most interesting part of current computer science and that it is still basically being left out of the mainstream. In the USA at least, people are wondering why they are losing students from computer science courses; one answer is that if you go into a bookstore and look at the computer science section you will find a stack of books on object-oriented C, databases and the other traditional computer science subjects, but virtually nothing on applied parallel computing. Even what is available is not much help. One recent book on parallel computing, a very fat one, essentially missed out all the important parts. It contains no experimental data and all the interesting issues have made mathematically abstract so that they are no longer related to the practicalities of parallelism - in short it has no relevance in training people to exploit parallelism.

This problem bears directly upon the importance of scalar speed, if only because the scalar performance must be good to make up for the fact that many users will not understand how to use vectors.

Once you have got the scalar problem solved, the next step is to add a vector unit and at this stage the sky is the limit as far as money is concerned. In Japan, where supercomputers' performance is usually measured in terms of vector power, manufacturers go for that target and promote their products as the world's fastest computers without elaborating on the conditions under which they will achieve the advertized gigaflops. I was in Japan when NEC announced the SX-3 and people were speculating as to whether that machine's four processors would be faster that the eight-processor Cray or the Cray-3. In fact, if you wanted to answer that question, all you had to do was to look at the scalar times.

If clock speed is the first issue of supercomputer design and scalar speed the second, the third rule is that you make it all flat, everything matters. Input/output matters, divide matters, it matters that you have scatter/gather for all the different data structures that occur, whether you are simulating a Connection Machine, working with sparse matrices, or whatever. Cache idiosyncrasies matter, as does everything and anything else that may be critical for a specific application because, once the machine is in use, there will always be some application that depends crucially upon it having one particular capability.

The fourth rule, which is in fact a general rule applicable to building any kind of machine, is that you put accelerators in wherever you can. In theory, of course, what you do is to select those bench marks or applications where your competitors do not perform well and concentrate on getting those to run as fast as possible. Then, when your potential customers ask about performance, you suggest they try this or that problem which you know you have taken good care of. Years ago, when the Whetstone benchmark was a widely accepted standard, the Vax was designed around it. So, we put in polynomial instruction and made sure all the functions went faster. That strategy was very succesful until people began to recognize the benchmark and realized they could answer the problems just by looking up the answers for the Whetstone.

The fifth issue concerns the address space. You must ensure that you do not run out of address bits as you progress from one generation to the next. The sixth, and final, rule is that you have got to be prepared to build a follow -on design because there are so many things that can go wrong in a supercomputer that virtually anyone who builds one has to build another just to correct all of the problems they did not foresee the first time round.

In a nutshell, that is what I have learned so far about building supercomputers. I would have learned more and learned it earlier if I had realized the machines were going to be so complex.

2.4   A SURFEIT OF PARALLEL COMPUTERS?

The next issue I want to address is the future prospects for the plethora of parallel computers that are now in development or on the drawing board. I try to keep a tally of startups, but I still keep finding new ones I had not heard about. The atmosphere is very reminiscent of the early days of the minicomputer, when there were something like a hundred startups in the USA alone. Of that hundred just three have survived the course and emerged as consistently successful businesses. Four or five years ago that figure would have been seven of eight, but the casualities have continued to accumulate.

My current tally of people building high-performance and/or parallel computers of one kind and another is also around one hundred. In the pedigree supercomputer field there is Cray, IBM and several Japanese companies plus three startups- and already, since 1980, three other startups have fallen by the wayside. In the minisuper area there are arguably four startups and another four ventures that have passed the five-year post. Of these latter ventures, Convex is certainly doing the best as a result of its policy of providing more power than its competitors, increasing that power step by step, and ensuring that the power is sufficient to compete with Cray.

Array processors are a development that I would regard as no more than an adjunct to traditional minicomputers and mainframes relevant mainly to fast scientific computing. Personally, I feel this was a dead-end which mainline computing has already bypassed and I do not think we will see more machines built to that formula.

My own view is that mainline computing applications, both high-performance transaction processing and time-shared data processing, will become dominated by multiprocessors with lots of microprocessors. Today one can build multiprocessors in the 100-200 mips range relatively cheaply, certainly more cheaply than other forms of computer. Currently there are perhaps twenty developments underway in this area, including the Hypercube in the USA and the Transputer in Europe. All involve machines which I would classify in the mono-program category.

When we look at the performance of these multiprocessors we find something of a paradox, in that they only provide an order of magnitude increase in performance per unit price. If you invest in one then you can, in effect trade off what you would have spent in time on a general-purpose machine against programming time. Economically speaking, exchanging human time for computer time is a good deal, and if you have a lot of people with time to spare it is a wonderful area to work in because it means every design is a challenge.

There are now two SIMD machines on the market and a third to come. These are very intriguing as research projects, but to me they are only interesting if they achieve the threshold of supercomputer power. To argue for them on the basis of the price/performance ratio is to ignore the fact that if they cannot match supercomputer power when it comes to your specific application, it will not be worthwhile using them.

The other main thrust of future development which I foresee focuses on the workstation - certainly if that term is widened to include the graphics supercomputers and personal supercomputers. I foresee a day when the workstation will be almost as ubiquitous as the PC - indeed they may become interchangeable in that the PC, if it continues to evolve at the same rate, will itself become a personal supercomputer. In this area I believe that the crucial consideration is not the performance which you get for a given price, but the fact that the user depends on the machine and must configure a part of his or her life around it.

So far I have not seen a machine in this category that has achieved suprcomputer standards of performance in any application. But I am sufficiently interested in the possibility to contribute some money towards its realization - though not very much money I hasten to add. Each year I award a prize for the best contribution to speeding up parallel processing. The first award went to a four-processor Cray, the next was won by some algorithms developed for two major new programs at NCAR and the last prize was won by Sandia running a 1000 node N-cube and it ran three problems (non-Cray problems) at an astonishing flop rate. It took the group concerned an appreciable part of their laboratory to run the problems, but they did succeed in obtaining a much faster solution. Last year no one entered the contest, and that reflects the fact that there has not been appreciable progress in this area recently.

However, I am anxious to continue monitoring progress at the leading edge, especially developments that may lead to really successful applications. I hope that progress will resume following DARPA's award of a contract to Intel for the development of a 2000-node multicomputer. I understand this is envisaged as a 64 megablock node kind of machine which should offer over 128 megaflops in a multicomputer configuration. To me, this sounds promising because one could envisage putting such a machine together in a large garage - it is not a particularly difficult engineering problem. Moreover, the relevant programming problems have already been worked out on smaller hypercubes, Transputer networks and similar systems which are not a major problem to build.

So the result might be a machine capable of over 100 gigaflops, delivered at around the same time as NEC and Cray are promising machines with something like 20 gigaflops. For the first time we may be able to look forward to a machine which can potentially solve problems too big for a traditional supercomputer. This is also the promise of the Connection Machine 2 which will, under the right circumstances, deliver ten gigaflops, a peak rate which no current supercomputer can match. In the end, unless parallel machines can offer the chance to solve hitherto insoluble problems, users are likely to stick with the tried and tested technology.

2.5   THE NEED FOR PROGRAMMING STANDARDS

The major requirement that will have to be satisfied if parallel computing is to progress is for a cleaning up of the situation so far as traditional programming languages are concerned. That probably implies the community committing itself to a language that many will never have heard of, or, if they have, only to hate it - Fortran. The Fortran X football has been kicked around for a long time now, and there are several conflicting theories as to whether the inclusion of explicit vector and data-structure reference operations would help or hinder progress of the parallelism. The head of our own compiler group, Randy Allen, whose work provides the basis of many of the parallel vectorizing compilers, believes that the question is unimportant. His attitude is that if you write it, then if it can be parallelized he will figure out how, make the vectors and run it in parallel.

But it must be true that anything would help which made the issue of parallelism more explicit, so that people would think of it as a unit operation. To see that this is so, one has only to imagine what would have happened to programming languages if real numbers were not put in hardware.

Vectors are here to stay. However I think the supercomputer people are tackling the issue in the wrong way, as are those concerned with minisupers. I think the designers are going about it the right way and that what we are doing is going to become the mainstream in the future. However, I would certainly like some help on the training front. I would also like to see a few text books; indeed I would like to see the existing textbooks changed to fully reflect the need for explicit parallel control, whether in the context of multiprocessors doing micro-tasking or multi-tasking or that of other paradigms. This would be helpful if you are concerned with machines that use message-passing as a means of communication, it would be relevant to the role of the multiprocessor and for multi computers and it would certainly be useful in relation to workstation clusters.

So far as I am concerned all these concepts are as important for, and as basic to, the future of people taking computer science courses today. I would, therefore, like to see textbooks and courses which addressed these issues and I would also like to see computer science departments start to use supercomputers.

If, as I would strongly urge, more people start researching in the supercomputing field, then once they have tried their hand at some programming and seen how the machines are used, they should examine other paradigms which offer alternatives to Fortran 77. Dataflow languages, dataflow extensions to Fortran and C should offer alternative ways of dealing with the implicit control of parallelism more effectively. Certainly, this is an area in which we badly need standards, new texts and more training.

2.6   SOME OTHER ITEMS ON THE SUPERCOMPUTING AGENDA

Apart from new programming standards and perhaps new programming paradigms, what else should be on the parallel computing agenda? The first need is for researchers and developers to get involved with actual problems. The Hypercube, and much else that was valuable, came out of CalTech because people in the computer science department there were working with users. These kinds of links with other disciplines are crucial - in fact if the computer science community is not going to develop them it should say so clearly. Then other departments in the universities will know that it is going to be their responsibility to train scientists and engineers in computing. The tragedy is that engineers and scientists still believe that if people take computer science courses they will learn something about programming. Sadly, that is not the case - but it could concievably become true.

The other thing I would like to stress - and, having been involved in building a graphics supercomputer, I obviously have an interest to declare here - is the importance of visualization. To me, one of the great attractions of parallel computing is that it promises us the chance to take a whole variety of data structures, representing anything from molecules to worms, or even abstractions like matrices, and produce visualizations which show how solutions develop and, equally importantly, the opportunity to interact with those visualizations. Indeed, I wouuld argue that all the programs that are in use in science and engineering should be thrown out and rewritten so that they are interactive. In this connection, it is interesting to note an analogy with electrical CAD; virtually none of the electrical engineering programs that were designed for mainframes and minis turned out to be useful to those designing ICs and digital systems. My feeling is that, in the same way, the old mechanical engineering or chemical engineering programs are going to have to be jettisoned and replaced by new ones if we are going to take full advantage of the possibilities of designing plant and machinery interactively on the screen.

Another important issue is networks. I think that for the machines of the future the existing networks will be inadequate, and I would like to see something done about that. I will not even comment on wide area networks, I cannot bear to think of the shape they are currently in. As far as LANs are concerned, the Ethernet of years gone by is certainly inadequate, even for today's workstation clusters, let alone the computers of tomorrow. Two years ago we needed a hundred megabits through those nets, soon we will need a gigabit. If we can begin to get those speeds then we will begin to realize the potential of multicomputer structures. If, as I have suggested, the workstation cluster has an important part to play, then we will only be able to make use of it if we crack the LAN problem.

2.7   CONCLUSION

Finally, another few words about my award. The original idea left it up to contestants to select not only their horse, but also the track they wanted to run it on and the race they wanted to compete in. Recently some people in Illinois pointed out to me that this was not, perhaps, the best basis for a fair contest. They suggested that they would provide the course and lay down the conditions for the race and then let others bring along their horses and race them against each other. So this year we are adding another category to the award. This is based on Kuck's work at the University of Illinois. He is working with a number of manufacturers and users on a Perfect Benchmark, which will consist of about fifteen large programs covering a variety of problems ranging from scalars to sparse matrices. All of them are programs which are valuable to users, mainly in science and engineering, and which are characterized by various kernels. The idea is that each year prizes will be awarded for the best performance in a range of categories - the fastest set of solutions, the one with the greatest degree of parallelism, the best price performance ratio, etc. There will also be awards for more specialized applications, really finely tuned algorithms that address specific applications.

3 Strategies for programming parallel architectures

R H Perrott

Department of Computer Science, The Queen's University of Belfast

3.1 INTRODUCTION

The 1970 s can be regarded as the decade in which a limited form of parallel computer became widely available. This was pioneered by the release of the Cray-1 in 1976; the parallelism of this machine was based on the overlapping of operations on vector operands within pipelined functional units. The ease of programming, the performance and the reliability of the machine ensured its acceptance among the scientific and engineering communities.

The method of programming the Cray-1 (CRAY-1 Computer Systems, 1981) was based on the technique of vectorization where existing sequential programs were examined to determine which parts could be executed on the vector units. The data structure which could be most easily vectorized was the array and the program structure which best facilitated vectorization was the DO loop. Hence it was the DO loops of a program which were examined in detail in order to determine which parts of the program could be executed in parallel. It was not necessary for the programmer to get involved with this exercise but if he did then further improvements in performance were usually forthcoming. For example, in the situation where there are nested DO loops it is the innermost loop that is examined for vectorisation. Hence the programmer should ensure that this is where the major part of the computation takes place; this may require loops to be restructured.

As the years passed the compilers responsible for vectorization became more efficient and capable of dealing with a more extensive range of programming situations. In addition, hardware improvements helped in other cases, such as scatter/gather operations.

Thus detection of parallelism was the main method used for programming vector processors and represented the first experience of many programmers of any form of parallel programming. There was little attempt at the time to provide a language with explicit features to program this type of machine. Subsequently the ANSI Fortran Standards committee have addressed this problem with their draft Fortran 8X standard.

One result of this approach was that programmers were cushioned from the problems of having to program in parallel and this hid many of the difficulties of that task and raised the expectations as to what could be achieved automatically.

These machines could not be regarded as general purpose parallel processors as their architectures favoured operations that could be performed with long vectors; this was reflected in the type of algorithms which performed efficiently on this type of machine. There is still room for further exploitation based on this technique but it is unlikely to be a factor of 100 improvement. To achieve this order of improvement requires a more adventurous form of parallelism. It appears that truly parallel machines are the only technology that offer a reasonable hope of a factor of 1000 or more over the performance of today's systems.

The 1980 s saw the introduction of truly parallel machines and it is estimated that there are now over 30 parallel machines being offered world-wide. A direct consequence has been the increasing involvement of many more people with parallel machines. This, in turn, has highlighted the problems of parallel programming and the difficulties that can occur in debugging parallel programs. There seem to be three major approaches in the provision of a parallel programming language and these are considered in the next sections.

3.2 LANGUAGE EXTENSIONS

In this scenario an existing language, usually Fortran, is extended with features that enable a programmer to express concurrency and synchronization. If this approach is adopted then there are several new features which must be provided such as:

1. A means of creating and terminating parallel processes. For example in Cray Multitasking Fortran (Larson, 1984) this is achieved using library routines. A task (process) is created whenever a call is made to the multitasking library routine TKSTART. It takes the form

CALL TASKSTART (ID, SUBNAME[,ARGS])

which creates a task with identification ID and entry point SUBNAME[,ARGS] where the SUBNAME is typically a subroutine and [,ARGS] is an optional list of arguments to the subroutine.

The called task ID completes when it executes a RETURN statement in the subroutine where it began execution. The calling task can wait until the called task has completed by using the library routine

CALL TSKWAIT (ID)

2.   Synchronization of parallel processes. This is perhaps the situation which requires most attention as it is necessary for the user to appreciate fully the difficulties that can arise when parallel processes interact. In effect they need to be carefully synchronized so that if a process requires a result not yet produced by another process it can be made to wait and resume at the appropriate time. Examples of the features which can handle this situation are also taken from Cray Fortran where the synchronization of tasks running in parallel is provided by the EVENT mechanism. EVENTS enable signalling between tasks and have two states: cleared and posted. The syntax of library routines concerning EVENTS is as follows:

CALL EVASGN (EVENT)

• identifies an integer variable that the programmer wishes to use as an event

CALL EVWAIT (EVENT)

• suspends the calling task until the status of the event variable EVENT is posted

CALL EVPOST (EVENT)

• changes the status of the event variable EVENT to posted

CALL EVCLEAR (EVENT)

• changes the status of the event variable EVENT to cleared

When an event variable is posted all of the tasks waiting for that event are reactivated. By means of these routines it is possible for a number of competing tasks to co-ordinate their activities to their mutual benefit.

3.   the identification of shared and private variables. In Cray Fortran any data appearing in a COMMON statement, appearing in a SAVE statement or passed

to a subtask in a calling sequence is known to all tasks. All other data is local; each task has its own copy of the data.

A user can set up critical regions of code to ensure that a variable is manipulated by only one process at a time this is achieved by means of the LOCK mechanism. When a task enters a critical region of code it sets a LOCK, this LOCK acts as a signal that the critical region is in use. Any other task attempting to execute the critical region is suspended until the LOCK is cleared by a task exiting the critical region. Thus only one task at a time may access this code.

The syntax of the library routines concerning LOCKS is:

CALL LOCKASGN (LOCK)

- identifies an integer variable that the programmer intends to use as a lock

CALL LOCKON (LOCK)

- suspends the calling task until the status of the lock variable LOCK is unlocked; then changes the status to locked.

CALL LOCKOFF (LOCK)

- changes the status of the lock variable LOCK to unlocked.

Tasks waiting for a lock variable to become unlocked are suspended on a queue in order of their arrival. When the lock status is changed to unlocked the task at the head of the queue is reactivated and the lock status is changed back to locked. Thus the user can control access to shared variables in a program.

The advantage of such an approach is that the extensions can be added by means of library subroutines. The number of extensions can then be increased or decreased in the light of experience. Programmers are already trained in the language and do not need to learn a new language only the extensions. In addition existing software can be transferred and executed without the extensions in the first instance. However, introducing multitasking to an existing program can lead to a significant amount of code restructuring which can lead to the introduction of errors. In certain circumstances the extensions may conflict with other features in the language.

Multitasking works best when the amount of work to be partitioned over multiple processors is large otherwise the synchronisation overhead may be significant. When the work is not easily partitionable into equal sized tasks load imbalance may occur producing lower speed ups than expected.

Other approaches have been implemented such as FORK/JOIN constructs. In these cases the execution model is sequential and dynamic processor allocation, process migration and load balancing are very difficult. There is some doubt if this method could be used for massively parallel computers as the experience has been gained with low N multiprocessor systems.

In addition there is no clear parallel debugging model since the sequential debugging methods of stepping through the code or tracing do not extend well into a multiprocessor environment.

3.3   AUTOPARALLELIZATION

For the naive programmer the most attractive and the approach which requires the least effort is to have an existing program automatically parallelized. This is a follow on from the approach used for the successful promotion and spread of vector processors. However the problems of detection for a multiprocessor are much more difficult to solve because of the problems of synchronization etc. In fact, only in the case of shared memory architectures have reasonable systems been implemented. The starting point for much of this work has been the work on vectorization carried out by Kuck (Kuck, 1980) and his associates.

The impetus to develop such systems is immense since many installations have large numbers of large codes which can benefit considerably from the application of parallel computers. At the same time it is neither feasible nor practical to rewrite these codes. Hence this approach has a considerable built-in advantage for that reason.

This approach requires a sophisticated compiler which can apply data dependence analysis techniques in order to determine the connections, if any, between parts of a program. The underlying architecture heavily influences the implementation since at an early stage it is important to know if the architecture is a shared or distributed memory model.

The technology for automatic problem decomposition now exists in a limited form; the techniques typically focus on loops. Different iterations are assigned to different processors and if there is no dependency between iterations then no synchronization is necessary. However data is often passed from one iteration to another requiring synchronization. This, in turn, will affect the final speed of the generated code.

The data dependence phase of the compiler determines when concurrent execution of a loop requires synchronization and one of the following synchronization methods might be used:

1. synchronize on every data dependence relationship, this may not be the most efficient method but does produce the most parallelism;

2. divide the loop into segments and synchronize after each segment;

3. insert barriers at various points in the loop so that no iteration can proceed until all iterations reach the barrier;

4. isolate critical sections, that is, areas where communication is concentrated.

If vectorization can be detected within a loop then it is possible with suitable hardware to assign vectorized loops to individual processors in a multiprocessor system. The iterations can be assigned to processors in numerical index order folding around the processors if necessary or the iterations may be scheduled in any order. The former is used when synchronization between iterations is needed. If the compiler detects a data dependence the compiler usually takes a conservative approach and does not generate parallel code. In order to introduce some user control into the system a set of compiler directives is provided. They enable the user to force parallelization if he is sure that it will not occur. The search is on to find techniques which can handle more situations automatically, there is no standard against which the techniques can be compared.

As an example of what can be achieved in a multiprocessor system consider the Alliant FX/8 (Perron and Mundie, 1986). A shared memory system consisting of eight processors where each processor has the characteristics of a vector processor. Each vector processor is directly connected to a concurrency control bus which is used for fast synchronization with a minimum of overhead. It is this extra hardware which provides a fast mechanism to enforce data dependencies between loop iterations so that loops can be executed in parallel.

The Alliant FX/Fortran compiler is an optimizing compiler which automatically detects the potential for vector and parallel processing in standard Fortran. Normally the compiler will take a nested set of loops, vectorize the innermost and parallelize the outermost. If only the innermost loop is eligible and has an iteration count larger than the vector register length the compiler will give each vector segment to a different processor. If none of these options can be performed the compiler will generate scalar sequential code for the loop. The compiler can handle some situations that contain data dependencies such as the following

```
DO 2 I = 1,N
    X = A(I)
    A (I + 1) = B(I) + C(I)
    - - -
2 CONTINUE
```

the dependence on the variable A would normally ensure that the loop was not vectorized because each iteration requires data from a preceding iteration. This means that the loop iterations could not be spread across the various processors for concurrent execution. However on the Alliant with the concurrency hardware, such a DO loop can be distributed. The compiler automatically detects the dependency and inserts synchronization instructions into the compiled code. There are some delays until the processors are synchronized after which the speed up approaches the number of processors installed.

The process of detection of parallelism can be controlled by means of the programmer inserting compiler directives. There are four different modes of processing that the compiler can generate code for:

1. scalar; code is generated to execute on a single processor;

2. vector; operations are performed in groups of 32 elements by special vector instructions;

3. concurrent; operations in different iterations of the same loop are performed by a number of processors;

4. vector concurrent; operations are performed in groups of up to 32 elements by a number of processors concurrently.

By skilful use of these directives the user can further enhance the parallel execution of his program. However it does require a clear and intimate understanding of many parts of the program. For example, there are situations when concurrency but not vectorization should be suppressed, for example storing multiple values into an array element where the order of the stores must be preserved. Suppressing vectorization may improve performance if the number of iterations is less than three or if there are sparsely distributed iterations. Suppressing concurrency may provide better performance if the outer loop is small, the loops are then vectorized.

The essence of these latter tasks are related to the characteristics of the machine and therefore require the user to understand them. Is this knowledge that a programmer should have or is it not just a distraction from the main task of programming?

Some people argue that such an approach takes away the fun of parallel programming as it does not require the programmer to learn new techniques. However it does allow users to make use of the machine immediately without extensive training and they can experiment by adding different amounts of concurrency.

The difficult question to answer is how much useful concurrency can these compilers find if their efforts continue to focus on loops. The next step is to look beyond subroutines boundaries. The problem here is that with subroutines data dependencies are harder to find because analysis of the program at compile time cannot always determine which variables will be passed to various subroutines.

Another question which is related to the underlying architecture is the size of the concurrency detected. On some systems with expensive processors it is important to assign large pieces of code in order to employ fully the processors and reduce the time required for synchronization overhead. The current techniques associated with loops ensure that the processors in any system are relatively equally used in the assignment of work to processors. However if the assignment of work is performed on a subroutine basis then load balancing will not be so easily achieved.

3.4   NEW LANGUAGES

From a computer science point of view it seems reasonable to develop and use a language with explicit parallel data and program structures whenever you move onto a parallel processor. In an ideal world this would be the most desirable approach, however, it ignores the dependence on existing software and the problems of training and programmer shortage. Such an approach although highly desirable is labour intensive and extremely expensive.

The approaches being followed can be divided into applicative and imperative languages.

In the case of imperative concurrent languages several models of computation have been proposed, one distinguishing feature is the method of process synchronization.

Two main techniques have been proposed for the solution of synchronization problems. The first technique is based on a monitor construct plus condition variables. In this solution the processes deposit shared information in a data structure and synchronize each other by means of queues using special operators. The second technique is based on processes passing information directly when they wish to communicate. There is no shared data structure and such a technique is referred to as a message passing technique.

Languages have been developed using both techniques. For example, Concurrent Pascal by Brinch Hansen (1975), Modula by Niklaus Wirth (1977) and Pascal Plus (Welsh and Bustard, 1979), all these languages are based on the monitor plus condition variable approach. To enable the user to control parallelism these languages provide a process which consists of a private data structure and a sequential program that can operate on the data. One process cannot operate on the private data of another process. A monitor defines a shared data structure and all the operations that can be performed on it. These operations are defined by the procedures of the monitor. In addition, a monitor defines an initialization operation that is executed when its data structure is created.

In general a process can access the shared data of a monitor by calling one of the monitor's procedures. If there is more than one call then only one of the calling processes is allowed to succeed in entering the monitor at any time; to guarantee that the data of the monitor is accessed exclusively. Only when a process exits the monitor is it safe for one of the calling processes which was delayed to enter the monitor.

It is also possible for a process to enter the monitor and discover that the information it requires has not yet arrived. In such a situation, it can join a queue associated with that condition and thereby release its exclusive access over the monitor. Another process is now able to enter the monitor. Eventually another process may enter the monitor and enable a delayed process to continue. The queues within a monitor are usually identified by condition variables and a process can append itself to a single condition variable queue by executing a wait operation. Another process executing a signal operation on a condition variable queue will cause a process delayed on that queue (if there is one) to be resumed.

The communication method used in Ada (Reference Manual, 1983) can be traced to notations like Communicating Sequential Processes (Hoare, 1978) and Distributed Processes (Brinch Hansen, 1978) which were proposed for the design of parallel systems. As in the previous languages a process or task in Ada terminology is used to indicate those parts of a system which can be executed in parallel. However there is no data structure like a monitor for the tasks to deposit data for later collection or in which to wait for data to arrive.

Instead the tasks first synchronize their activities and then communicate directly without the help of an intermediate data structure. Hence one process may have to wait for another process to arrive, when it does the processes can exchange messages directly; such an encounter is referred to as a rendezvous. In addition non deterministic selection has been introduced to Ada tasks so that given a choice between several alternatives one is chosen at random. It is felt that this more accurately reflects the unpredictable nature of events in the real world. The monitor is more easily implemented on a shared memory multiprocessor system while the message passing system favours local memory configurations for efficiency of implementation.

Although the experience that has been accumulated in the use of these languages is limited there does appear to be some guidelines emerging. It appears relatively easy to write programs for shared memory machines while debugging is difficult - a consequence of the changing a value of a shared variable. Writing programs for local memory machines is not straightforward or well understood but the debugging is relatively easy - a consequence of the effects of changing a variable being localized.

Applicative languages are more recent and are designed to enhance the visibility of concurrency without requiring programmer management of synchronization. A distinct advantage is that they do not rely on any particular model of computer architecture and could be used for either a shared memory or message passing machine. This could have significant consequences for program portability.

Applicative languages are based on the simultaneous evaluation of all input arguments to a function; every executable action is a mathematical function. Any number of functions can execute simultaneously so long as their input arguments do not depend on each other. A programmer focuses on the mathematical structure of the solution and the concurrency implied by that structure. There is no need to be concerned about processor assignment or synchronization; these are problems for the compiler or the architecture.

The compilers for such systems are therefore responsible for partitioning, mapping and synchronization and are still in their infancy and not achieving a desirable level of efficiency. For example a major problem is the dynamic memory management problem which requires large amounts of memory.

One of the main reasons for such an approach is that a parallel notation is more likely to exploit the underlying parallel architecture more effectively than trying to achieve that with a sequential notation. The experience with sequential notations on vector and multiprocessors is that some user reordering or rewriting is necessary to improve performance. In addition a parallel notation is more likely to lead to the discovery of new algorithms which is an important if not a crucial aspect of parallel programming.

3.5   SUMMARY

Experience indicates that the behaviour of short parallel programs can be very complex; the fact that it functions correctly for one or more executions is no guarantee that it will not fail on some future occasion with the same data. The tracking down of a bug can be frustrated due to a combination of logical complexity, non repeatable behaviour and our present lack of tools.

The rapid increase in the number of parallel machines means that concurrent rather than sequential is becoming the normal mode of programming.

This has meant that many more programmers are having to convert an existing program for a parallel environment or to learn a new parallel programming language.

Several systems are now appearing which can help with the automatic parallelization of a sequentially written program on shared memory machines. However it will be several years before compilers can capture all the parallelism in a sequential program. An even more severe problem exists for automatic parallelization of sequential programs for message passing systems.

Languages with explicit parallel features make parallelism easier to detect and extract. However, it does require substantial relearning by programmers. In addition such a notation facilitates the discovery of new parallel algorithms.

REFERENCES

1. Ada (1983) Reference Manual for the Ada Programming Language. (ANSI/MIL-STD 1815). United States Department of Defense, Washington DC

2. Brinch Hansen P. (1975) The programming language Concurrent Pascal. *IEEE Trans. Soft. Eng.,* 1, 199- 207.

3. Brinch Hansen P. (1978) Distributed processes: A concurrent programming concept. *Comm. ACM,* 21, 934-940.

4. CRAY-1 Computer Systems. (1981) *Fortran (CFT) Reference Manual.* Publication No SR-0009, Rev H.

5. Hoare, C. A. R. (1978) Communicating sequential processes. *Comm. ACM,* 21, 666-667.

6. Kuck, D. (1980) High speed multiprocessing and compilation techniques. *IEEE Trans. on Computers,* C-29, 763-776.

7. Larson, J. L. (1984) An introduction to multitasking on the Cray X-MP multiprocessor. *Computer,* July, 62-69.

8. Perron, R. and Mundie, C. (1986) The architecture of the Alliant FX/8 Computer. *Compcon (Spring)* IEEE Computer Society Press.

9. Perrott, R. H. (1987) *Parallel Programming* Addison- Wesley.

10. Welsh, J. and Bustard, D. W. (1979) Pascal Plus - another language for modular multiprogramming. *Software Practice and Experience,* 9, 947-957.

11. Wirth, N. (1977) Modula: a language for modular multiprogramming. *Software - Practice and Experience,* 7, 3-35.

4 Who should think parallel?

Chris Wadsworth

SERC Rutherford Appleton Laboratory

4.1 INTRODUCTION

In fact the advent of parallel programming may do something to revive the pioneering spirit in programming, which seems to be degenerating into a rather dull and routine occupation.

Plus ca change, plus ca meme chose! Hardware of course has always been parallel, e.g. overlapped I/O, parallel adders, and gate logic, but the user has not needed to be aware of this. The hardware, or in some cases the systems programmer, does all the work for him.

From the mid-1950s to the late 1970s a number of experimental parallel machines were designed, but none were a commercial success. Progress in parallel programming was relatively limited during this period (though of course there was much interesting work done on the theoretical basis for concurrency and on the discovery of parallel algorithms for particular problems).

The 1980s has seen an explosion of commercially available parallel machines with a wide variety of architectures, e.g. array processors, hypercubes, transputer systems, and shared-memory multiprocessors. Almost overnight the VLSI revolution in particular has made parallel processing affordable; indeed the systems mentioned now typically offer improvements in price/performance of an order of magnitude or better compared to conventional uniprocessors.

Advances in parallel programming have not been so sudden (or dramatic)! Programming the new parallel machines was certainly initially difficult. Early examples were perhaps too tightly coded for a particular machine. Gradually a body of experience, knowledge, approaches, and techniques has been built up, both of applications apparently best suited to one style of architecture (see, e.g., Fox [1] [2]) and methods and parallel thinking of a more generic nature.

This paper gives an overview of the unifying ideas that have emerged, with some remarks on probable future trends in parallel programming and on the implications for parallel languages and (virtual) architectures. We seek to stress generic ideas, common paradigms, and abstraction. Our concern in fact is with a separation of concerns: distinguishing the rightful concerns of the user from those of the system (whether provided by hardware or by software). From the user's point of view provision of the right abstractions is regarded as somebody else's problem [9], though no less important or interesting for that.

4.2   WHY PARALLEL PROCESSING?

Let us be in no doubt at the outset: parallel processing is a means to an end. The end-user is typically motivated by one or more of the following main potential benefits:

- cheaper

- faster

- bigger (problems)

- more (functionality)

In short, better performance in one direction or another. At this level the motivation for parallel processing is no different from that for any other advance in computing technology (or indeed from that for computerizing some task in the first place).

The bottom line is economics. The economics of mass produced VLSI components is increasingly favouring parallel systems built from many cheap processors. Current systems are already achieving a price/performance advantage in the range from 10 to 30 times better than traditional minicomputers, mainframes, and supercomputers; e.g. a parallel CFD program developed by Rolls-Royce/Top Express gives 20% of Cray performance on a transputer system costing 100 times less [6].

This last comparison, needless to say, is based on hardware (purchase) costs alone. The costs in developing parallel programs, both in time and effort, are as yet not well understood; indeed there appear to be few studies which address the issues at all, though Tucker [15] points to some of the commercial issues. A related difficulty is that of balancing extra development effort against run-time gains. One thing has become clear, however, from the experience gained in recent years: there are now a growing range of applications and styles of parallelism for which parallel programming is no longer so terribly difficult.

4.3   PROBLEM PARALLELISM

Problems vary widely in the degree to which parallelism is evident in the problem itself.

4.3.1   Obvious parallelism

Sometimes parallelism does not need to be teased out of a problem at all, it is staring the user in the face. Problems involving large, regular data spaces are often trivially solved by partitioning the data into pieces that can be processed concurrently, Ray tracing [12] is a typical example. In many cases the degree of parallelism evident in the data far exceeds the number of processors that are currently affordable. Such problems have been referred to as being embarrassingly parallel [1].

Other examples in this category are found in real-world systems consisting of many interacting agents, e.g. a control system for an industrial plant with multiple sensors and controllers. The real-world system is inherently parallel; it is far simpler and more natural to follow this parallelism than to squeeze a solution onto a single processor. It may well be the best way to ensure that any real-time demands are met. Scalable performance is often of lesser importance in this area.

The user concerns in this category are predominantly threefold:

1.   to have a convenient means of expressing the obvious parallelism;

2.   to have the work spread evenly across the available processors;

3.   to have any real-time constraints satisfied.

4.3.2   Discovered parallelism

More commonly a problem has no obvious parallelism, or the obvious parallel algorithm turns out to be a poor solution. The human, however, knows or is able to devise a good strategy by discovering parallelism in an approach to a solution.

There are many such examples in the literature, e.g. in linear algebra, sorting algorithms, and graph problems. Another example is the travelling salesman problem; here the obvious parallel search of all permutations is not feasible, but a technique based on simulated annealing [2,p.215] yields a good solution (in this case an approximate one).

The key point about this category is that human ingenuity will always discover clever parallel algorithms that are unlikely to be found by automatic means (at least for the foreseeable future!). The user concerns, once a parallel strategy has been devised, are much the same as for the previous category, except that the user may need to be more conscious of balancing the work load in his design. With current understanding also the algorithm may well need to be chosen with the specific target architecture in mind; the best parallel algorithm for say, matric multiplication on a DAP may well be unsuitable for a transputer system, or *vice versa*.

4.3.3   Implicit parallelism

A third approach is to ignore a parallelism! The user programs in a language without explicit parallel features and the system compiles into parallel code as it knows how. In principle, this approach has clear portability advantages.

Foremost in this category is the use of declarative languages, such as functional and logic languages. Their strength in this context derives from the fact that these languages remain uncommitted about matters of order of evaluation, leaving the system free to make choices appropriate to an implementation (whether parallel or not). As yet, however, parallel implementations of declarative languages are not competitive, though there is much active research, e.g. Peyton-Jones [13] for a recent progress report. A major focus in this research is the design of novel target architectures, e.g. dataflow and graph reduction, and possibly special hardware.

At an opposite extreme are the conventional sequential languages such as Fortran, C, and Cobol. A large body of (large) programs written in these languages has been built up over the last 30 years or so, the so-called dusty-deck problem. Such programs may be characterized as being embarrassingly serial. It is impractical in the short term to contemplate any wholesale rewriting into a parallel language. More attractive is the possibility of compilers which detect and extract parallelism automatically. There are now quite good compilers for shared-memory machines, the Alliant Fortran compiler for instance is based on a range of advanced techniques for data-dependence analysis, but for distributed memory machines automatic parallelization is still a research topic. Other papers in this conference discuss the progress in software migration aids which can assist the task of porting existing sequential software by hand without extensive rewriting.

4.3.4 Discussion

The first two categories, explicit parallelism, are clearly distinct from the third, and are at a more advanced stage of development and exploitation. Implicit parallelism promises substantial benefits for the future, but for the time being explicit parallelism holds sway for real applications work on grounds of efficient implementation, and to some extent on grounds of familiarity.

The situation with efficiency here is not unlike that which pertained when the first high-level language compilers were appearing. Many felt that a compiler would never produce as good code as hand-written assembler. We all know which way that argument went, only in special circumstances does anyone program in assembler these days.

It is too soon to predict that the same may happen to explicitly parallel programming. Perhaps it never will completely; many will feel that parallelism is too far-reaching to be automated. But need the user be concerned with so much of the fine detail?

Current languages for expressing parallelism explicitly may be broadly classified into two families:

1. (new) process languages, e.g. Occam, Ada;

2. parallel extensions to sequential languages, e.g. several variants of parallel C, Fortran, Lisp.

Both offer a pragmatic way forward in the short term, the first perhaps more general than the second, but the current languages do have a number of drawbacks to them. Occam [7], for instance, though it provides excellent support for a theoretically-proven model of concurrency, is rather spartan in its normal programming features (no data structures, no recursion, no data abstraction, no type parameterization, no modules, etc). In the second family, the examples of parallel extensions we have seen seem to us methodologically unsound, both as exercises in language design and in making the task of producing safe, reliable software harder rather than easier. There is also the problem of incompatible, non-standard variants among extensions of the same language.

Occam's experience has an important lesson for the promotion of new languages. There has been strong resistance to Occam from the applications user community just on the basis that it is a new language. Occam is also seen as being too closely associated with one architecture, the transputer. New languages must, in our view, be integrated as part of a coherent development methodology with a full environment of necessary support tools from the start. (Alternatively, they must have the backing of a big funding agency!)

4.4   SOLUTION PARADIGMS

There are by now a number of common paradigms for parallel implementations of many applications. The classification which follows is drawn from Hey [5] with two additions.

4.4.1   Farm parallelism

This paradigm applies to problems whose data space is partitioned into many pieces, which we shall call packets, that can be processed independently. A master, or farmer, process farms out packets to each of several identical worker processes. The workers return the results to the master, which then sends a further packet. By partitioning the data into rather more packets than there are workers, the master is able to keep all the workers busy even if some packets take much longer to compute than others. In other words, this solution load balances automatically.

In this case there is no need for communication between the worker processes. The only communication is that between the master and the workers for distributing the work and returning the results. Depending on the problem, these distribution costs are negligible provided the packet size can be chosen large enough to amortize the distribution time.

Ray tracing [12] is the best-known example. Another is high-energy physics programs that run many simulations on multiple events sets [4].

4.4.2   Geometric parallelism

In this case, as the name suggest, there is a geometric structure to the data space, e.g. volumes in a fluid dynamics problem. Unlike farm parallelism, however, the computations for each region are not independent and may now depend on that of their immediate neighbours (only).

This case is naturally modelled by assigning each region to a different processor (statically). Typically the same code is run on each processor, though not necessarily. Provided the compute times (between communications) for each region are roughly balanced, and the frequency of communication is not too high, the solution works well.

Again, there is a choice about the size (and shape) of the regions. It is not necessary either that the processor topology matches the dimensionality of the problem, e.g. a 3D-problem can be solved on a 2D-array by projecting one dimension onto each processor, or a 2D-problem can be projected onto a linear chain of processors. Extensions to irregular meshes, e.g. in finite element problems, are also possible.

A toy example is the game of life, in which successive states of point in a grid are determined as a combination of preceding states of their neighbours. The commonest real applications arise in numerical integration of partial differential equations, e.g. for problems in electromagnetics, fluid dynamics, and weather forecasting.

4.4.3   Long-range parallelism

Life gets more difficult when the rules are changed! Suppose the propagation rule is made more complicated, with next states depending on the previous states of all points in the system. What we have then is essentially the n-body problem in astrophysics (motion under gravity), or multi-particle dynamics in molecular modelling.

Effective solutions have been developed based on a ring of processors [10]. Much as before, the particles are divided (equally) among the processors. On each timestep, each processor starts a packet around the ring, carrying information about its own particles and accumulating the effect of the forces due to other. On return to the home processor the states are updated. A simple optimisation is easily added; by exploiting symmetry of forces (and packets), packets need only travel half-way round the ring, then take a short-cut home.

4.4.4   Algorithmic parallelism

Having exhausted the easy cases of data parallelism, we are left with partitioning the program. This is algorithmic parallelism, which is much less regular in structure.

One well-known example is processes connected in a pipeline with the output from each passing as input to the next. This generalizes, through splitting and merging, to a process net, but no other common subcases have been identified. Systolic arrays are essentially a special formulation of process nets, as are other novel approaches such as dataflow and demand flow.

4.4.5   Dynamic parallelism

Each of the above involves only static parallelism, i.e. the partition into processes is fixed at design-time (some would say compile-time). There are many problems for which this is not possible, or at least not easily so. In dynamic parallelism new processes are generated at run-time in a data-dependent fashion.

There are few generally useful paradigms in this case. One that has been studied is divide-and-conquer (-and-combine) [11]. Each subject problem spawns zero or more sub-problems, each of which is solved recursively then combined to solve the subject problem. The number of sub-problems, and hence sub-processes in the natural parallel implementation, is dependent on the data values in the subject problem.

One solution in this case is to simulate the dynamic parallelism by using a paradigm-specific kernel on each processor. The kernel used in [11] included experiments with process-stealing rules whereby idle processors steal work from their neighbours.

4.4.6   Discussion

The classification is useful but incomplete. Static data parallelism is well covered though there are no doubt other useful sub-paradigms waiting to be discovered. It is also well catered for practically with a range of standard harnesses available — program templates which set up the overall process structure and do all the communications, into which the problem-specific code (which may be purely sequential) is slotted. The user either uses a standard harness as is or may extend it for additional facilities, e.g. monitoring.

Dynamic parallelism and algorithmic parallelism need further refinement into useful sub-paradigms.

4.5   VIRTUAL ARCHITECTURE

There are too many parallel architectures! The best way forward is to define an abstract programming model based on a virtual architecture, with systems software implementing the abstractions as appropriate across a variety of parallel hardware choices.

It would be unrealistic to suggest that one single virtual architecture will suffice, e.g. how would novel approaches such as dataflow or neural nets fit in. We shall limit out attention to the dominant examples of MIMD machines, and their expected successors, for which there are already indications of convergence to a common programming model.

Our discussion is oriented to distributed memory machines, but we see no reason why the model should not be applied to shared memory. Indeed it may actually be easier to implement on a shared-memory machine. The challenge for shared-memory architectures is in a different direction: scalability to large numbers of processors.

We shall look at four areas -- communications, processing, libraries, and memory — roughly in the order in which we expect abstract models with good solutions to emerge.

4.5.1   Virtual communications

Most MIMD machines use point-to-point communication links and are well suited for algorithms involving only local communications. General communication between distant processors is far less efficient, because of the software overheads in each intermediate processor. It is also cumbersome for the programmer to be concerned with routing messages passing through as well as his own communications. Software harnesses have been developed for doing this but remain poor in efficiency.

The desirable abstract model is obvious: that of a logically totally-connected network in which the user need not be concerned about routing. The challenge is to devise routing methods for which distant communications are as efficient as local.

Recently Intel[8] launched their second generation hypercube, the iPSC-2, which includes special hardware for "direct connect" through routing of messages. There are also strong indications from Inmos that the next generation transputer will provide some form of through routing. Convergence to a common model is thus well underway in this area.

What is less clear is the entity addressed by a message: a processor, a process, or a (logical) channel between processes? Another choice is the semantics of message passing: synchronized or not? guaranteed delivery or not? buffering? It is up to the user to pull the providers in the preferred direction.

4.5.2   Virtual processing

Placement of (logical) processes onto (physical) processors, and specification of interconnect topology (when configurable), is currently done manually by the user, either at the outermost program level as in Occam, or outside the programming language at the operating system level in a configuration file. Both methods work, but are notoriously tricky and tedious. Placement of an Occam channel, for instance, at a particular link number is very low level, analogous to allocating a variable at a particular memory location.

The user does not normally care how his processes are allocated to processors when these are drawn from a pool of identical processors. There are exceptions, however. Sometimes several processes must be placed on the same processor, e.g. decoupled communications and compute processes; or it may be that not all processors are identical, e.g. a process for controlling a particular device can only be run on the processor to which that device is attached (graphics, input sensors, disks, etc). Current mechanisms may be seen as an overkill: because it is necessary for some placements to be specified by the user, the method requires the user to specify all.

What is needed is a means for the user to express only the essential placement constraints. Beyond that it should be the responsibility of the system. A good solution for virtual communications should make automatic placement much more straightforward.

The above covers static allocation only. For dynamic parallelism, allocation at run-time becomes essential. Process migration also needs to be considered to balance the load between processors. Some studies of dynamic allocation and migration strategies have been conducted, but there is no definitive solution yet. One example is Equus[14].

4.5.3 Virtual libraries

Virtual is something of a misnomer in this case. It is standard practice on uniprocessors to have standard libraries in which the individual routines are implemented differently on different machines.

It is trivial to extend the practice to parallel machines, except for one complication: reconfigurability (including scalability). On a reconfigurable machine, different routines may run best on different configurations (ring, grid, tree, or whatever). When several library routines are used in the same program, either the routines need to be parameterized for the configuration must be done at run-time and not be too slow.

What is the library implementor, who cannot know the programs in which the library routines will be used, to do? A better answer should follow from solutions in the previous two areas.

4.5.4 Virtual memory

This again is standard on uniprocessors and is generally provided in conjunction with multi-tasking and/or multi-user timesharing. In that context virtual memory fulfils two distinct functions:

1. memory protection: protecting the address space of each user (or task) against those of others (including the system kernel);

2. large address space: enabling a user program to have a virtual address space (much) larger than the available physical memory.

(The second alone is often taken as virtual memory, but provision of both is almost always via the same mechanism of a memory management unit.)

On a parallel machine with shared memory, it is straightforward to extend the implementation from that on a uniprocessor, just some choice perhaps whether the memory management unit is centralized close to the memory (and swap-space on disks) or distributed closer to the processors.

With distributed memory, the need for memory protection is best avoided by assigning users to different (sets of) processors. Why share a processor between users when there are lots (of processors)? Support for large address spaces is much more difficult to provide. Few processors will be directly connected to disks; that would destroy the economics of massive parallelism. So where would one page to, and how? Paging across the communication network would be too slow. This seems to us a particularly difficult nut for the system designers to crack.

Perhaps there is another way of thinking about applications whose memory requirements exceed the total physical memory of all the processors. Certainly there will always be users with such demands! For the time being, they may have to revert to defining their own overlays.

4.5.5 Discussion

The virtual architecture we have sketched is obvious enough; the challenge is implementing the functionality without sacrificing performance. To some extent what we have given is a wish list. We (are led to) believe that effective solutions are likely in the near future.

At least the first and last areas will clearly need hardware support. The second is to do with user languages (placement constraints) and system software tools (automatic placement). Libraries may become trivial when the others are solved.

4.6 A FUTURE RED HERRING?

A little controversy to close ... The literature on parallel processing is almost obsessed with performance in a narrow sense, that of efficiency of processor utilization. This is understandable for current parallel systems which, though relatively cheap, are costly enough. Efficiency matters when resources are scarce or expensive. Few of us have that many processors! Even now there are not that many systems with 100 processors, let along 1000 or more.

If the industry hype is to be believed, processing will soon become a cheap, plug-in resource just like memory. Predictions have been made that office workstations with perhaps 1000 processors, and central installations perhaps 100 times larger, will be commonplace before the end of the century. Processor utilization then becomes a secondary issue of concern to the system provider perhaps but little to the user. After all, who really worries about memory utilization any more?

Of course the user cannot afford to be grossly inefficient. He must choose a good parallel algorithm, just as for a sequential sorting algorithm he would choose, say, an $0(n \log n)$ algorithm rather an $0(n \ 2)$ algorithm. But that is another story ....

4.7 CONCLUDING REMARKS

We have argued that by examining styles of parallelism, common paradigms for parallel solutions, the parallel programming model, and the capability of current and predicted parallel hardware, we can arrive at a better separation between matters which are the proper concern of the user and functionality desired from the system. A virtual architecture for future MIMD machines has been outlined.

There are many further issues -- granularity, scalability, synchronization, deadlock, correctness, for instance -- each of which gives rise to similar questions about the relative roles of the user and the system. When we get the answers right, parallel processing will have come of age. It would be very surprising, however, if there is a unique answer.

To Gill's chagrin (1985) perhaps, parallel programming is now emerging from its pioneering stage, though the prospect ahead is certainly not dull!

REFERENCES

1   Fox, G.C. (1988a)   What have we learnt from using real parallel machines to solve real problems, *3rd Conference on Hypercube Concurrent Computers and Applications,* JPL Pasadena, California.

2   Fox, G.C. et al. (1988b) *Solving Problems on Concurrent Processors.* Prentice-Hall, Englewood Cliffs, N.J..

3   Gill, S.(1958)Parallel programming. *Computer J.,* vol 1.

4   Glendinning, I. and Hey, A.J.G. (1987) Transputer arrays as Fortran farms for particle physics, *Report SHEP 86/87-7,* University of Southampton.

5   Hey, A.J.G. (1987) Parallel decomposition of large scale simulations in science and engineering, *Report SHEP 86/87-2,* University of Southampton.

6   Holman, A. (1988) At the leading Edge, *Parallelogram 4.*

7   Inmos Ltd.,(1987) *Ooccam2 Reference Manual.* Prentice-Hall, Hemel Hempstead.

8   Intel Scientific Computers, (1988) *iPSC-2,* Intel International Ltd., Swindon.

9   Jesshope C.R. and   Panesar, G. (1988) P1085: Somebody else's problem. *Proc CONPAR 88,* Cambridge University Press, Cambridge, UK.

10   Meiko Ltd., (1987) *Achieving results.* Bristol.

11   McBurney, D.L. and   Sleep, M.R.(1987) Transputer-based experiments with the ZAPP Architecture. *Proc PARLE Conference* (Eindhoven), Springer-Verlag LNCS 258.

12   Packer, J. (1987) Exploiting concurrency: A ray tracing example. *Inmos Technical Note 7.* Inmos Ltd., Bristol.

13   Peyton-Jones, S.L. (1989) Parallel Implementations of functional programming languages. *Computer J.* vol 32, pp. 175-186.

14   Sahiner, A.V. Sherman, A. and Kindberg, T. (1989) Horsebox (article on Equus). *Parallelogram.*

15   Tucker, N. (1989) Commercial issues: Parallel processing and the transputer. *Microprocessors and Microsyst.* vol 13, Special Issue: Applying the transputer.

Part Two

Algorithms

5 Super parallel algorithms

D. Parkinson

Active Memory Technology Limited and Queen Mary College London

5.1 INTRODUCTION

Parallelism in computers exploits the fact that we want to be able to perform multiple operations! Hence at one level the desire to perform not just one multiply but many multiplications gives us the opportunity to apply some special architecture to the task of speeding up the set of multiplications. The two common routes to parallelism are the vector pipeline and multiple processors. In both types of system the time to multiply a single pair of numbers is not a good measure of the time to create the product of a number of pairs of numbers.

It is well known that a vector pipeline has a start-up time (or latency) so the time for multiplying N pairs of numbers is $(s + Nt_v)$, where s is the start-up time and tv is the beat time for the pipeline. Hence a first level approximation to the time for performing N repeats of a single operation is $(s + Nt_v)$. This is however an over-simplification for in practice there is a maximum length of vector that any given vector architecture can perform in a single activation. If this maximum is p_v then we must express N as $M_v p_v + q_v$ with $0 \le q_v < p_v$. The time to perform the total task is therefore $M_v(s + p_v t_v) + (s + q_v t_v) = (M_v + 1)s + N t_v$.

If we have a multi-computer configuration with pm processors each with an operation time of t_m then, if $N = M_m p_m + q_m$, the operation time on a multiple processor is $(M_m + 1)t_m$.

Let us define the speed-up due to parallelism (S) as the ratio

S = (time to compute N results singly) /

        (time to compute the results using the parallel facilities).

For vector pipelines we have

$$S_v = N(s + t_v) / ((M_v + 1)s + N t_v)$$

which is approximately $1 + (s/t_v)$ if $p_v > > 1$. Hence the benefits of the vector pipeline approach are greatest when the start-up time is long compared with the beat time. For multiple processor systems we have

$$S_m = N_m/(M_m + 1)$$

which is approximately p_m. The qualitative difference between S_v and S_m is one of the reasons why vector processing and parallel processing should be considered as separate (and parallel) areas of study.

So far we have only considered using parallel processing for a trivial single vector type of problem. The usual parallel algorithm design study is based on the use of parallel machines to solve a more complex problem e.g. sorting, matrix multiplication, polynomial evaluation, solving sets of linear equations, etc. There is a large and continually growing literature of this type of study.

A major flaw in most studies is that they concentrate on trying to evaluate the maximum number of processors that can be used to implement the given task. For example there is a well known result that matrix multiplication can utilize not more than n^3 processors; therefore, providing one ignores the intercommunication costs, a time proportional to log2n can be expected when multiplying n*n matrices.

These types of result are somewhat pure mathematical existence theorems, often with little practical relevance. For matrix multiplication, in particular, the neglect of inter-processor communications has been criticized by Gentleman[1]. Other problems with these types of result include the failure to give any hint of what to do in the case when the number of processors is not equal to that indicated by the method.

In practice two cases are of interest

1.   The number of processors is less than the number suggested i.e. we only have n or n2 processors available for matrix multiplication. This is going to be the usual case when we are interested in large matrix manipulations. The increased parallelism will encourage us to attempt to solve larger applications, and matrices of size 200*200 will not be considered especially large. Theoretically we can use 8 million processors for multiplying such matrices but it is unlikely that we shall have them. It is more likely that we will have access to only 40 000 or 200 processors.

2. The converse of the previous case is also of great interest. The size of matrices that we are dealing with may be only say 4*4 and we have 40 000 processors. The question is now one of an embarrassment of riches, how can we utilize the excess number of processors? This paper is about that problem.

The question of utilizing a larger number of processors is in many ways just the next layer of parallel thinking above the basic question of how we utilize a few processors. The parallelism as discussed initially came from the realization that we had lots of multiplications to perform and the fact that there were lots of multiplies could allow us to use parallel computational facilities. The same argument can be applied now to the problem of our 4*4 matrix multiplications. Many of the applications for which 4*4 multiplication time is important will require us to compute many matrix multiplications, and so we can try and perform many of them simultaneously. In other instances we may wish to perform different operations such as polynomial evaluations, FFTs etc. In the terms of programs this may mean that we are examining outer loops as the source of parallelism. This statement appears to me to be rather obvious and banal but seems to be forgotten by some people who artificially seem to limit their consideration of parallelism to just one algorithmic level above primitive operations, such as add, multiply, compare etc.

5.2 EMBARRASSINGLY PARALLEL

The most trivial examples of the use of higher level parallelism occurs in the so-called embarrassingly parallel problems where one uses the parallel multiple processors to simply perform many repeats of a serial algorithm. Much of the embarrassment seems to be for those people who have not expected their application to be amenable to parallel processing. Embarrassingly parallel problems occur very frequently and should always be searched for. A particular advantage of embarrassingly parallel algorithms is the fact that they operate by performing many repetitions of a serial algorithm simultaneously; for this reason they are often called multi-serial algorithms.

The only snag with embarrassingly parallel problems is sometimes a need for access to large amounts of data, a requirement which might be unsatisfactory, in say real time signal processing, due to an effective increase in the latency. A typical example is in FFT analysis performed on input data streams. If we have to perform FFTs of length say 256 on input signals and we have 10000 processors then, in one sense, the optimal algorithm is to perform one FFT per processor over a set of 10000 samples. Such a strategy implies the collection of 10000*256 measurement points before processing can start. If the data were complex at 4 bytes precision real and imaginary, then 40 Mbytes of data would need to be collected before this " computationally optimal" algorithm can be started. Such a demand might imply a latency time unacceptable for the application.

5.3   MULTIPLE PARALLEL ALGORITHMS SUPER PARALLEL   ALGORITHMS

For the above reasons it is often the case that we wish to perform simultaneously a number of repeats of a given sub-task using a given processor set. The practical application task confronting somebody implementing an application is therefore of the form:

> What is the best strategy for solving N repeats of sub-problem Y using P, processors where each of the sub-problems Y has a characteristic size parameter M?

P is usually a fixed number for a given system at a given time, but the programmer may wish to write a program which will be portable across a range of processor sizes. For small degrees of parallelism it may be reasonable to assume that P can change in steps of unity, but for massively parallel systems (such as the DAP or Connection Machine) P will only change by multiplying factors such as 4.

The problem is, as posed, characterized by a minimum of three parameters (N,M,P) and sufficient is known about parallel algorithm design to suggest that different algorithms are optimal in different parts of the parameter space:

- If P=1 we are in the serial regime and the best serial algorithm is optimal.

- If P=N we are in the embarrassingly parallel regime and again the serial algorithm is optimal.

- If N=1 then we are in what we might call the Classical Parallel Algorithm design regime and the literature alluded to above gives many clues about optimal algorithms.

- Special cases exist if P divides N exactly or if P has a nice relationship with M.

Currently there seems to a rather naive view prevalent that somehow one should be able to express in a high level language this maximally parallel algorithm, and that clever compilers will be able to optimize the implementation onto any particular target set of P processors. The fallacy in this viewpoint is evident when one realizes that such a compiler should, by definition, be able to optimize the use of a single processor and therefore should be able to deduce the optimal serial algorithm from the maximally parallel algorithm! Such a faith in the cleverness of compiler technology is very touching, it is particularly strange to find that faith so prevalent in the high performance Fortran community who for years have investigated the tricks which will bluff Fortran compilers into producing efficient code.

The task we are interested in is therefore that of writing algorithms which solve not just one instance of a problem but solve in parallel many instances of the problem. We call these algorithms super parallel. A typical scenario in which the need for super parallel algorithms arises naturally is that of solving sets of tri-diagonal equations. The solution of a set of tri-diagonal linear equations is a common sub-task in many problems derived from partial differential equations arising from 3-point approximations to second derivatives. An efficient tri-diagonal solver is therefore a useful tool for many applications. Parallel algorithms for solving tri-diagonal linear equations have been extensively studied, Hockney and Jesshope[2] is a good source for discussion of the problem. Indeed Hockney and Jesshope do discuss the problem of solving m sets of tri-diagonal systems with n equations, although their study is more closely related to the problem of choosing the optimal algorithm for vector processors. The optimal parallel algorithm for solving one set of tri-diagonal linear equations given n processors is the Cyclic Reduction Algorithm and uses N processors.

Our concern here is as much with programming as with theoretical analysis, so we consider a tri-diagonal set of linear equations as being defined by four one-dimensional arrays A(N),B(N),C(N),D(N) which define a set of tri-diagonal equations which we write algebraically as

$$b_i x_i = a_i x_i\text{-}1 + c_i x_i + 1 + d_i \qquad\qquad i = 1\ldots\ldots\ldots n$$

with $\quad a_1 = c_n = 0.0$

The cyclic reduction algorithm transforms these equations into a new set by the operations

$$A_i = a_i/b_i$$
$$C_i = c_i/b_i$$
$$D_i = d_i/b_i$$

then

$$a'_i = A_i A_i - 1$$
$$c'_i = C_i C_i + 1$$
$$b'_i = 1 - A_i C_i - 1 - C_i A_i + 1$$
$$d'_i = D_i - A_i D_i - 1 - C_i D_i + 1$$

The equations we now have are

$$b'x_i = a'x_i - 2 + c'_i + 2 + d'_i$$

The algorithm repeats this transformation log2n times to produce the result.

Programming the algorithm in Fortran 88 is instructive since the operations all take place on the data structures a,b,c,d. We can write the inner loop as

```
         K=1
                  DO 10 ISTEP=1,LOG2N
         A=A/B
         C=C/B
         D=D/B
         B=1-A*EOSHIFT(C,1,-K)-C*EOSHIFT(A,1,K)
         D=D-A*EOSHIFT(D,1,-K)-C*EOSHIFT(D,1,K)
         A= A*EOSHIFT(A,1,-K)
         C=                    C*EOSHIFT(C,1,K)
         K=2*K
   10    CONTINUE
```

The solution is D/B.

If the Fortran community is prepared to accept a WHILE statement, we could program the above as

```
   K=1
   WHILE(K.LT.N) THEN
         A=A/B
         C=C/B
```

```
        D = D/B
        B = 1 -  A*EOSHIFT(C,1,-K) -  C*EOSHIFT(A,1,K)
        D = D-   A*EOSHIFT(D,1,-K) -  C*EOSHIFT(D,1,K)
        A =      A*EOSHIFT(A,1,-K)
        C =                           C*EOSHIFT(C,1,K)
        K = 2*K
ENDWHILE
```

The benefit of this version is the elimination of the need to compute the variable LOG2N.

One way of describing the functioning of the cyclic reduction algorithm is to consider that each step doubles the number of zeros between the central diagonal and the off-diagonal terms. After log2n steps the off-diagonal terms disappear (become all zero) and we can alter the program to reflect this view to the following:

```
K = 1
WHILE(ANY(A.NE.0.OR.C.NE.0)  THEN
        A = A/B
        C = C/B
        D = D/B
        B = 1-   A*EOSHIFT(C,1,-K)-  C*EOSHIFT(A,1,K)
        D = D-   A*EOSHIFT(D,1,-K)-  C*EOSHIFT(D,1,K)
        A =      A*EOSHIFT(A,1,-K)
        C =                          C*EOSHIFT(C,1,K)
        K = 2*K
ENDWHILE
```

As Hockney and Jesshope point out one can, if the equations are diagonally dominant, consider replacing the tests versus zero with a test versus some tolerance factor. The code we have produced has a more surprising property when we realize that there is no explicit reference to the number of equations being solved! At first glance this may seem to be a minor quirk with no great significance, but it hides an observation of much greater significance.

The code that we now have will not only solve one tri-diagonal system it will solve any number of tri-diagonal systems of any combination of lengths, and the number of times that the loop will be traversed is given by the logarithm of the size of largest system in the set!

Although we originally set out to write an algorithm to solve a single instance of our problem we have developed an algorithm which solves multiple instances of the same problem. An algorithm with this property is a SUPER PARALLEL algorithm.

A given tri-diagonal system is defined by the four linear data structures a,b,c and d. A set of tri-diagonals is usually considered to be defined by sets of these data structures. We can however concatenate all of these small sets into a grand set; typically, in diagrammatic notation, we would have a matrix of the following structure:

This structure has an overall tri-diagonal structure but does in fact define three distinctly separate tri-diagonal systems with 5,6 and 4 elements respectively. Applying the general algorithm to the above grand matrix solves the 3 subsets after the loop has been traversed three times.

At first glance the result may seem like magic, but a little thought shows that we should have expected the effect. It is well known that the first step of the cyclic reduction algorithm splits the input problem of solving a system of N equations into two separate systems of about N/2 equations, one set of equations connecting the even numbered unknowns and the other system connecting the odd numbered unknowns. The parallel cyclic reduction algorithm does not exploit this reduction but solves the two distinct sets simultaneously. It is therefore no great surprise that the algorithm handles multiple sets of equations.

One advantage of the above approach comes from the observation that tri-diagonal systems seldom occur in single sets but occur naturally in multiples Solving multi- dimensional partial differential equations by ADI methods naturally gives rise to sets of tri-diagonal systems.

5.4 OTHER EXAMPLES OF SUPER PARALLEL ALGORITHMS

It is not difficult to find other examples of Super Parallel examples; most recursive doubling type of operations are ideal candidates. Hence we can use the above methods to solve sets of recurrence relations of the type $x_i = a_i x_i \text{-} 1 + b_i$, $x_i = (a_i x_i \text{-} 1 + b_i)/(c_i x_i \text{-} 1 + d_i)$

The characteristic of these types of operations that we are exploiting is the self- contained nature of the definition, or the possibility of defining the boundary conditions as part of the problem.

Consider the case of first order recurrence relations. One can consider the equations as either a set of relations $x_i = a_i x_i \text{-} 1 + b_i$, $i = 1.....n$ with x_0 specified, or as a set of relations $x_i = a_i x_i \text{-} 1 + b_i$, $i = 0......n$ with $a_1 = 0, b_1 = x_0$. This second approach is better for parallel processing.

Those super parallel algorithms that we have so far discovered exploit the fact that there is some data structure in the problem which can be used to control the operations. Although there are algorithms which have the recursive doubling structure, they do not have such a control data structure. An example is the FFT algorithm. Although the FFT algorithm functions by splitting the problem of computing an N point FFT into two disjoint problems of size N/2, there does not appear to be a variable which would allow us to easily extend the algorithm to have the super parallel property.

REFERENCES

1 Gentleman, W. M. (1987) Some complexity results for matrix computations on parallel processors. *JACM* 25 112-115.

2 Hockney, R. W. and Jesshope, C. R. (1988) *Parallel Computers 2* Adam Hilger.

6 Strategies for developing algorithms for massively parallel machines

S. Zenios *

University of Pennsylvania

6.1 INTRODUCTION

Over the last several years parallel computing has emerged as the only viable approach for the solution of very large problems that appear in several areas of applications: engineering, social and physical sciences, economics, operations research and so on.

Among the several designs for parallel computing architectures, massively parallel systems (like for example the Connection Machine) stand out. They seem to offer the highest potential for significant speedup factors − even if it has not yet been realized in several applications − together with the intellectual challenge for developing the required algorithms.

A discipline that stands to gain significantly from massively parallel computers is operations research with its numerous applications in engineering design, economic planning, financial modeling, transportation and so on. Progress has already been made is several important problem areas, utilizing parallel systems like the Connection Machine or the DAP. For example, on the Connection Machine we have the work of Goldberg[Goldberg87] on max-flow problems, Gerasch and Weidman[GW88] and Gerasch et al.[GWW89] on 0/1 knapsack problems, Zenios and Lasken on nonlinear networks[ZL88] , Phillips and Zenios on assignment problems[PZ89] , Wein[Wein88] on min-cost network flow problems, Zenios on

* Research partially supported by NSF grant CCR-8811135 and AFOSR 89-0145. Computing facilities were made available through ACRF Argonne National Laboratory, CRAY Research Inc., and the NPAC Centre at Syracuse University.

matrix balancing problems[Zenios88a] and Censor and Zenios on interval constrained matrix balancing [CZ89] . On the DAP we have seen the work of Frize *et al.* [FYHP89] on assignment problems and Yadegar *et al.* [YPFH89] on shortest path problems. The results have been quite impressive in several of these applications although not for all. Difficulties appear either due to the lack of adequate data structure for the parallel implementation or by algorithms that, while exhibiting high degree of parallelism at the initial stages, execute only sequentially towards the end.

In this report we discuss strategies for implementing algorithms for graph-based problems on a Connection Machine. We draw from our experiences with some diverse problem areas — assignment problems, nonlinear networks and entropy optimization problems — to develop data structure for both sparse and dense implementations of network problems. We also report on computational experiences with all the problem classes on a Connection Machine CM−2 and offer some comparisons with the performance of similar algorithms on vector supercomputers.

The rest of this paper is organized as follows: section 6.2 provides a brief description of the environment of the Connection Machine. Section 6.3 introduces data structures for three kinds of network problems: dense transportation problems, sparse transportation problems and sparse transhipment problems. Section 6.4 summarizes the results with three classes of optimization problems: assignment problems, matrix balancing problems and nonlinear network problems. Some conclusions are provided in the final section 6.5.

6.2 THE CONNECTION MACHINE ENVIRONMENT

In this section we introduce the characteristics of the Connection Machine that are relevant to the parallel algorithms of subsequent sections. Further details on the architecture of the CM can be found in Hillis [Hillis85] and system documentation. Key aspects of the programming languages C* and C/Paris that are relevant to our work are discussed briefly.

6.2.1 The Connection Machine system

The basic component of the CM is an integrated circuit with sixteen processing elements (PE) and a router that handles general communication. A fully configured

CM includes 4096 chips for a total of 65536 PE. The 4096 chips are wired together as a 12-dimensional hypercube. That is, assuming the chips are assigned addresses from 0 to 4095, two chips are connected by a wire if and only if the binary representation of their addresses differ in exactly one bit. Each processor is equipped with local memory: 512 bytes with each PE for model CM-1 and 8Kbytes for model CM-2. In the former model processors are bit-serial while in the later a floating point accelerator for each cluster of 32 PE handles floating point arithmetic.

The Connection Machine is attached to a front end sequential processor which holds the programs and executes any sequential segments of code. Operations by the PE are under the control of a microcontroller that broadcasts instructions simultaneously to all the elements for execution. A flag register at every PE allows for no-operations; i.e., an instruction received from the microcontroller is executed if the flag is set 1 and ignored otherwise. Input/output operations can be handled either through the front end computer or via a high performance I/O bus with transfer rate 500 Mbits/second. Since local memories are in the address space of the front end it is possible to load and read data one at a time. For large amount of data this is impractical. The front end can instruct the PE to load local memories directly from the disk via the bus. Figure 6.1 illustrates the overall organization of the CM.

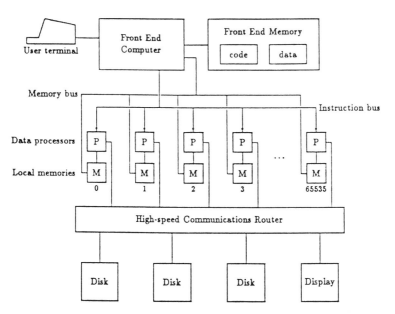

Figure 6.1 Organization of the Connection Machine.

Parallel computations on the CM are in the form of a single operation executed on multiple copies of the problem data. The machine is an SIMD (Single Instruction stream, Multiple Data stream) computer. All processors execute identical operations, each one operating on the data stored in its local memory, possibly accessing data residing in the memory of other PE or receiving data from the front end. This mode of computation is termed data level parallelism in contradistinction to control level parallelism whereby multiple processors execute their own control sequence, operating either on local or shared data. The later paradigm is adopted in MIMD computers (Multiple Instruction stream, Multiple Data stream). If the instructions of the control sequence are independent they can be scheduled for execution on multiple processors of an MIMD system. On the other hand if large amounts of data are also independent then operations on these data can be carried out in parallel by multiple simple processors. This form of parallelism was introduced by Hillis [Hillis85] and the CM is the first hardware realization of a data level parallel computer.

To achieve high performance with data level parallelism one needs a large number of processors that could operate on the multiple copies of data concurrently. While the full configuration of the CM has 65536 PE this number is not large enough for several applications. For example, in balancing matrices of dimension 512 x 512 we need over 260K processors. Solving discretized image reconstruction problems of size 1024 x 1024 pixels we need over 1M processors. The CM provides the mechanism of virtual processors (VP) that allows on PE to operate in a serial fashion on multiple copies of data. This is equivalent to having multiple PE each operating on their own copy of the data. VP are specified by slicing the local memory into equal segments and allowing the physical PE to loop over all slices. The number of segments is called the VP ratio (i.e., ratio of virtual to physical PE). Looping by the PE over all the memory slices is executed, in the worst case, in linear time. The set of virtual processors associated with each element of a data set is called a VP set. VP sets are under the control of the software and are mapped onto the underlying CM hardware in a way that is transparent to the user.

6.2.2 Communications

The CM supports two addressing mechanisms for communication. The send address is used for general purpose communications via the routers. The NEWS address describes the position of a VP in an n-dimensional grid that optimizes communication performance.

The send address indicates the location of the PE (hypercube address) that supports a specific VP and the relative address of the VP in the VP set that is currently active. NEWS address is an n-tuple of coordinates which specifies the relative position of a VP in an n-dimensional Cartesian-grid geometry. A geometry (defined by the software) is an abstract description of such an n-dimensional grid. Once a geometry is associated with the currently active VP set a relative addressing mechanism is established among the processors in the VP set. Each processor has a relative position in the n-dimensional geometry and NEWS allows the communication across the North, East, West and South neighbours of each processor, and enables the execution of operations along the axes of the geometry. Such operations are efficient since the n-dimensional geometry can be mapped onto the underlying hypercube in such a way that adjacent VP are mapped onto vertices of the hypercube connected with a direct link. This mapping of an n-dimensional mesh on a hypercube is achieved through a Gray coding.

Finally we mention that it is possible to communicate among processors in different VP sets. This can be achieved by translating the relative address of the processors from the NEWS coordinates in the two sets into send addresses and then routing the messages through the hypercube. In general, however, communication along send addresses is expensive and computations should be structured, if possible, around a NEWS grid.

6.2.3 Elements of the C* Programming Language

The C* programming language is an extension to C++ of Stroustrup [Stroustrup86]. It was designed for the CM in order to support data level parallelism at a high-level of abstraction. A reference for the language is C* Reference Manual (1988). The abstract machine model upon which C* is designed assumes a large number of processors each capable of running a C++ program. Each processor has its own local address memory. C* supports pointers much in the same spirit of C with a subtle extension that is the key to parallelism: a processor can, through indirection, access any part of memory. This mechanism enables communication between the processors in arbitrary patterns (although communication along, for example, a mesh are much more efficient). Finally C* assumes a synchronous model of computation. All instructions are issued from a single source (a distinguished processor called the front end). Remaining processors are called data processors and operate under instructions from the front end. Three new language features allow for parallel computations:

1. two new data type attributes poly and mono;

2. an extension to the concept of a class called domain ;

3. a selection statement for the activation of multiple processors.

A poly data type attribute is used for data that can be processed in parallel. Data declared poly reside on the memories of the data processors. Mono data types reside on the front end. In general poly data are operated upon by the data processors while mono data are operated upon by the front end. Since, however, the abstract machine model assumes a uniform address space it is possible for the front end to operate serially on poly data. Data processors can also operate on a mono datum, if the front end broadcasts a copy to each. The mono and poly attributes apply to pointers as well, and can be used for interprocessor communication. Poly and mono data attributes do not play a significant role in the work reported here, and we skip additional details.

The second feature that supports parallelism is that of a domain. A domain is an extension of the concept of a class in C + + (in turn an extension of a structure in C). A domain groups together a set of data objects and functions. Each instance of a domain can be viewed as a small program with its own data set (member variables) and code (member functions). The key extension of domain over classes is that multiple instances of a domain reside on the data processors with identical memory layout. This implies that each processor can execute the instructions of a member function to its member variables.

The third extension of C* is that of a selection, used to activate multiple instances of a domain. In effect what is activated are the VP where the selected domain instances are stored. Conditional statements can be used to reduce the set of active processors. With this done a member function of the active domain can be applied in parallel to member variables. Operations on member variables are not restricted only to member functions and are executed in parallel. In the terminology introduced earlier member variables are poly. The notion of domains and selection statements is central in the C* implementation of RAS discussed later in this paper.

A number of rules resolve issues of contention and guarantee correctness of results when multiple processors have to communicate. For example, how are poly variables combined with mono variables in a reduction operation? The C* model enforces an as-if-serial rule that enforces a parallel operator to be executed as if in some serial order. This rule removes the burden from the programmer to explicitly code synchronization mechanisms and prevent memory contentions.

While the C* paradigm allows us to program the CM at a high-level of abstraction it has a severe drawback. Due to the requirement for uniform address space and arbitrary interprocessor communication the language is unable to take advantage of the efficient communication patterns along the NEWS network. Instances of a domain are not necessarily laid out in a pattern that optimizes communications. Any indirect addressing among processors (i.e., communications) takes place through the more general, but less efficient, send address mechanism. A set of macros — the GRID package explained in Supplement to C* Manual (1988) — allows programmers to layout instances of domain on a NEWS grid. At this point, however, one may wish to write directly at the low-level instruction set Paris, which we introduce next.

6.2.4   Elements of the parallel instruction set Paris

Paris is the lowest level protocol by which the actions of the data processors of the CM are controlled by the front end. It is intended primarily as the base upon which higher-level languages can be built and provides the most efficient mechanism for developing programs for the CM. Interfaces with languages like C, Fortran or Lisp allow users to develop a program in the language of their choice and then use Paris instructions to control the execution of parallel operations. Paris supports operations on signed, unsigned and floating-point numbers, message passing operations both along send and NEWS addresses and mechanisms for transferring data between the host and the data processors.

Before invoking Paris instructions from a program the user has to specify the VP set, create a geometry and associate the VP set with the geometry. Thus a communications mechanism is established (both along send and NEWS addresses). Paris instructions — parallel primitives — can then be invoked to execute operations along some axis of the geometry (using NEWS addresses), operate on an individual processor using send addresses, or to translate NEWS to send addresses for general interprocessor communication or communication with the front end. Parallel primitives that are relevant to our implementation are scans and spreads. Blelloch [Blelloch87] provides details on these, and other, primitives of the CM.

Scan is also known in the literature as parallel prefix. The $\otimes$-scan primitive, for associative, binary operator $\otimes$ takes a sequence $\{x_0, x_1, ..., x_n\}$ and produces another sequence $\{y_0, y_1, ..., y_n\}$ such that $y_i = x_0 \otimes x_1 \otimes ... \otimes x_i$. On the Connection Machine, for example, add-scan takes as an argument a parallel variable (i.e., a variable with its i-th element residing in a memory field of the i-th VP) and returns at VP i the value of the parallel variable summed over $j = 0, i$. User options allow the scan to apply only to preceding processors (e.g. sum from $j = 0, ..., i-1$) or to perform the scan in reverse. The $\otimes$-spread primitive, for associative, binary operator $\otimes$ takes a sequence $\{x_0, x_1, ... x_n\}$ and produces another sequence $\{y_0, y_1,..., y_n\}$ such that $y_i = x_0 \otimes x_1 \otimes ... \otimes x_n$. For example, add-spread takes as an argument a parallel variable residing at the memory of n active data processors and returns at VP i the value of the parallel variable summed over $j = 0, n$. An add-spread is equivalent to an add-scan followed by a copy-scan in the opposite direction. Spreads, however, are significantly more efficient than the combined add- and copy-scans.

Another variation of the scan primitives allows their operation within segments of a parallel variable or VP. These primitives are denoted as segmented-$\otimes$-scan. They take as arguments a parallel variable and a set of segment bits which specify a partitioning of the VP set into contiguous segments. Segment bits have a 1 at the starting location of a new segment and a 0 elsewhere. A segmented-$\otimes$-scan operation re-starts at the beginning of every segment. Figure 6.2 illustrates the use of segmented-add-scan and segmented-copy-scan on a small example. When processors are configured as a NEWS grid, scans within rows or columns are special cases of segmented scans called grid-scans. Because the communication pattern needed to perform the calculations can be predetermined, grid-scans use the hypercube wires directly, bypassing the router.

Processing Element	= [	0	1	2	3	4	5	6	7	8	9	]
X	= [	5	1	3	4	3	9	2	6	1	0	]
Segment Bits (Sb)	= [	1	0	1	0	0	0	1	0	0	1	]
Y = add-scan (X,Sb)	= [	0	5	6	3	7	10	19	2	8	9	]
copy-scan (Y,Sb)	= [	0	0	0	6	6	6	6	19	19	19	]
reverse-copy-scan (Y,Sb)	= [	6	6	19	19	19	19	9	9	9	9	]

Figure 6.2 The segmented add-scan and copy-scan primitives.

6.3   DATA STRUCTURE DESIGNS FOR NETWORK PROBLEMS

We now discuss the mapping of several network problems on the CM. We start with the case of dense assignment problems which have a natural mapping on a NEWS grid. We proceed with the more challenging representation of sparse transportation problems and conclude with representation of sparse transhipment problems of arbitrary topologies. Our discussion essentially explains how to map the nodes and edges of a graph to the underlying configuration of processing elements. The representation, however, of a network problem is not quite complete until we specify the data that are stored at every processor. To complete this specification we would have to examine the operations of the underlying algorithm and this discussion goes beyond the scope of this paper. Once we describe the representation of the graph we point readers to published references that use the graph representation to execute certain numerical optimization algorithms. Additional information is provided in section 6.4. However, readers that are not familiar with developments of parallel numerical optimization may find the details of the implementation inadequate and are referred to the cited publications or the survey article by Zenios[Zenios89a] .

6.3.1   Dense transportation problems

Dense transportation problems have a very natural mapping on a CM configured as an nxn NEWS grid, where n is the number of origin nodes or, equivalently, the number of destination nodes rounded up to the closest integer that is a power of 2. Processor with NEWS coordinates (i,j) represents the corresponding edge of the graph. It holds data both for the from − and the to-node of the edge as well as data for the edge itself. It also holds pointers that identify the processor by the origin node i and the destination node j.

6.3.2   Sparse transportation graphs

To represent sparse problems the CM is configured as a one-dimensional NEWS grid. Every VP on this grid operates only on the existing edges of the underlying graph, thus preserving sparsity. We store edges twice: once by the from-node (or tail) and once by to-node (or head). This format allows simultaneous operations on both origin and destination nodes of the graph and the efficient comunication between nodes that are connected via an edge. This scheme has some redundancy, but allows the efficient use of segmented-scan operations along the axis of the NEWS grid.

Figure 6.3 illustrates the sparse representation of a small transportation network. The problem is represented as a sparse matrix on the top of the figure: rows of the matrix represent origin nodes and columns represent destination nodes. The non-zero entries of the matrix correspond to the edges that exist in the network. The memory fields allocated to each VP in order to represent the problem are described below. Since a bipartite (transportation) graph can be represented as a matrix of dimension number of origin nodes x number of destination nodes in our discussion we refer to nodes as rows and columns of the matrix and edges as entries of the matrix.

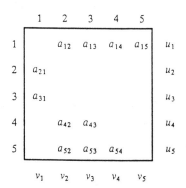

NEWS address

of VP	1	2	3	4	5	6	7	8	9	10	11	12
S–ROW	1	0	0	0	1	1	1	0	1	0	0	1
A–ROW	a_{12}	a_{13}	a_{14}	a_{15}	a_{21}	a_{31}	a_{42}	a_{43}	a_{52}	a_{53}	a_{54}	
R–TOTAL	u_1	u_1	u_1	u_1	u_2	u_3	u_4	u_4	u_5	u_5	u_5	
P–ROW	3	6	9	11	1	2	4	7	5	8	10	
P–COL	5	6	1	7	9	2	8	10	3	11	4	
C–TOTAL	v_1	v_1	v_2	v_2	v_2	v_3	v_3	v_3	v_4	v_4	v_5	
A–COL	a_{21}	a_{31}	a_{12}	a_{42}	a_{52}	a_{13}	a_{43}	a_{53}	a_{14}	a_{54}	a_{15}	
S–COL	1	0	1	0	0	1	0	0	1	0	1	1

Figure 6.3 Representation of a sparse transportation network.

1. A 1-bit field s-row of segment bits. It is used to delimit the VP set into segments such that VP in the same segment correspond to entries of the same row.

2. A 32-bit field a-row that holds the value of the entry a_{ij} . The matrix entries are allocated row-wise: entries of the same row belong to the same segment as indicated by s-row.

3. A 32-bit field r-total holds the row total values u_i. All VP that correspond to the same row (i.e., are in the same segment as delimited by s-row) hold identical values in this field.

4. A second 1-bit field of segment bits s-col arranges the VP set into segments, such that VP in the same segment correspond to entries of the same column.

5. A 32-bit field a-col holds the value of the entry a_ ij in column-wise order. This field provides redundant information, since the non-zero entries have already been stored row-wise in field a-row.

6. A 32-bit field c-total holds the column total values v_j. All VP that correspond to the same column (i.e., are in the same segment as delimited by s-col) hold identical values in this field.

7. A 32-bit field scale holds temporarily the scaling factors for each row or column.

8. Two 16-bit fields p-row and p-col hold pointers to map the non-zero entries from the row-wise field a-row to the column-wise field a-col and *vice versa*.

6.3.3 Sparse transhipment graphs

The representation of sparse transhipment problems is a generalization of the sparse transportation structure introduced above. Again each arc is represented twice — one by from- and once by to-node — in order to allow grouping of arcs into segments by node and to allow for efficient communication between nodes.

Figure 6.4 shows the representation of a small sparse network. Every arc in the network is associated with two processing elements (PH_{ij} and PT_{ij}) where PH and PT indicate processors at the head and tail of an arc repectively and the subscript indicates arc $(i,j) \in \varepsilon$. Processors corresponding to a node i are designated as a segment defined by $SEG_i = \{PT_{ij} , PH_{ki} \ \forall \ (i,j)$ and $(k,i) \in \varepsilon \}$.

The data stored at each processor PH_{ij} and PT_{ij} include:

1. Arc data like upper and lower bounds, the flow of the edges and the objective function coefficients.

2. Dual variables at the nodes at both ends of the arc: π_i and π_j,

3. The address of the processor at the other end of the arc; PH_{ij} stores the address of PT_{ij} and vice versa.

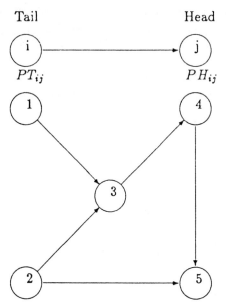

Processor (P)	Address $ad(P)$	Data Stored Locally
PT_{13}	0000	$ad(PH_{13})$, d_1, π_1, π_3 and data for arc $(1,3)$
PH_{13}	0011	$ad(PT_{13})$, d_3, π_1, π_3 and data for arc $(1,3)$
PT_{23}	0001	$ad(PH_{23})$, d_2, π_2, π_3 and data for arc $(2,3)$
PH_{23}	0100	$ad(PT_{23})$, d_3, π_2, π_3 and data for arc $(2,3)$
PT_{25}	0010	$ad(PH_{25})$, d_2, π_2, π_5 and data for arc $(2,5)$
PH_{25}	1000	$ad(PT_{25})$, d_5, π_2, π_5 and data for arc $(2,5)$
PT_{34}	0101	$ad(PH_{34})$, d_3, π_3, π_4 and data for arc $(3,4)$
PH_{34}	0110	$ad(PT_{34})$, d_4, π_3, π_4 and data for arc $(3,4)$
PT_{45}	0111	$ad(PH_{45})$, d_4, π_4, π_5 and data for arc $(4,5)$
PH_{45}	1001	$ad(PT_{45})$, d_5, π_4, π_5 and data for arc $(4,5)$

$SEG_1 = \{PT_{13}\}$ $SEG_2 = \{PT_{23},\ PT_{25}\}$
$SEG_3 = \{PH_{13},\ PH_{23},\ PT_{34}\}$ $SEG_4 = \{PH_{34},\ PT_{45}\}$
$SEG_5 = \{PH_{25},\ PH_{45}\}$

Figure 6.4 Representation of sparse network problems.

6.4 NUMERICAL OPTIMIZATION EXPERIENCES

In this section we report numerical experiences with three classes of optimization problems: linear assignment problems, entropy maximization problems from matrix balancing and nonlinear network problems. The algorithms illustrate the use of the data structure for the three types of graphs introduced in section 6.3. The assignment problems are solved using the dense representation of transportation graphs, the matrix balancing algorithm is implemented using sparse transportation data and the nonlinear network algorithm is executed on a sparse transhipment graph.

6.4.1 Assignment problems

We implemented the auction algorithm for assignment problems due to Bertsekas[Bertsekas88] Readers are referred to Phillips and Zenios[PZ89] for a detailed discussion of the algorithm and its parallel implementation. In a globally optimal solution to the assignment problem any given person may not be assigned to the object which is most valuable to him. For any optimal assignment it is possible to assign to each object j a price π_j such that if each person i views the profit of being assigned to object j as $v_{ij} - \pi_j$, then every person is assigned to the most profitable object. An assignment is ε-optimal if each person is assigned to an object that is no more than ε less profitable than its most profitable object.

The auction algorithm is performed as follows. We start with $\varepsilon = \max_{i,j} v_{ij}$ and find an ε-optimal assignment. Keeping the prices π generated in that round, we reduce ε and find a new assignment optimal for that ε, and so on until $\varepsilon > 1/n$ where n is the number of people. At this point the assignment is optimal. In practice we scale all values by $n+1$ to allow integer calculations. Each inner loop (finding an ε-optimal assignment) can be viewed as an auction where all currently unassigned people bid on the most profitable object, the price of the object is raised to the highest bid and the object is temporarily assigned to the highest bidder. The auction algorithm is defined as follows:

Step 0: We keep a copy of in each processor. Using a global max operation and a broadcast, set $\varepsilon \leftarrow (n+1)*\max(v)$. In each processor set $\pi \leftarrow 0$ and assigned-here $\leftarrow$ False. We keep another Boolean variable person-assigned which is True in all processors of row i if person i is assigned to an object. Set person-assigned $\leftarrow$ False. Also scale all values of v by $n+1$.

Step 1: Determine if everyone is assigned (global or of the person-assigned variable). If a person is unassigned proceed to Step 2. If every person is assigned to an object and $\varepsilon \leq 1$ the algorithm terminates. If $\varepsilon > 1$ reduce its value, unassign everyone whose current assignment is no longer ε-optimal for the new and proceed to Step 2.

Step 2: Select processors associated with unassigned people. Set profit $\leftarrow v - \pi$. Within each row i find the column index j_i of the most profitable object: form the concatenation of the profit and column number in each processor and do a grid max-scan. Set best $\leftarrow j_i$. Turning off processor (i, best) use grid scan to find the profit p of the next best object and set next-best $\leftarrow$ p. Person i bids on object best by setting the variable bid in processor (i,best). The value of the bid is computed as follows: Let $w_{(i,best)}$ be the maximum profit from all objects except best. The bid from i to best is $v_{(i,best)} - w_{(i,best)} + \varepsilon$.

Step 3: Using a max grid-scan within all columns, determine the maximum price bid on each object and update the prices π within the columns. For all objects bid upon, assign the object to the highest bidder by setting the assigned-here variable. Update the person-assigned variable using or grid-scans within the rows. Go to step 1.

At the start of each auction with a new ε, many people bid simultaneously, but the number of people bidding decreases monotonically during the auction. In our implementation we use an ε-scaling heuristic to reduce the tail-effect. For a given value of ε the auction terminates when k% people have been matched. k increases as ε decreases until k = 100% when $\varepsilon < 1$. ε is decreasing from its initial large value to less than 1 by dividing after each iteration by a parameter ndecr.

The auction algorithm, implemented in *LISP, was used to solve the assignment test problems shown in the Appendix. Table 6.1 summarizes the performance of the algorithm. All runs were performed on a CM-2 with 16K processors running at 6.69 MHz clock cycle. The solution time will improve by a factor of 3 with the use of a 64K machine. The estimated solution time on a 64K machine is summarized in the last column of the table.

Table 6.1 Solution of assignment problems (CM sec)

| Problem | CM time | Best CM time | | VP | CM time |
| | | | | ratio | Estimate |
	ndecr $=2, k=.9$	CM time	ndecr/k		on 64K CM
ASSIGN1	108.48	28.60	5/0.80	64	9.1
ASSIGN1a	53.88	33.77	5/0.80	64	10.7
ASSIGN1b	52.90	36.92	2/0.80	64	11.7
ASSIGN1c	223.08	76.25	2/0.95	64	24.1
ASSIGN1d	43.87	43.87	2/0.90	64	13.8
ASSIGN2	16.16	10.57	2/0.80	16	3.3

6.4.2   Matrix balancing problems

The matrix balancing problem we are interested in can be defined as follows. Given an $m \times n$ non-negative matrix A and positive vectors u and v of dimensions m and n, respectively, determine a nearby non-negative matrix X (of the same dimensions) that satisfies:

$$\sum_{j=1}^{n} x_{ij} = u_i, \text{ for } i = 1, 2, \ldots, m,$$

$$\sum_{i=1}^{m} x_{ij} = v_j, \text{ for } j = 1, 2, \ldots, n,$$

and $x_{ij} > 0$ only if $a_{ij} > 0$.

One of the earlier algorithms for solving MB problems is RAS that dates back to the Russian architect Sheleikhovskii in the 1930s. See Schneider and Zenios[SZ86] for a discussion of RAS-related literature and a classification of MB applications.

6.4.3   The RAS Algorithm

The algorithm is formally defined as:

The RAS Algorithm

Step 0: (Initialization) Set $k = 0$ and $A^0 = A$.

Step 1: (Row Scaling) For $i = 1, 2, ..., m$ define

$$\rho_i^k = \frac{u_i}{\sum_j a_{ij}^k},$$

and update A^k by

$$a_{ij}^{k+1} = a_{ij}^k \sigma_j^k, \; i = 1, 2, \ldots, m \quad \text{and} \quad j = 1, 2, \ldots n.$$

Step 2: (Column Scaling) For $j = 1, 2, ..., n$ define

$$\sigma_j^k = \frac{v_j}{\sum_i a_{ij}^k},$$

and define A^{k+1} by

$$a_{ij}^k \leftarrow \rho_i^k a_{ij}^k, \; i = 1, 2, \ldots, m \quad \text{and } j = 1, 2, \ldots n.$$

Step 3: Replace $k \leftarrow k + 1$, and return to Step 1.

The algorithm terminates either after a maximum number of iterations has been reached or when the maximum row and column error is reduced below some acceptable tolerance. The error at iteration k is computed by:

$$\max_{i,j} \left\{ \frac{\left| u_i - \sum_j a_{ij}^k \right|}{u_i}, \frac{\left| v_j - \sum_i a_{ij}^k \right|}{v_j} \right\}.$$

Using the sparse representation of the transportation problems we can implement RAS in C/Paris as shown in Fig. 6.5. First the permutation arrays p-row and p-col — that are pointers to the NEWS addresses — are translated into send addresses. This allows transferring of data between the row and column representation using the routers. A segmented-add-scan operation on field a-row (over the row segments) computes the sum of the entries in each row. This partial sum is then used to divide the row total field r-total thus computing the scaling factors. Note that only the last processor in each segment has the sum of all the entries in the row and hence only the scaling factor of the last VP is the correct one. A reverse segmented-copy-scan is used to copy the correct scaling factor to all VP in the same segment. Finally, each VP proceeds to multiply its copy of the matrix value with its local copy of the scaling factor. Thus a complete iteration over all the rows is completed in four Paris steps.

Before the algorithm can proceed with the column scaling the non-zero entries, just scaled following a row operation, have to be copied from the row-wise to the column-wise representation. This is a rearrangement of the contents of the memory field a-row according to the sparsity structure of the matrix. The NEWS addresses stored in the pointer field p-row have already been converted into send addresses and router communications are used to copy the non-zero entries of the matrix from the row field a-row to the column field a-col. The algorithm then proceeds with a column scaling, which is identical to the row scaling described above. See Zenios [Zenios88a] for further details and alternative parallel implementations.

The algorithm was tested on the problems shown in the Appendix. Test problems were derived from regional input/output tables. Our source is the National table for the USA for 1977. This set of data consists of the Make and Use matrices, with a classification scheme of over 500 sectors. We are also using a very small problem (STONE) obtained from Byron[Byron78].

```
/* Get send address coordinates for permutation arrays */

CM_deposit_news_coordinate_1L (vec_geometry          , send_row          ,
                        vec_axis_news[axis]      , p_row     , LINT  );

CM_deposit_news_coordinate_1L (vec_geometry          , send_col          ,
                        vec_axis_news[axis]      , p_col     , LINT  );


/* ROW SCALING */

CM_scan_with_f_add_1L(scale          , a_row          , axis_news[axis]  ,
                    S_REAL        , E_REAL        , CM_upward        ,
                    CM_inclusive, CM_start_bit, as_head              );

CM_f_divinto_2_1L    (scale          , r_total        , S_REAL , E_REAL );

CM_scan_with_copy_1L (scale          , scale          , axis_news[axis]  ,
                    REAL          , CM_downward , CM_inclusive       ,
                    CM_start_bit, cs_head                            );

CM_f_multiply_2_1L   (a_row          , scale          , S_REAL , E_REAL );

/* Copy matrix values from row to column representation   */

CM_send_1L           (a_col          , send_row       , a_row  , REAL , 0);


/* COLUMN SCALING */

CM_scan_with_f_add_1L(scale          , a_col          , axis_news[axis]  ,
                    S_REAL        , E_REAL        , CM_upward        ,
                    CM_inclusive, CM_start_bit, as_tail              );

CM_f_divinto_2_1L    (scale          , c_total        , S_REAL , E_REAL );

CM_scan_with_copy_1L (scale          , scale          , axis_news[axis]  ,
                    REAL          , CM_downward , CM_inclusive       ,
                    CM_start_bit, cs_tail                            );

CM_f_multiply_2_1L   (a_col          , scale          , S_REAL , E_REAL );

/* Copy matrix values from column to row representation   */

CM_send_1L           (a_row          , send_col       , a_col  , REAL , 0);
```

Figure 6.5 C/Paris sparse implementation of RAS.

The results are summarized in Table 6.2. The CM time is more than 99% of the total solution time. Communications is a significant part of this implementation, accounting for as much as 50% of the CM time. The results in Table 6.3 show the time spent in communication.

Table 6.2 Performance of sparse implementation of RAS in C/Paris (CM sec)

Problem	Error	No. itns.	CM time 8K CM-2	CM time 16K CM-2	CM time 32K CM-2
STONE	10^{-6}	63	0.59	–	–
USE537	10^{-6}	27	1.33	0.70	0.45
MAKE537	2.5×10^{-4}	300	4.47	3.45	–
MAKE537	10^{-4}	1000	14.69	11.41	–

Table 6.3 Time for communications in sparse C/Paris implementation of RAS (CM sec)

Problem	Error	No. itns.	CM time 8K CM-2	CM time 16K CM-2	CM time 32K CM-2
STONE	10^{-6}	63	0.05	–	–
USE537	10^{-6}	27	0.86	0.35	0.15
MAKE537	10^{-4}	1000	5.22	2.36	–

6.4.4 Solution of nonlinear network problems

A relaxation algorithm for strictly convex network problems proposed by Bertsekas, Hossein and Tseng[BHT87] was shown by Bertsekas and El Baz[BB87] and Zenios and Mulvey[ZM88] to be well suited for massively parallel computations. Zenios and Lasken[ZL88] provide the first study of the algorithm on massively parallel hardware (the CM-1). Using the sparse representation of section 6.3.3 and the segmented-scan operations one iteration of the algorithm can be executed as follows:

Step 0: Choose starting prices $\{\pi^0 = \pi_1^0, \pi_2^0, ..., \pi_n^0\}$ (Fix one price to zero).

Step 1: Compute values of x_{ij} satisfying complementary slackness conditions:

$$x_{ij} = u_{ij} \quad \text{if} \quad \pi_i - \pi_j > \frac{\partial f_{ij}(x_{ij})}{\partial x_{ij}} \Big|_{x_{ij}=u_{ij}} \tag{1}$$

$$x_{ij} = l_{ij} \quad \text{if} \quad \pi_i - \pi_j < \frac{\partial f_{ij}(x_{ij})}{\partial x_{ij}} \Big|_{x_{ij}=l_{ij}} \tag{2}$$

$$x_{ij} = \hat{x}_{ij} \quad \text{if} \quad \pi_i - \pi_j = \frac{\partial f_{ij}(x_{ij})}{\partial x_{ij}} \Big|_{x_{ij}=\hat{x}_{ij}} \text{ for } l_{ij} < \hat{x}_{ij} < u_{ij}. \tag{3}$$

This calculation is executed concurrently for all arcs $(i,j) \in \varepsilon$, PH_{ij} and PT_{ij} compute identical values for x_{ij}. Perform a Segmented-Plus-Scan operation over the flows of all processors to compute the deficit at all nodes, defined by

$$d_i = \sum_{(i,j)\in\varepsilon} x_{ij} - \sum_{(k,i)\in\varepsilon} x_{ki}$$

If the maximum deficit is less than some tolerance the algorithm terminates.

Step 2: The dual variable for all nodes is adjusted such that the flows corresponding to complementary slackness conditions result to zero deficit. This step is performed concurrently for all nodes by the underline last processor in every segment. (After the Segmented-Plus-Scan at Step 1 only the last processor in a segment has the correct value of the deficit.) A Segmented -Reverse-Copy-Scan operation copies the dual price to all processors in a segment. Finally each processor broadcasts its dual value to the processor at the other end of the arc using a *PSet operation. Return to Step 1.

This algorithm run on a CM−1 and a CM−2 using the test problems of the Appendix. The same test problems were solved using the primal truncated Newton algorithm of Ahlfeld *et al.* [ADMZ87] on an IBM 3081−D, an IBM 3090--600/VF and an Alliant FX/8 . On the last two machines significant effort went into modifying the software to take advantage both of the vector and parallel features of the hardware. Figure 6.6 summarizes the results.

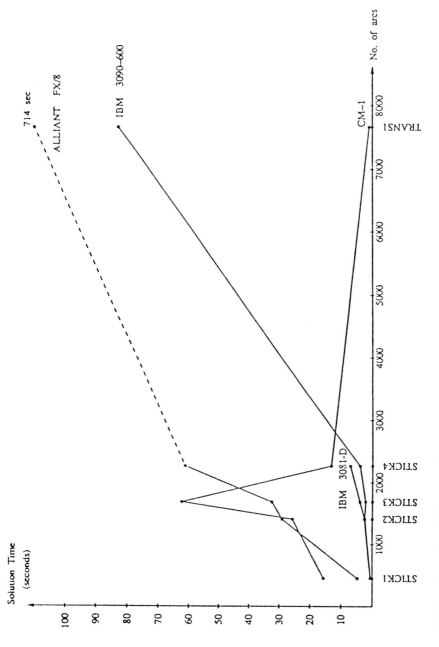

Figure 6.6 Benchmarks with the solution of nonlinear networks.

6.5   CONCLUSIONS

In this paper we have described several strategies for the implementation of graph-based algorithms on massively parallel computers of the SIMD type. Computational results are very encouraging, especially for the nonlinear problems (matrix balancing and network optimization). It appears that the combinatorial nature of the assignment problem is a source of inefficiency in the parallel implementation. An algorithm that is apparently ideal for massive parallelism is executed almost sequentially for a significant part of the computation. It is also very encouraging to observe that the sparse implementation is only marginally inferior to the dense implementation — at least for the problems presented here. SIMD architectures have been criticized for a lack of flexibility. This has not been the case with the problems we have been addressing so far.

APPENDIX A :   TEST PROBLEMS

ASSIGN1	2000	10^6	Cost range $1-10$
ASSIGN1a	2000	10^6	Cost range $1-10$
ASSIGN1b	2000	10^6	Cost range $1-100$
ASSIGN1c	2000	10^6	Cost range $1-1000$
ASSIGN1d	2000	10^6	Cost range $1-10000$
ASSIGN2	1000	25×10^4	Cost range $1-1000$

Assignment Test Problems

Problem	No. of rows x columns	No. of non-zero entries
STONE	5 x 5	12
USE537	507 x 471	50000
MAKE537	490 x 505	9340

Matrix Balancing Test Problems

Problem	Nodes	Arcs	Comments
STICK1	209	454	Stick percolation
STICK2	650	1412	problems from
STICK3	782	1686	Ahlfeld *et al.*[ADMZ87]
STICK4	832	2264	
TRANS1	2500	7668	Randomly generated
			transportation problem

Nonlinear Network Optimization Test Problems

REFERENCES

1. *C*Reference Manual,* Version 4.0A, Thinking Machines Corporation, Cambridge, MA., 1988.

2. *Supplement to C* Reference Manual,* Version 4.3, Thinking Machines Corporation, Cambridge, MA., May 1988.

3. Ahlfeld, D. P. Dembo, R. S. Mulvey, J. M. and Zenios, S. A., (1987) Nonlinear programming on generalized networks. *ACM Trans. on Mathematical Soft.,* 13,4 350 – 368.

4. Bertsekas , D. P. and El Baz, D. (1987) Distributed asynchronous relaxation methods for convex network flow problems. *SIAM J. Control and Optimization,* 25,1   74 – 85.

5. Bertsekas, D.P. (1988) The auction algorithm: a distributed relaxation method for the assignment problem. *Parallel Optimization on Novel Computer Architectures Annals of Operations Research,*   14(eds.)., R.R. Meyer and S.A. Zenios.

6. Bertsekas, D.P. Hossein, P. and Tseng, P. (1987) Relaxation methods for network flow problems with convex arc costs. *SIAM J. Control and Optimization,* 25, 1219 – 1243.

7. Blelloch, G.E. (1987) The scan model of parallel computation. *Proc. Int. Conf. Parallel Processing,* August. 1987.

8. Byron, R. P. (1987) The estimation of large social account matrices. it *J. R. Statistical Society A*, 141, Part 3,359–367.

9. Censor, Y. and Zenios, S.A. (1989) *Interval Constrained Matrix Balancing with Range-RAS*. Working paper, Decision Sciences Department, The Wharton School, University of Pennsylvania, Philadelphia, PA.

10. Frize, A.M. Yadegar, J. El-Horbaty, S. and Parkison, D. (1989 to appear) Algorithms for assignment problems on an array processor. *Parallel Computing*.

11. Gerasch, T.E. Wang, P.Y. and Weidman, S.T. (1989) SIMD knapsack approximation algorithms. *The Impact of Recent Computing Advances on Operations Research*, Elsevier Science Publishing.

12. Gerasch, T.E. and Weidman, S.T. (1988) Massively parallel computing applied to 0/1 knapsack problems. *Supercomputing'88*, International Supercomputing Institute.

13. Goldberg, A. V. (1987) *Efficient Graph Algorithms for Sequential and Parallel Computers*. PhD thesis, Electrical Engineering and Computer Science, Massachusetts Insitute of Technology, Cambridge, MA, February 1987.

14. Hillis, W. D. (1985) The Connection Machine. The MIT Press, Cambridge, Massachusetts.

15. Phillips, C. and Zenios, S.A. (1989) Experiences with large scale network optimization on the connection machine. *The Impact of Recent Computing Advances on Operations Research*, Elsevier Science Publishing.

16. Schneider, M. H. and Zenios, S. A. (1989 to appear) A comparative study of algorithms for matrix estimation. *Operations Research*.

17. Stourstrup, B. (1986) *The C^{++} Programming Language*. Addison-Wesley, Reading, MA.

18. Wein, J. (1988) *Technical Report*, (private communication).

19. Yadegar, J. Parkinson, D. Frize, A.M. and El-Horbaty, S. (1989) Algorithms for shortest path problems on an array processor. *Proc. Int. Conf. Supercomputing' 89*.

20. Zenios, S. A. and Lasken, R. A. (1988) Nonlinear network optimization on a massively parallel Connection Machine. *Annals of Operations Research,* 14,147–165. *Parallel Optimization on Novel Computer Architectures* (eds R.R. Meyer and S.A. Zenios).

21. Zenios, S.A. (1988) *Matrix Balancing on a Massively Parallel Connection Machine.* Report 88–09–04, Decision Sciences Department, The Wharton School, University of Pennsylvania, Philadelphia, PA.

22. Zenios, S.A. (1989) Parallel numerical optimization: current status and an annotated bibliography. *ORSA J. on Computing,* 1,1,20–43.

23. Zenios, S.A. and Mulvey J.M. (1988) A distributed algorithm for convex network optimization problems. *Parallel Computing,* 6,45–56.

7 Distributing computations

T. Lake

GLOSSA

7.1 INTRODUCTION

This paper will include an overview of various distributed computation schemes, but the new material is related to the porting and implementation of serial computations on distributed memory systems. I will show you how data placement can be the key step in moving from a serial to a distributed program. This is still work in progress, and will undoubtedly be subject to change.

I believe that it will be useful to embody some of these ideas in program restructuring software. In advance of this I will at least have given you a means of designing the distribution of your programs and a way or writing out those designs. It would be most useful if we could agree on standard language extensions along the lines that I shall propose, because we could then cooperate on providing the appropriate software tools for the different architectures current today.

Professor Tony Hey of Southampton University recently told us that there was a software crisis in parallel processing. That's not hard to believe, since there is always a software crisis anyway and distributed parallel processing is no easier than serial computing. The essence of the crisis is the lack of tools for expressing computations in a familiar and widely useful way which are at all suitable for implementation on concurrent processors. So this is a problem of computer languages and mechanisms. It makes this seminar very timely indeed.

The applications that I am going to address are the engineering and scientific applications where large mathematical and database computations need to be carried out. Now it may be that the writers of such packages are going to leave their maths and data manipulation to standard libraries and database packages. In that case what I have to say about languages will not be of wide interest. But I think that they are not ready to do so yet.

The architectures that are contending most strongly in this area are the shared memory multiple vector processors like CRAY, IBM 3090VF and Alliant/Cedar, distributed memory systems like the Meiko and Parsys Transputer systems, the NCube and the Intel iPSC and the massively parallel SIMD machines like the AMT DAP and the Connection machine.

7.1.1   Shared memory vector processors

The shared memory vector processors are suited to a relatively small degree of parallelism of very powerful processors. They have the characteristic that the communication bandwidth through the shared store is very high but the cost of the process switch is very high owing to the pipelining and the processor design.

The software that is being proposed for these processors currently involves adding tasking and synchronization extensions to Fortran. It is the hope of the suppliers that automatic parallelization will be sufficient for most purposes: I don't think that this point has been reached yet. An alternative approach is for interactive program restructuring to be provided. A third approach is to provide a lower level language more suited to the machine and let the application analysts choose the appropriate mix of restructuring and writing for the machine. I believe this to be the best way. A Fortran for this environment is being defined by the Parallel Fortran Consortium in the USA.

I believe that the constructs that are being proposed in PFC, VOLATILE data and complex synchronization, are too error-prone to be used except within automatic parallelysers. The current multiple vector processor machines are very complex in architecture, with storage hierarchies and concurrency entirely visible to the user. Dumping the problems into the programmer's lap will not be the best way for the United States to meet the Japanese competition.

An alternative approach in many of these areas is that of the functional languages. There is real effort at last being put into the implementation of functional systems on vector processors. The advantages are that the simpler and better defined semantics of the functional language give much more and better scope for automatic program restructuring. However, the community have found that doing without variables is not all plain sailing and that the advantages are not as clear-cut as they might once have seemed. This approach is undoubtedly the Pretender, waiting to seize the crown should Fortran falter.

7.1.2   Distributed memory processors

The processors which do without the concept of uniform shared address space can offer more cost effective processing at the operation level. The local store can be tightly linked to the processor, perhaps even on-chip. There is opportunity for high degrees of parallelism here. We are seeing systems with hundreds and even a thousand processors used effectively. The bottle-neck in these systems is communication; a characteristic that will not go away with increasing logic density. The existing software regimes have concentrated on explicit message-passing as the chief operation of concurrency.

Looking at the transputer based systems in particular the choice of Occam as the machine-level language provides non-deterministic concurrency within each processor and a degree of independence of the program from its placement. In practice this is far from the orthogonality that we require between placement and the meaning of the program. For programmers of embedded systems responding to a variety of inputs this is fine and necessary. But for those of us interested in distributing computations ported from serial processors we have the tail wagging the dog. It is distribution that we require. We know that concurrency on each processor is a necessary aid to that distribution. But Occam plays down the placement or distribution aspects and emphasizes the concurrency.

From observation of programmers working on distributed systems it is clear that the distributed application has to be translated into an implementation which uses local non-deterministic concurrency as an implementation mechanism. My observations of non-real-time Occam programmers at work on distributed systems suggests that they behave this way. They design their programs from the start with an implementation layer of message-handling harnesses and then distribute the meat of the computation in a manner just like that of the distributed Fortran programmer who is obliged to use a communications harness. Recently, people have found that they can get better performance by building these harnesses and message-handlers in transputer assembler so they don't use Occam there. The data placement approach outlined in section 7.2 is proposed as a simpler means of describing this sort of program.

7.1.3   SIMD processors

SIMD processors are in some ways the most revolutionary, although in program development terms they are the most familiar. They suffer from the fact that programs don't port from serial processors very effectively although applications port very well. I believe that we are likely to see networks of SIMD processors, possibly within heterogeneous systems as attractive. Communication will be at the level of passing an image or a large data structure. Once we are using nets of these processors we have solved the problem of gentle performance upgrade. The only puzzle that I see is why they are not already being used much more for image handling applications, especially satellite data reduction.

There is a great deal that distributed programming can learn from SIMD programming styles, notably the importance of regular mappings of data to processors and of mapping transformations involving wholesale redistribution of data.

The data distribution approach described below applies to SIMD as well as MIMD systems.

7.2   DISTRIBUTION

If we are interested in high performance computing we need to think about distribution before thinking about local concurrency and make local concurrency the servant of distribution.

We want to have distribution be independent of program results so we need to choose a notation in which distribution is orthogonal to the other components. The notation that I choose is data placement. We are going to include in our language the place at which each data item is to be held. This should make no difference to the results that are obtained (provided that they are determined by the program alone) but could make quite a lot of difference to the time taken by the computation (either way!).

Data placement is of most practical interest for distributed memory systems, but, interestingly enough, the same notation can be used to express distribution for systolic systems, SIMD systems and distributed memory MIMD systems. There has been interest in data placement in the functional language community. It is straightforward to add expression placement to functional languages. The point of interest is whether we can provide a sound and flexible intermediate and programming language based on adding data placement to conventional imperative languages.

Once we start thinking seriously about distribution we shall come up with the same approaches that have been seen in other applications of distributed computing. We shall see a place for replicated data and concern about synchronization of irreversible operations (transaction commitment).

I assume that we have a system in which there is no global address space. Each processor has its own address space and a separate communication space consisting of ports or links. For the scientific and engineering problems process to process communication seems the most useful. Different addressing models are possible.

7.3 RESOURCE ALLOCATION

To allocate a task to a processor and make the necessary transfers of data to allow it to proceed can be expensive but need not be prohibitively so. Dynamic allocation of tasks can take place effectively on distributed memory systems, as in the common 'farming' of independent tasks across processors. But in some applications it is too expensive, and it is necessary for the data to be distributed statically and appropriate work to be performed on the data wherever located.

Professor Hey's group at Southampton have identified three particularly useful structures of parallelism: pipelining (functional distribution), geometrical distribution and farming of independent tasks (see D. Pritchard's contribution to these proceedings). In each case what would be sequential structure in a serial program is rearranged into distributed structure. In pipelining, sequential operations on a stream of repeated data are partitioned between two or more processors. In geometrical and 'farm' distribution the repeated data are shared out between the processors, in one case with a static arrangement, in the other with a dynamic arrangement. The static case has the advantage that paths between neighbouring elements are statically known. The dynamic case allows better load balancing in the case that different data require different amounts of processing. I shall show below that hybrids between these schemes can be described using data placement.

It is clear that static allocation of a data can enhance performance, since less decisions remain at run time. Scalable structures like grids have the additional advantage that a grid of unknown size can be mapped to one of known size with little run-time overhead. This gives us the three options for time of allocationof data: compile-time allocation, compile-time structured but run-time sized, and run-time allocation.

7.4   DATA PLACEMENT IN CONVENTIONAL LANGUAGES

My intention is to introduce data placement into conventional imperative languages to indicate the distribution of processing.

We introduce the placement statement:

PLACE   X   AT   P

or for arrays, we can allow the data to be spread over processors according to some integral-linear expression on the subscripts:

DIMENSION X(20,40)

PLACE X(I,J) AT   (I-1)/4 + 1

This allows us to write pipelined computations in a simple dataflow style.

INTEGER A, B, C

PLACE A AT 1

PLACE B, C AT 2

B = A*A

C = SQRT(1 + B)

or, more to the point,

INTEGER A, B, C

PLACE A AT 1

PLACE B, C AT 2

READ A

B = A*A

C = SQRT(1 + B)

WRITE C

These are to be interpreted in a dataflow sense. The interpretation is that each processor effectively executes the whole program, skipping any operations that don't pertain to its local data. This might not sound like a very good route to parallelism. In order to get high performance we have to be able to let processors skip most of the programs (by compile-time analysis). Provided that the program contains enough information on placement, compile-time analysis will be able to detect, at least in favourable cases, what parts of the program are specific to which processors. There are two very favourable cases, which we shall look at in more detail below. Where data is geometrically distributed, loops over the whole data can be narrowed down to cover just the local data without loss. Where a routine is local in action the control can be 'localized' to that processor.

In order to get high performance from the system we have to evade Amdahl's Law which tells us that the program time cannot be less than the time required for the central control to be executed. We need to distribute the control to minimize the time for central control and we should do it by compile-time optimizations starting with the notion of all processors executing the whole program but with the data distributed.

7.4.1 Language implications

In order to be able to carry out localization of control at compile time the compiler needs good information about data distribution, not only for data declared in a routine but also for its parameters. This in turn demands run-time strong typing in respect of placement, which is the only alternative to a global dynamic address space. Having strong typing means that different parts of a program need to be held in a program library and that some parts may need to be recompiled when others are changed. This approach is required in any case by inter-routine dataflow analysers which are the basis of the powerful program parallelysers now being developed and offered.

With such a distributed Fortran we can write a single routine which performs distributed processing on an array spread over many processors. (Multi-processor routines have been introduced previously by Banatre under the name multi-functions.)

7.5 THE MULTI-PROCESSOR INTERPRETATION OF DISTRIBUTED FORTRAN

There is a canonical interpretation of Distributed Fortran which seems the most natural. In addition to the placement described above it allows for REPLICATED data. The coefficients appearing in placement expressions may be replicated data values as well as constants.

A DO index variable is automatically replicated. This is possible because the DO index can only be updated by the loop control mechanism. It allows DO control to be localized readily.

The standard interpretation of multi-processor Distributed Fortran is that the program is executed at each processor but only local or replicated data is updated. When values are required from another processor communication must take place. It is not necessary for replicated data to be broadcast; it is just updated in every processor. (This may require a broadcast if the value to be assigned is local).

Any interpretation that gives the same results as the standard interpretation is valid. The whole subject is of interest because optimized interpretations do exist in useful cases.

Consider the interpretation of:

```
INTEGER A, B, C
PLACE A AT 1
PLACE B, C AT 2

DO 10 K = 1,100
READ  A
B = A*A
C = SQRT(1+B)
WRITE  C
10 CONTINUE
```

This is interpreted as:

On processor 1:

```
DO 10 K = 1,100
READ A
WRITEMESSAGE(A*A)
10 CONTINUE
```

On processor 2:

```
DO 10 K = 1,100
RECEIVEMESSAGE(B)
C = SQRT(1+B)
WRITE C
10 CONTINUE
```

Similarly the program:

```
INTEGER X, Y
DIMENSION  X(100), Y(100)
PLACE X(I) AT (I-1)/10+1
PLACE Y(I) AT (I-1)/10+1

DO 10 K = 1,99
Y(K) = X(K) + X(K+1)
10 CONTINUE
```

can be interpreted as:

On processor M:

```
DIMENSION X(10),Y(10)
INTEGER X, Y, Z
IF (M.NE.1) WRITEMESSAGELEFT(X(1))
DO 10 K = 1,9
Y(K) = X(K) + X(K+1)
10 CONTINUE
IF (M.NE.10)  THEN
RECEIVEMESSAGERIGHT(Z)
Y(10) = X(10) + Z
END IF
```

Transformations of this kind are carried out by the SUPERB interactive restructurer for the SUPRENUM system, though the SUPERB system makes a full dataflow analysis of the program and is able to assist the programmer interactively.

7.6 CONCURRENCY

The data placement notation used so far does not affect the results of the program. It is useful to introduce notations specifying where concurrency is permitted. These define a concurrent program which is to be distributed. The meaning of the concurrent program will not generally be the same as that of the serial program obtained by deleting all the concurrency annotations.

7.6.1 Independent loop instances

Independent loop instances can be considered to be performed concurrently. They can safely be farmed out to remote processors. This can be described in a distributed Fortran in the following way. The loop is annotated with a concurrency indicator, for example DO may be replaced by DOPAR. The data items which are to be available to the remote task are declared LOCAL to the loop instance. This declaration takes place at the head of the loop as within a block in a block-structured language.

```
                INTEGER B(100), KK

                PARDO 1 K = 1,100
                    LOCAL BB, KK
                KK = K
                BB = KK*(1+3*KK*KK)
                B(K) = BB
        1 CONTINUE
```

The intended implementation is for the body of the loop to be executed in a separate processor, with the local to non-local assignments indicating communications, usually, but not necessarily at top and bottom of the loop body.

This form of loop is more general than the simple farm. The loop body can communicate with the other parts of the computation although different instances of the same loop cannot communicate directly. The loop executions could be distributed themselves.

It may also be useful to declare sections of code concurrent. This would allow effects like buffering of data in a pipeline to be described explicitly.

Lastly, it can be useful to have an I/O mechanism which accepts transfers in any order, rather than retaining the order of the serial interpretation.

7.7 SUMMARY

I have attempted to show that data placement combined with appropriate strong typing, can be useful a annotation to a serial program, giving enough information to allow a restructuring to distributed form. These annotations do not alter the meaning of the program. Concurrency extensions to the serial programming language can also be accommodated and can lead to better utilization of the processor at the cost of explicit expression of concurrency. I have not given details here of the type checking necessary between caller and called to achieve consistent access to distributed data.

With data placement and concurrency extensions, imperative programs may be specified which have a wide range of distributed computing behaviours, allowing both SIMD-like computations or the automatic distribution of independent program components. I believe that this is a good basis for a parallel Fortran.

It is clear that this approach will work with a range of languages although the inclusion of pointers seems to demand a global address space, which is contrary to the approach taken here. Apart from inclusion of pointers this approach would work well (better!) with the 8X extensions to Fortran.

An important feature of this approach is the presence of subprograms which operate upon distributed data and parameters. I feel sure that these will have a part in our future computing environment.

Part Three

Autoparallelization

8 Automatic vectorization and parallelization for supercomputers

H. Zima

Institut für Statistik und Informatik, University of Vienna, Austria

8.1 INTRODUCTION

In this paper we investigate automatic tools for the transformation of numerical Fortran 77 application programs into programs for a supercomputer. We will discuss the problem of vectorization - which essentially can be considered as solved - and then discuss parallelization for shared-memory and distributed-memory multiprocessing systems. We are interested in massive parallelism; as a consequence, our search for parallelism focuses on DO-loops whose iterations may be run in parallel.

We will consider arbitrarily nested loops. All discussions related to transformations for loops will be based upon the concept of dependence, as originally introduced by Kuck and further developed by Kennedy and Allen and co-workers [3,4,5,13,15,22]. A statement S_2 is said to be dependent on S_1 T, if S_1 T is executed in the sequential program before S_2 T, both statements access the same variable v, and at least one statement writes the variable. If S_1 T writes and S_2 T reads, we speak of a true dependence; if S_1 T reads and S_2 T writes, of an anti dependence; and if both statements write, of an output dependence. An important classification of dependences which is orthogonal to the one just mentioned has been proposed by Allen and Kennedy [5]: a dependence is loop-carried if it exists across iterations of a loop, otherwise it is said to be loop-independent. The levels of a loop nest are numbered from 1, beginning with the outermost loop. Dependences represent the semantically relevant restrictions for the order of statement instances.

Vectorization aims to rewrite statements in a loop as vector statements. For example, the DO-loop

DO I = 1,N
    A(I) = B(I) + C(I)
END DO

can be validly transformed into the Fortran 8x vector statement

A(1:N) = B(1:N) + C(1:N),

in which all component additions and assignments are performed concurrently. The transformation is valid if the statement to be rewritten is not contained in a dependence cycle. A vector statement can be easily mapped to a sequence of vector instructions for an arbitrary vector computer.

Parallelization maps the iterations of a loop to different processes. Let us first consider shared-memory systems (SMS). We introduce two kinds of parallel loops: DOALL and DOACROSS. Their iterations can be executed asynchronously as independent processes; the difference between the two constructs lies in the role of synchronization: while the iterations of DOALL-loops are assumed to be completely independent, DOACROSS-loops allow synchronization between iterations. For example, in the loop

DO I = 1,100
    A(I) = B(I) + C(I)
    IF (A(I) < 0) THEN A(I) = A(I) + B(I)
END DO

all iterations are mutually independent; it can therefore be transformed into the DOALL-loop

DOALL I = 1,100
    A(I) = B(I) + C(I)
    IF (A(I) < 0) THEN A(I) = A(I) + B(I)
ENDALL

Consider now the loop

DO I = 1,100
    S: A(I) = B(I)*C(I) + D(I)
    S′: B(I) = C(I)/D(I-1) + A(I-3)
END DO

This loop contains a loop-carried dependence from S to S′; thus it cannot be transformed into a DOALL-loop. However, a DOACROSS-loop can be generated:

DOACROSS I = 1,100
    S: A(I) = B(I)*C(I) + D(I)
        SEND_SIGNAL(S)
        WAIT_SIGNAL(S,I-3)
    S′: B(I) = C(I)/D(I-1) + A(I-3)
ENDACROSS

The execution of SEND_SIGNAL(S) in iteration i signals to the other processes that statement S has been executed in that iteration and thus A(i) has been defined. The process performing iteration i + 3 has to wait for this signal; the required synchronization is expressed by the statement WAIT_SIGNAL(S,I-3).

Processes in a distributed-memory multiprocessing system (DMS) may only access their local address space directly: in order to satisfy a true dependence across processes it is then necessary to physically transmit the data (in the above example, the value of A(i) together with the iteration number i) to the local memory of the process that is the target of the dependence. Communication in a DMS is significantly more time-consuming than in an SMS, which makes its optimization an absolute requirement. An approach to the solution of that problem is based on the partitioning of the data domain of the sequential program, such that the elements of the partition can be mapped to the local memories of processes, and the processes essentially execute the same program on disjoint portions of the data domain.

The rest of the paper is organized as follows: In section 8.2, automatic vectorization will be shortly reviewed. Section 8.3 deals with parallelization for SMSs, and section 8.4 treats parallelization on the basis of data partitioning for a DMS. The paper concludes with bibliographical references.

8.2   VECTORIZATION

We provide an informal overview of the basic approach to automatic vectorization.

The objective of vectorization is to rewrite a statement in a sequential loop as a vector statement, in which all instances are executed concurrently, subject to the constraint of a fetch before store semantics (FS-semantics), i.e. under the condition that all values needed for the execution of any instance are determined before the first result is computed. This models the properties of vector instructions.

Vectorization is semantically valid if all dependences of the original program are retained. This is satisfied for the example given in the introduction. Statement S below, on the other hand:

$$DO\ I = 1,N$$
$$S:\ A(I+1) = A(I)*B(I)$$
$$END\ DO$$

is contained in a cyclic true dependence. The statement instances are executed sequentially as follows:

$$S(1) \quad :\ A(2) = A(1)*B(1)$$
$$S(2) \quad :\ A(3) = A(2)*B(2)$$
$$\cdots$$
$$S(N) \quad :\ A(N+1) = A(N)*B(N).$$

As we see when we unroll the loop, the values of all A(i), 2 i N+1, are determined in the loop and subsequently used in it. If we were to vectorize S, then the products A(i)*B(i) would be computed using the values A(i) held prior to entering the loop. Since this would generally produce different results, vectorization is invalid.

However, an existing dependence need not always prevent vectorization as the next example shows. In loop L,

$$L: \quad DO\ I = 1,100$$
$$S:\ D(I) = A(I\text{-}1)*D(I)$$
$$S':\ A(I) = B(I)+C(I)$$
$$END\ DO$$

S depends on S'. S' could be vectorized immediately, but not S. However, both statements can actually be vectorized: since exchanging the textual order of the two statements does not modify the program semantics, we swap them. This reordering transformation yields the loop:

```
L1:     DO I = 1,100
            S':A(I) = B(I) + C(I)
            S: D(I) = A(I-1)*D(I)
        END DO
```

The dependence arc for this loop points downwards and we can perform loop distribution as shown below:

```
L21:    DO I = 1,100
            S':A(I) = B(I) + C(I)
        END DO

L22:    DO I = 1,100
            S: D(I) = A(I-1)*D(I)
        END DO
```

Loop distribution has converted the loop-carried dependence from S' to S in L1 into a loop-independent dependence. There are no dependences within L21 and L22, and vectorization is possible:

$$S'(1{:}100){:}\ A(1{:}100) = B(1{:}100) + C(1{:}100)$$
$$S(1{:}100){:}\ D(1{:}100) = A(0{:}99) * D(1{:}100).$$

Roughly speaking, we can vectorize a statement S if it is not contained in a cycle of the dependence graph. On the other hand, if S is contained in a dependence cycle, then an order must be retained for certain instances of S, which makes vectorization in general invalid.

A vectorizing compiler could be based on this principle, i.e. rule out vectorization when a dependence cycle has been found. But this is unnecessarily restrictive. Consider the following loop:

```
DO I = 1,N
    DO J = 1,N
        S:C(I,J) = C(I-1,J)-D(I-1,J+1)
    END DO J
END DO I
```

This loop has a cyclic loop-carried dependence at level 1 involving S, but no dependences in the inner loop: If we do not modify the outer loop, then the dependence is satisfied and the inner loop may be executed as a vector statement.

The loop may thus be transformed into:

$$DO\ I = 1,N$$
$$C(I,1:N) = C(I-1,1:N)-D(I-1,2:N+1)$$
$$END\ DO\ I$$

Thus even cyclic dependences may not altogether prevent vectorization when the level at which the dependence occurs is taken into account.

The fundamental transformations required for vectorization are statement reordering, loop distribution, and vector statement generation. Statement reordering changes the textual position of two adjacent statements; it can be validly applied if no loop-independent dependences exist between these statements. Loop distribution splits a loop with two or more statements into a sequence of loops by distributing the loop control over single statements or statement groups. It can be applied validly if there are no loop-carried dependences pointing backward. Vector statement generation rewrites a perfectly nested loop with just one statement as a vector statement.

Suppose that S is a statement at level n of a loop L. If S is not contained in a dependence cycle, then we can generate vector code for S at all levels. Otherwise, we can determine the smallest number c_0 such that the serial execution of the c_0 outermost loops suffices to break the dependence cycle; the innermost $n-c_0$ loops, if any, can then be executed in vector mode. The Allen-Kennedy algorithm for vector code generation is based on this principle [3,4,5]. The algorithm operates on the dependence graph and uses its strongly connected components to distinguish between sequential and vectorizable regions.

8.3   PARALLELIZATION FOR SHARED-MEMORY SYSTEMS

We first outline an approach to the generation of parallel code that is based on the requirement that the iterations of a loop can be excuted independently. An algorithm for this transformation was developed by Callahan, Kennedy and Allen [2,7].

The underlying theory is quite simple and closely related to that for vectorization: a loop can be executed as a DOALL-statement if it does not contain a loop-carried dependence. However, whereas vectorization is applied to the inner loops of a nest, parallelization attempts to execute the outermost loop in parallel in order to minimize the overhead of scheduling and synchronization. Loop fusion can be used (under appropriate conditions) to further increase the size of the code section that is to be executed in parallel.

The program produced by the algorithm consists of serial code and DOALL-loops. Processes can be synchronized outside DOALL-loops by barriers, which must be executed by all processes before any one can proceed.

We illustrate this by an example:

```
LL₁:    DO I = 1,N
            DO J = 1,N
                S₁: A(I,J) = A(I,J-1)
                S₂: B(I,J) = A(I,J-2) + 2
            END DO J
        END DO I


LL₂:    DO I = 1,N
            DO J = 1,N
                S₃: C(I,J) = C(I-3,J) + A(I,J)*2
            END DO J
        END DO I
```

It can be easily shown that S_1 can be executed in parallel at level 1, S_2 at both levels, and S_3 at level 2. The algorithm generates the following code:

```
        DOALL I = 1,N
            DO J = 1,N
                S₁: A(I,J) = A(I,J-1)
                S₂: B(I,J) = A(I,J-2) + 2
            END DO J
        ENDALL I
        BARRIER
        DO I = 1,N
            DOALL J = 1,N
                S₃: C(I,J) = C(I-3,J) + A(I,J)*2
```

ENDALL J
IF I < N THEN BARRIER
END DO I

If parallel code is to be generated for loops with loop-carried dependences, then the DOACROSS-statement must be used, and the dependences must be satisfied by inserting the proper synchronization statements. An example for this was shown in the introduction; we do not go into further details here. The problem has been discussed by Wolfe, Polychronopoulos, and others [16,23].

A final remark is in order here. In theory, every loop can be rewritten as a DOACROSS-loop, but this transformation is of practical value only if a thorough analysis of the degree of parallelism in the DOACROSS-loop, and the associated overhead for synchronization and scheduling is made [16].

8.4   PARALLELIZATION FOR A DISTRIBUTED-MEMORY MACHINE

The approach to parallelization discussed in this section differs fundamentally from the one we have considered previously; we call it parallelization by data partitioning. We are now dealing with a DMS; an essential difference between this and an SMS is the high cost of communication: whereas communication can be realized on an SMS by synchronizing processes via special registers or the global memory, on a DMS, data involved in a true dependence may have to be physically transferred from one local memory to another via the communication network. Depending on how the network is realized and how efficient the operating system is, the time taken to transmit a single data item between two processors may reach the order of a millisecond. So it becomes vital to control communication effectively: we must attempt to reduce the total number of communication statements to be executed, and increase the amount of data transferred during one communication, even at the cost of lowering the degree of parallelism.

We describe here the salient features of the interactive parallelization system SUPERB [10,12,25,26,27], which was developed at Bonn University and is the first automatic tool to support parallelization for a DMS. The target machine of SUPERB is the SUPRENUM computer [6]. The validity of the approach described here extends, however, to general DMSs and is not restricted to this particular architecture.

We assume a DMS consisting of a kernel system with a large number of processing nodes, and a host that controls I/O and performs global management tasks. Each node contains a local memory; there is no global memory in the system.

Our target language is a superset of Fortran 77, which provides a new type of program unit which is called a task unit. A process is created when a task unit is activated. Different processes have disjoint local address spaces; communication with other processes may be established using message passing primitives SEND and RECEIVE. The abstract machine outlined here can be mapped to a real DMS in an obvious way.

The parallelization system takes as input a sequential Fortran program, together with a specification of data partitioning, and produces a parallel program for a DMS (see fig.8.1). Parallelization is performed in three steps:

Step 1: Splitting

The program is split into an initial task unit which includes all I/O and is executed on the host, and a kernel task unit that describes the actual computation. The activations of the kernel task unit create the processes of the kernel system.

Step 2: Partitioning the data domain

The data domain of the sequential program is partitioned interactively under the control of the user. The partition is determined by subdividing arrays into rectangular blocks, and mapping the blocks to processes. The mapping establishes which process owns each block - storage for the block is allocated in the local address space of its owner and any assignment to an element of a block must be performed by its owner.

The way we partition our data determines the process structure of the resulting parallelized program. When we select a suitable partition, we must take into account, among other things, the size of the application, the ranges of DO-loops, and the structure of the dependences between the statements of a loop.

Step 3: Transforming the kernel task unit

The choice of a partition determines a set of requirements for the transformation of the kernel task unit. Its assignment statements must in general be masked in order to guarantee that they write exclusively into the local address space of the executing process, loop bounds must be adjusted, and communication statements have to be inserted in order to satisfy dependences between statements executed in different processes.

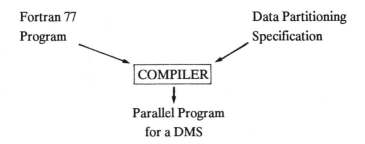

Figure 8.1 Compiling for a DMS.

Given a program and a partition, the generation of the subtask with the objective of minimizing communication is a difficult problem which has to be approached heuristically. The following optimization transformations are considered in this context:

1.   moving communication out of loops;

2.   reordering statements with the objective of sending at the earliest, and receiving at the latest possible time;

3.   increasing the volume of data transmitted for one communication by fusing communication statements.

We conclude by reviewing related work. In parallel to the development of SUPERB, Callahan and Kennedy independently developed a similar scheme in the ParaScope system, based on user-supplied annotations of Fortran programs by DECOMPOSE and DISTRIBUTE statements, which provide language features for a (static) data partitioning scheme. A closely related approach is being currently explored at Cornell University [17].

The method works in principle for arbitrary programs - i.e., it correctly translates any sequential program, for which data partitioning has been specified, into an equivalent parallel program for a DMS - but a reasonable efficiency of the target program can only be achieved under certain conditions. The approach is specifically oriented towards the parallelization of numerical algorithms that can be characterized as follows:

1. the programs work on a mesh or mesh-like data domain;

2. the computations at the mesh points are local, i.e. depend only on the values of a small number of points in the neighbourhood;

3. the size of the data domains may be very large: a typical program may operate on up to 10^9 grid points.

Koelbel, Mehrotra, and Rosendale [14] translate BLAZE, an explicitly parallel language, into E-BLAZE, a language with low-level process manipulation features. Their work uses a compilation mechanism that is basically analogous to the one developed in SUPERB and ParaScope.

Kennedy and Zima generalize the static partitioning schemes of SUPERB, ParaScope, and BLAZE by defining a data partitioning language that allows dynamic array decomposition and distribution, and correspondingly extending the compilation method [11]. This expands the range of applications to include adaptive methods and other problem solutions in which the distribution pattern of data changes dynamically (as, for instance in systolic matrix algorithms). In addition, they explore methods for the analysis of sequential programs to automatically derive elements of a data partitioning strategy.

The parallelization systems for DMSs, as discussed above, can all be seen as tools that provide the user with the abstraction of a virtual shared-memory for a DMS. Such abstractions can also be realized by using a suitable language. We mention three language-based approaches (C*, Linda, Dino) below.

C*, developed for the Connection Machine [19], is an SIMD-language. Programmers declare replicated variables, which can be manipulated as aggregates in an extension of the C language. Explicit message passing is eliminated in the virtual machine provided by the system.

Linda, developed at Yale [8], supports virtual shared data structures, but forces the programmer to use special primitives for the access of these structure. Each node has to be programmed explicitly.

DINO, developed at the University of Colorado, Boulder [18], allows the programmer to specify distributed data structures and invoke replicated functions on these data structures. Programmers must mark variable references that indicate updates and thus are forced to program message passing.

8.5 CONCLUSION

In this paper we gave an overview of automatic vectorization and parallelization of numerical Fortran programs. A systematic in-depth treatment of this topic is given in [29]. We have considered both shared-memory as well as distributed-memory architectures. While vectorization and some basic strategies for parallelization that have been developed are successfully applicable to a wide range of problems, there are still many problems for which only partial solutions exist at this time. These include interprocedural data flow and dependence analysis [9,21], incremental analysis [20,24], optimization of synchronization and communication [23,27], and the integration of parallelization tools in interactive programming environments [1,28].

REFERENCES

1. Allen,R.*et al* (1986) PTOOL: A semi-automatic parallel programming assistant. *Proc.1986 Int. Conf. on Parallel Processing,* 164-170.

2. Allen,J.R.,Callahan,D.,Kennedy,K.(1987) Automatic decomposition of scientific programs for parallel execution. *Proc.14th Ann.ACM Symp.on Principles of Prog.Languages (POPL),* 63-76 (January 1987).

3. Allen,J.R.(1983) *Dependence Analysis for Subscripted Variables and its Application to Program Transformations.* Ph.D.Thesis, Rice University, Houston, Texas.

4. Allen,J.R. and Kennedy,K (1982) PFC: A program to convert Fortran to parallel form. *Proc.IBM Conf.Parallel Comp. and Scientific Computations.*

5. Allen,J.R., and Kennedy,K.(1987) Automatic Translation of FORTRAN programs to vector form. *ACM TOPLAS* 9,4, 491-542.

6. Behr,P.M.,Giloi,W.K.,and Muhlenbein,H.(1986) SUPRENUM: The German supercomputer architecture - rationale and concepts. *Proc.1986 International Conference on Parallel Processing.*

7. Callahan,D.(1987) *A Global Approach to Detection of Parallelism.* Ph.D.Thesis, Rice University, Houston, Texas.

8. Carriero,N., and Gelernter,D.(1988) *The S/Nets Linda Kernel.* Research Report YALEU/DCS/RR-383, Yale University, Dept.of Computer Science.

9. Cooper,K.,Kennedy,K., and Torczon,L.(1986) The impact of interprocedural analysis and optimization in the R^n Programming Environment. *ACM TOPLAS* 8, 4, 491-523.

10. Gerndt,M. and Zima,H.P.(1987) MIMD-Parallelization for SUPRENUM In eds E.N.Houstis, T.S.,Papatheodorou, C.D.Polychronopoulos, *Supercomputing. Proc.first Conference,Athens,Greece,June 1987 Lecture Notes in Computer Science* 297, pp278-293 Springer Verlag, Berlin.

11. Kennedy,K., and Zima,H.P.(1989) Virtual shared memory for distributed-memory machines. *Proc.Fourth Hypercube Conference,* Monterey, CA.

12. Kremer,U., Bast,H.-J., Gerndt,M., and Zima,H. (1988) Advanced tools for automatic parallelization. Proc. second Int. SUPRENUM Colloquium. *Parallel Computing* 7, 387-393.

13. Kuck,D.J.,Kuhn,R.H.,Leasure,B., and Wolfe,M.(1984) The structure of an advanced retargetable vectorizer In:*Tutorial on Supercomputers: Design and Applications,* (Ed. K.Hwang,) 967-974, IEEE Press, New York.

14. Koelbel,C.,Mehrotra,P., and Rosendale,J. (1987) Semi-automatic domain decomposition, in *BLAZE Proc.1987 Int.Conf.Parallel Processing.*

15. Padua,D.A., and Wolfe,M.J.(1986) Advanced compiler optimizations for supercomputers. *Comm.ACM* 29,12,1184-1201.

16. Polychronopoulos,C.D.(1986) *On Program Restructuring, Scheduling, and Communication for Parallel Processor Systems.* Ph.D.Thesis,CSRD Rpt. No.595,Center for Supercomputer Research and Development, University of Illinois at Urbana-Champaign.

17. Rogers,A., and Pingali,K. (1989) Process decomposition through locality of reference. *Proc.ACM SIGPLAN 1989 Conference on Programming Language Design and Implementation.*

18. Rosing,M., and Schnabel,R.B.(1988) *An Overview of DINO - A New Language For Numerical Computation on Distributed-Memory Multiprocessors.* Technical

Report TR CU-CS-385-88, Dept.of Computer Science, University of Colorado, Boulder, Colorado.

19. Rose,J., and Steele,G.(1988) C* *An Extended C Language for Data Parallel Programming.* Technical Report PL87-5, Thinking Machines, Inc.

20. Ryder,B.G., and Paull,M.C.(1988) Incremental data-flow analysis. *ACM TOPLAS* 10,1, 1-50.

21. Triolet,R.(1985) *Interprocedural Analysis for Program Restructuring with Parafrase* CSRD Report 538, Center for Supercomputing Research and Development, University of Illinois at Urbana-Champaign.

22. Wolfe,M.J.(1982) *Optimizing Supercompilers for Supercomputers.* Ph.D.Thesis,Rep.82-1105,Dept.of Computer Science,University of Illinois at Urbana-Champaign.

23. Wolfe,M.J. (1987) *Multiprocessor Synchronization for Concurrent Loops.* Technical Report, Kuck and Associates.

24. Zadeck,F.K.(1983) *Incremental Data Flow Analysis in a Structured Program Editor.* Ph.D.Thesis, Dept.of Computer Science,Rice University,Houston, Texas.

25. Zima,H.P.,Bast,H.-J.,Gerndt,M., and Hoppen,P.J.(1986a) Semi-Automatic Parallelization of Fortran Programs, in: Handler,W. *et al.* (Eds.): *CONPAR 86 Conference on Algorithms and Hardware for Parallel Processing Lecture Notes in Computer Science* 237,287-294 Springer Verlag,Berlin.

26. Zima,H.P.,Bast,H.-J.,Gerndt,M., and Hoppen,P.J.(1986b) *SUPERB: The SUPRENUM Parallelizer.* Bonn Research Report SUPRENUM 861203, Bonn University.

27. Zima,H.P.,Bast,H.-J., and Gerndt,M.(1988) SUPERB: A tool for semi-automatic MIMD/SIMD parallelization. *Parallel Computing* 6, 1-18.

28. Zima,H.P.(to appear) An advanced programming environment for a supercomputer. *Proc.1988 Tromso Conf.on Vector and Parallel Computing.*

29. Zima,H.P. (1989) *Advanced Compiling for Supercomputers,* Addison-Wesley (to appear in late 1989).

9 Fortran compilers for parallel processors

John Barr

System Software Factors

9.1 OVERVIEW

This paper discusses Fortran compilers for parallel architectures. The classes of parallel architectures under discussion are outlined, followed by an examination of where we find parallelism within Fortran programs. A range of parallelization techniques used by compilers are outlined, and this is followed by some examples of compilers in action. Finally, we take a look at future opportunities for the exploitation of parallelism by more sophisticated compilers.

9.2 PARALLEL ARCHITECTURES

Like all fashion goods parallel architectures come in a variety of shapes, sizes and styles.

9.2.1 Array Processors

Array Processors (APs) are not mainstream parallel machines, but they do exhibit parallel features, and many of the compilation techniques used in this environment are also applicable to larger scale parallel systems.

A typical AP comprises multiple floating point function units, an integer processor, one or more address generators, a multi-port register file, and a full or partial interconnect linking the many individual processing units. Any of these function units can be pipelined, with data fetches and floating point operations often taking several cycles to complete. To achieve reasonable performance on an

AP, a program must use the multiple function units simultaneously, and keep the pipelines full whenever possible. There is an additional problem on microcoded architectures as each area of the instruction word may have several different uses. An AP compiler is tasked with juggling the use of all of these resources in order to maximize a programs performance.

9.2.2   Vector processors

Vector processors are similar to APs in many ways. Their most distinctive feature is that they support vector processing by having vector instructions which can be applied to special vector registers (or sometimes to main memory). The penalty for starting a pipelined vector instruction is paid once when the first element is processed, and results become available every cycle when the pipeline has been filled.

9.2.3   Shared memory multiprocessors

The next level of parallelism is obtained through the replication of complete processors. Within this class of architectures there are a number of trade-offs to be made in terms of the scale of the system, its peak theoretical performance, the complexity of processor and memory interconnection, and the ease with which the system can be programmed. Shared memory systems permit a relatively straightforward programming model to be used, with much of the compiler technology from array and vector processors having some application. These systems are not, however, scalable beyond certain limits, as memory bandwidth is quickly saturated.

9.2.4   Message passing systems

The problem of scalability is solved by moving to a message passing architecture, but a new set of problems is introduced. Although system bandwidth grows as more processors are added to the system, this bandwidth is not always available where it is required by a program. Fortran is a sequential language, and to apply it to parallel architectures compilers must work very hard. To take the large step from using a shared memory model to providing automatic support of distributed data structures increases that workload still further.

9.3   PARALLELISM IN FORTRAN PROGRAMS

Parallelism can be found in many places in Fortran programs. At a high level different parts of a program may be independent, and so they can be executed concurrently. This is also true of independent code threads at the Fortran block level. However, while the exploitation of these styles of parallelism can be effective on an array processor, the benefits to be gained are limited on large-scale parallel architectures. DO loops are an obvious place to search for parallelism, as many operations are performed in sequence on a collection of data items. Potential parallelism is also found at the lowest levels. Multiple operations within a Fortran statement may be executed in parallel, and pipelined architectures allow for a number of similar operations to be under way simultaneously on the same function unit. The problem is not so much "Is there any parallelism?, but how best to exploit the parallelism.

The parallelism found within DO loops can be exploited to good effect on all styles of parallel architectures, while the benefit to be gained from the other styles of parallelism is more limited.

9.4   TECHNIQUES USED BY FORTRAN COMPILERS

9.4.1   Dependence analysis

An accurate analysis of data dependence within Fortran programs is fundamental to the efficient vectorization and/or parallelization of loops. If one statement depends on another, then the relative order of execution for these statements is very important, and care must be taken to apply only valid program transformations. There are a number of different types of data dependence.

(a)   True dependence

Statement S1 defines a variable which is later accessed by S2.

$$S1: \quad A = B + C$$
$$S2: \quad D = A * 2.0$$

A true dependence can be limited to a single iteration of loop code, or can affect other iterations.

Loop independent dependence

This type of dependence must be maintained within the transformed program, but does not preclude separate iterations of the loop from being executed in parallel, despite the fact that S2 depends on S1. Any program transformations are valid as long as the order of the dependent statements is maintained.

```
        DO I   = 1, N
S1:     A(I)   = B(I) + C(I)
S2:     D(I)   = A(I) * 2.0
        ENDDO
```

Loop carried dependence

Parallel transformation of loops which contain this style of dependence are not valid, as a variable defined in one iteration of the loop is accessed by the next iteration. Although this dependence is obviously sensitive to the order in which the iterations of the loop are executed, the order of the statements within the loop is not important. Each execution of S1 is dependent on the execution of S2 during the previous iteration.

```
        DO I   = 2, N
S1:     A(I)   = B(I) + C(I)
S2:     D(I)   = A(I-1) * 2.0
        ENDDO
```

(b)   Antidependence

S1 accesses a variable which is later defined by S2.

```
        S1:    D = A * 2.0
        S2:    A = B + C
```

(c)   Output dependence

Both S1 and S2 define (output) the same variable.

```
        S1:    A = B + C
        S2:    A = D * 2.0
```

(d)   Control dependence

The preceding dependencies are all data dependencies. Control dependence occurs when the behaviour of one statement can cause a change in the flow of control which determines whether or not the dependent statement is executed. In the example, S2 is dependent on S1.

S1:   IF (A .GT. B) GOTO 100

S2:   X = Y + Z

9.4.2   Instruction scheduling

Instruction scheduling enables a compiler to make the best use of pipelined, multiple function unit architectures. The internal representation of a program is not broken up into the individual source statements, but is sequentially structured only in accordance with control and data dependencies. Code generation for a given code fragment may target instruction words which have already been used, provided that the instruction field to be written is available, and no dependencies are violated.

This example shows the type of code which would be produced for an array processor with a single memory address register and a three stage add pipeline.

Source code :

A = B + C

Generated code :

```
1      FETCH      B,    R1
2      FETCH      C,    R2
3                             ADD   R1, R2, R3
4                             ADD   (push)
5                             ADD   (push)
6      STORE      R3,   A
```

Two adds do not take twice as long as a single add, as the above example uses only one function unit on each instruction, leaving spare capacity for later operations.

Source code :

A = B + C

D = E + F

Generated code :

1	FETCH	B,	R1		
2	FETCH	C,	R2		
3	FETCH	E,	R4	ADD	R1, R2, R3
4	FETCH	F,	R5	ADD	(push)
5				ADD	R4, R5, R6
6	STORE	R3,	A	ADD	(push)
7				ADD	(push)
8	STORE	R6,	D		

The number of additional instructions to perform the second add is only two, and for register to register operations it comes down to a single instruction. For these memory to memory operations the limiting factor on performance is the ability to get data to and from memory. Most array processors use a pair of memory address registers in order to overcome this limitation.

Scheduling can go much further than this simple example. The performance of pipelined architectures is crippled every time a change in control flow is encountered, as pipelines are generally flushed before a branch, and take a number of instructions to refill. A clever compiler will note where a label can be reached from, and will attempt to fill the pipelines for computations after a jump, as it is draining the pipelines before the jump.

9.4.3   Vectorization

Vectorization is the transformation of a number of sequential scalar operations within a Fortran DO loop, to a single vector operation (or operations) which is applied to a set of data items. This transformation is beneficial as many high performance architectures support efficient vector processing, whether it is achieved by vector instructions, the generation of tightly rolled microcode, or by calling efficient mathematical library routines which have been hand coded in assembler. Vectorization is important because many compute- intensive codes spend a significant proportion of their execution time inside a relatively small number of loops, and if these loops can be executed optimally, then the program run-time can be minimized.

An important part of the vectorization process is the use of program transformations to remove dependencies, and to therefore allow the vectorization of previously unvectorizable loops. These transformations include :

- scalar expansion

- loop interchanging

- fission by name

- loop fusion

- strip mining

- loop collapsing

9.4.4   Parallelization

For shared memory multiprocessors many of the vectorisation techniques are used to parallelize loops. The most common technique used is strip mining, which allocates a portion of the algorithm to be computed to each processor. For many algorithms strip mining provides for automatic load balancing. Nested loops can be processed efficiently by distributing the outer loop across multiple processors, and vectorizing the inner loop.

9.4.5   Language extensions

Particularly for distributed memory architectures, the problem of automatic program parallelization is often too onerous for current compiler technology, and parallel language extensions are used to help the compiler to produce parallel code.

(a)   DOACROSS

This language extension directs the compiler to execute the first iteration of the loop on the first processor, the second iteration on the second processor, and so on. DOACROSS is used when synchronization is needed between iterations of the loop.

(b)   DOALL

This is another type of loop that a compiler is expected to distribute across available processors, but no restrictions are placed on the order of iteration execution.

(c)   FORTRAN 8X

The proposed Fortran 8X standard includes extensions to the syntax for describing arrays of the form :

$$A(\,I:J:K\,)$$

where A is an array, I is the first element, J is the last element, and K is the subscript stride. A simple vector add, which is described by the following loop in Fortran 77 :

```
DO I = 1,N
    A(I) = B(I) + C(I)
ENDDO
```

becomes simply :

$$A = B + C$$

in Fortran 8X.

9.5   COMPILER EXAMPLES

The vector add algorithm will be used as a simple example to demonstrate the behaviour of compilers for the different types of parallel architecture under discussion. The Fortran 77 code is :

```
DO I = 1, 50
    A(I) = B(I) + C(I)
ENDDO
```

The first task of the compiler is to recognize that the functionality of the DO loop can be represented by a single vector operation. Even the most naive of vectorizing compilers can recognise that this loop is a candidate for vectorization. The use of the proposed Fortran 8X array assignment syntax can help to express the vector operations in a more easily recognized form for the compiler, particularly for complicated operations. The Fortran 8X representation of this algorithm is :

$$A(1:50) = B(1:50) + C(1:50)$$

9.5.1 Array processors

The vector operation is isolated using the vectorization techniques outlined earlier in this paper. The compiler can then replace the code with a call to the vector add routine, or generate rolled microcode.

9.5.2 Vector processors

Once the vector operations have been isolated, code generation becomes very straightforward. For vector register machines the code is something like :

```
MOV         VL, 50
VLOAD       V1, B(1), 1
VLOAD       V2, C(1), 1
VADD        V1, V2, V3
VSTORE      V3, A(1), 1
```

For memory to memory vector operations the code is even more simple :

```
VADD        A(1), B(1), C(1), 50
```

9.5.3 Shared memory multiprocessors

The compiler can schedule a portion of the algorithm for execution on individual processors. This can be represented by the DOALL construct :

```
DOALL I = 1, 50
    A(I) = B(I) + C(I)
ENDDO
```

The loop can be distributed across processors by stride, or by contiguous sub-vectors, the effective loop code being as follows :

Distribution by stride:

```
DO I = proc, 50, nproc
    A(I) = B(I) + C(I)
ENDDO
```

Distribution by sub-vector:

$$DO\ I = (50/nproc) * (proc-1) + 1, (50/nproc) * proc$$
$$A(I) = B(I) + C(I)$$
ENDDO

Code generation for each individual processor is then for the array or vector processor as before.

9.5.4   Message passing systems

Compilers which efficiently target serial Fortran code at distributed memory systems are not yet available. The problem is not so much one of program analysis and code generation, we have already seen that this can be achieved, but is one of distributing data across the distinct areas of memory in the system. To further clarify this point, data can indeed be distributed, but the real problem is caused by the cost of that distribution. A distributed data model for Fortran programs must be developed before dusty decks can make use of message passing systems without significant operator intervention, or the use of language extensions which describe the data distribution.

Message passing extensions have allowed the development of efficient Fortran environments on a number of message passing architectures, but this solves the problem for only some types of application.

9.6   FUTURE DEVELOPMENTS

A number of organizations are working in the area of the automatic parallelization of standard Fortran programs. Both Illinois and Rice Universities support long-standing research projects which have provided many of the techniques used by others for vectorization. Their work now extends into the field of parallelization. The OACIS group at the Oregon Gradutate Centre are working on an interactive Fortran parallelizer, and System Software Factors is tasked with the development of automatic parallelizing compiler technology within the ESPRIT Supernode II project.

9.7 CONCLUSIONS

Efficient parallel code generation techniques for array and vector processors are well understood, and have been successfully implemented in a large number of commercial compilers. It seems that as soon as compiler technology catches up with current hardware, new architectures are being developed which cause compilers a whole new set of problems. Automatic parallelization techniques for small-scale shared memory systems are maturing, and a number of tools are being developed to assist with the problem on message passing systems.

It seems likely that when automatic parallelization has become commonplace, new machines will appear which support memory heirarchy of mind-numbing complexity, all in the name of peak performance. Compiler writers must accept that the goalposts have been moved yet again, and think themselves lucky that they have so many interesting problems to tackle.

REFERENCES

1 Allen, R. *et al* (1986) *PTOOL : A Semi-automatic Parallel Programming Assistant.* Rice COMP TR86-31.

2 Barr, J. (1989) Parallel power generation. *Systems International,* May 1989, 47-48.

3 Bast, H.J. and Gerndt, M. (1989) SUPERB - the Suprenum parallelizer. *Supercomputer,* March 1989, 51-57.

4 Cox, S. (1988) Fortran loop optimiser functional specification. *System Software Factors.*

5 Ellis, J.R. (1985) *Bulldog : A Compiler for VLIW Architectures,* MIT Press, London.

6 Hockney, R.W. and Jesshope, C.R. (1988) *Parallel Computers,* 2nd Edition. Adam Hilgar, Bristol.

7 Johnson, T. and Durham, T. (1986) *Parallel Processing: the Challenge of New Computer Architectures,* Ovum, London.

8   Levesque, J.M. and Williamson, J.W. (1989) *A Guidebook to Fortran on Supercomputers,* Academic Press, London.

9   Padua, D. and Wolfe, M. (1986) Advanced Compiler Optimisations for Supercomputers, *CACM,* 29, 12, 1184-1201.

10 Solchenbach, K. (1989) Suprenum Fortran - an MIMD/SIMD language. *Supercomputer,* March 1989, 25-30.

11 Wolfe, M.   (1989) *Optimizing Supercompilers for Supercomputers,* Pitman, London.

10 Parallel processing at Cray Research, Inc.

M. Furtney

Cray Research Inc., USA

10.1 INTRODUCTION

Cray Research Inc. introduced its first multiprocessor supercomputer in 1982, the dual-CPU Cray X-MP/2. To support individual programs using both CPUs, a library of synchronization primitives was introduced (macrotasking), and it became the *defacto* industry standard. In 1984, the Unicos operating system, based on AT&T's Unix System V, was introduced. This system provided new, easy-to-use tools (background processes, pipes) for utilizing multiple CPUs to accomplish complex tasks. As users and developers gained experience with macrotasking, several unexplored avenues for parallel exploitation were opened. The collection of these techniques (microtasking) addressed some of the weaknesses of macrotasking, was generally easy to use, and provided good performance in both batch and dedicated computing environments. Microtasking evolved from macrotasking, and provides substantial advantages over macrotasking; it still required that programmers occasionally do some detailed data dependence analyses to use it safely. Unlike vectorization with Cray Fortran compilers, microtasking is not automatic, and that is the next evolutionary step. Autotasking has grown from the excellent performance experiences with microtasking, and provides an automatic mechanism for exploiting parallelism without programmer intervention. Since there will probably never be a replacement for the experienced Fortran programmer, Autotasking provides a variety of techniques by which the knowledgeable user can fine-tune a program and exploit levels of parallelism not visible to the Autotasking system.

Section 10.2 describes briefly the macrotasking libraries, and experiences with macrotasking. Section 10.3 describes microtasking and how it has addressed some of the shortcomings of macrotasking. Section 10.4 discusses Autotasking: how it evolved from microtasking, how it fits in the compiling system, and how it can be used. Some of the benefits of the Autotasking system are discussed, and the results of Autotasking several large Fortran programs are reported in this section also. A short Summary section concludes this paper.

10.2 MACROTASKING

Macrotasking is a technique whereby programs are modified with explicit calls to a special Fortran-callable library of synchronization routines (these routines are also callable from C and other languages). This collection of routines, termed the macrotasking library, provides the primitives necessary to allow a single program to execute correctly on multiple CPUs. These library routines interact directly with the operating system for the creation of extra tasks, and with the hardware to provide the necessary synchronization between concurrently-executing tasks. The macrotasking library contains four sets of routines: one (tasks) for task creation and manipulation, and three for synchronization (locks, events, barriers).

Macrotasking works best when the amount of work to be partitioned over multiple processors is large. When the work to be partitioned is not large compared to the synchronization time, excess synchronization time may become noticeable. When applying macrotasking to an existing code that did not consider multiprocessing as one of its design considerations, it may be necessary to do a significant amount of code restructuring. This can lead to an opportunity to introduce new errors. When the work is not easy to partition into equal-sized tasks, load imbalance may occur, producing lower speedups than anticipated. Further, macrotasked programs may display markedly different performance characteristics when comparing batch versus dedicated executions. Because of these and other reasons, macrotasking of existing large engineering and scientific applications codes did not appeal to many programmers. Microtasking is the direct result of efforts to address some of the characteristics of macrotasking that made it unpopular.

10.3 MICROTASKING

Microtasking is a technique for multiprocessing programs which is based on exploiting parallelism in DO-Loops. The primary design goals of microtasking have been to provide good performance over a wide range of problem sizes, to make it easy to use, and to work well in both batch and dedicated environments. Microtasking employs a master/slave relationship between CPUs. When the master processor enters a region that can benefit from parallel execution, it alerts the slaves, which may then enter the computation.

Programmers who employ microtasking determine where parallelism exists, then place comment directives in the text of their programs. See the bottom half of Table 10.2 for a description of the microtasking directives. A preprocessor reads these directives, and translates them and their associated DO-Loops into a form acceptable to the compiler. Code is generated that allows the program to use extra CPUs if they are available. If idle CPU cycles are available on the system, microtasked codes can use them as accelerators for completing a particular loop. If idle cycles are not available, the microtasked code (executing in the master processor) does not slow down to summon them or to wait for them. Loop iterations are handed out to the next CPU ready for work (self-scheduling), resulting in excellent load-balancing. The code that performs this protected handling out of iterations is extremely efficient, around 40 clock periods on a Cray X-MP system. This permits the profitable exploitation of very fine-grained parallelism. Microtasking also makes good use of other Cray X-MP features (like hardware deadlock detect) to provide very fast mechanisms for getting CPUs to join a fray (a code segment that may utilize multiple CPUs) and to remove CPUs from a potential busy-wait situation (for example when a CPU is withdrawn from a fray by the operating system and the other CPUs must wait for a DO-Loop to be completed before continuing).

When microtasking on the Cray-2 system (which does not have such a rich set of parallel synchronization hardware), alternate methods were developed to handle these situations. These methods have proven to be so powerful that they are being moved to the Cray X-MP microtasking design for comparison.

Although microtasking generates its computional efficiency by spreading DO-Loop iterations over multiple CPUs, it is based on subroutine boundaries, not loop boundaries. This has been done because subroutines provide a natural break in a code where the scope of variables (which subroutines and tasks can see particular instances of particular variables) can be easily manipulated into a form that permits correct parallel execution. This implies that some portions of microtasked subroutines are executed redundantly by whichever CPUs show up. In many instances, this redundant computation merely sets up a local context in which the parallel loop may execute (without slowing the master processor down by forcing it to broadcast local context).

On other occasions, there may be a fair amount of redundant code, or the code not inside parallelizable. DO-Loops may not be safe to execute by multiple CPUs. This is the first of the drawbacks to microtasking. The second drawback is that programmers must still find the parallelism, and sometimes this can be difficult. Just as microtasking evolved from macrotasking and grew on its strengths while addressing its weaknesses, so Autotasking has evolved from microtasking. Autotasking retains the many advantages of microtasking, and relieves some of the shortcomings.

10.4 AUTOTASKING

Autotasking is a technique whereby the compiling system detects opportunities for parallel exploitation, and generates code to execute these parallel regions on multiple CPUs. Autotasking retains the many advantages of microtasking (self-scheduling for good load-balancing, very low synchronization overhead, uses idle CPU cycles when available, excellent performance in both batch and dedicated environments, original source code unmodified, etc.), while adding several new advantages. Autotasking can be completely automatic, where the compiling system does all the analysis and generates parallel code, or it can work with the programmer to provide support for potentially higher levels of parallelism exploitation. Autotasking works on DO-Loop boundaries, but is easily expandable to parallel regions and to subroutine boundaries.

Autotasking inside the compiling system can be thought of as a three-phase operation: dependence analysis, translation, and code generation (as illustrated by fig. 10.1). Programmers may optionally pass directives to any of the three phases (see Tables 10.1 and 10.2 for an outline of these directives). For example, a programmer may know that a certain large program segment accounts for only a percent or two of total run-time, and so may choose to disable the extensive dependence analysis done in this region of the code because there will be no payoff (and to save compilation time). Or, a programmer may know that a DO-Loop that contains an external call may be safe to execute in parallel, and wish to alert the compiling system to that fact (the dependence analyser does not look beyond subroutine boundaries). Sections 10.4.2 and 10.4.4 describe these directives.

Table 10.1 Directives to the dependence analyser phase

CFPPS	Directive description
CONCUR	Enable concurrency analysis
NOCONCUR	Disable concurrency analysis
INNER	Enable concurrency analysis for vectorizable loops
NOINNER	Disable concurrency analysis for vectorizable loops
VECTOR	Enable vectorization analysis for innermost loops
NOVECTOR	Disable vectorization analysis
SKIP	Disable dependence analysis

Table 10.2 Directives to the translator phase

CMICS Directive	Description
CASE	Independent code block separator
CONTINUE	Parallelism extension to extemal
GUARD	Start a critical section
DO ALL	Independent DO-Loop iterations where the DO-Loop is the entire Parallel Region
END CASE	Independent code block terminator
END DO	Termination point for Reduction
END GUARD	Critical section terminator
END PARALLEL	Parallel Region terminator
PARALLEL	Start of a Parallel Region
DO PARALLEL	Independent DO-Loop iterations where the DO-Loop is inside a Parallel Region
SOFT EXIT	GOTO on next line cause a branch out of a parallel region
ALSO PROCESS*	Independent code block separator
CONTINUE*	Parallelism extension to external
DO GLOBAL*	Independent DO-Loop iterations
END GUART*	Critical section terminator
END PROCESS*	Independent code block terminator
GUARD*	Start a critical section
MICRO*	microtasking subroutine follows
PROCESS*	Start of a code block
STOP ALL PROCESS*	GOTO on next line cause a branch out of a parallel region

*Microtasking directive

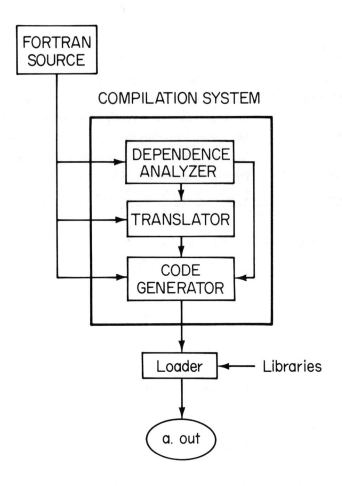

Figure 10.1 3-Phase compiling system

10.4.1 Functions of the dependence analyser

The dependence analyser performs a wide variety of program optimizations. It looks for parallel constructs and may perform some source code transformations to produce faster-executing code. Payoffs from dependence analysis come in four major areas:

1. enhanced vectorization

2. recognition and generation of parallel constructs (concurrentization)

3. automatic in-line expansion

4. special code sequence recognition

(a)   Enhanced vectorization

The dependence analysis phase recognizes vectorization opportunities and uses a host of techniques to try to produce vectorizable code. These techniques include statement reordering, ambiguous subscript resolution, reference reordering, splitting calls out of loops, loop nest restructuring, and loop exchange (to get stride of one and/or longest vector length on the innermost loops). In a recent vectorization study [1] of 100 loops, the vectorized loop count went from 51 to 72 when using the new compiling system, showing a substantial improvement.

(b)   Concurrentization

The dependence analysis phase recognizes parallelization opportunities, and inserts directives to the next phase (translation), which tell it how to exploit this inherent parallelism. Again, the dependence analyser may do some code transformations to produce parallel opportunities. In general, it will attempt to concurrentize on the outermost loop possible.

(c)   Automatic in-line expansion

Automatic inlining of subroutines by the dependence analyser also has a big payoff. Not only does in-line expansion remove the overhead of the call, it also can then possibly concurrentize on a more outer loop (from the original code before in-line expansion). In many cases this is very profitable.

(d)   Specific code sequence recognition

The dependence analyser also recognizes some special code sequences, including matrix multiply, first and second order linear recurrences, dot product, and search for maximum or minimum. It then generates calls directly to optimized library routines, which can perform these functions in parallel.

10.4.2 Parallel processing directives (to the dependence analyzer)

Directives to the dependence analyser begin with CFPPS in columns 1-6 and run from columns 7-72. Upper case and lowercase may be used freely in the directive text. Optional parameters to individual directives are declined by brackets []. The following is a full list of the directives and their optional parameters with a discussion of each.

CFPP$ CONCUR [(n)] [s]

CFPP$ NOCONCUR [s]

CFPP$ INNER [(n)] [s]

CFPP$ NOINNER [s]

CFPP$ VECTOR [s]

CFPP$ NOVECTOR [s]

CFPP$ SKIP [s]

Throughout this section, the optional parameter s refers to the scope of the directive, and n refers to the concurrency threshold. As directives are encountered in the Fortran source text, these parameters are treated as if they were in a pushdown stack. The allowable values for s are:

s	Description
L[OOP]	For the next DP-Loop (but not its inner Loops)
R[OUTINE]	For the rest of the current subprogram
F[ILE]	For the rest of the file

When s is not specified, the default scope for a directive is LOOP. The concurrency threshold parameter, n, must be a positive integar constant. When n is specified, and dependence analyser can determine the DO-Loop tripcount, concurrency analysis is enabled only when (tripcount $>$ =n). When n is specified and tripcount cannot be determined, concurrency analysis is enabled, but the dependence analyser must generate the (tripcount $>$ =n) test in the if clause of the DO ALL or DO PARALLEL directive (see next section).

CFPP$ CONCUR [(n)] [s]

CFPP$ NOCONCUR [s]

The CONCUR directive enables concurrency analysis, telling the dependence analyser phase to look for parallelization opportunities over the scope (s parameter) specified. When n is not specified, concurrency analysis is enabled unconditionally. When n is specified, the rules outlined above are followed. At the beginning of a file sent to the compiling system, the default in CONCUR FILE. When concurrency analysis is enabled, the INNER directives are activated. The NOCONCUR directive disables concurrency analysis over the scope (s parameter) specified. Note that both CONCUR and NOCONCUR imply VECTOR (see below). That is, vectorization analysis changes.

CFPP$ INNER [(n)] [s]

CFPP$ NOINNER [s]

The INNER directive enables concurrency analysis for innermost vectorizable DO-Loops over the scope (s parameter) specified. The INNER directive is only recognized when concurrency analysis is enabled. That is, when the dependence analyser phase cannot find exploitable parallelism on an outer DO-Loop, and INNER is enabled, and it detects an innermost vectorizable DO-Loop, the dependence analyser will issue a DO ALL or DO PARALLEL directive for that loop. (See the next section for a discussion of the DO ALL and DO PARALLEL directives). The NOINNER directive disables concurrency analysis for innermost vectorizable DO-Loops over the scope (s parameter) specified. At the beginning of a file sent to compiling system, the default is NOINNER FILE. Note that the INNER-NOINNER directives refer only to vectorizable innermost DO-Loops. Nonvectorizable innermost DO-Loops are subject to concurrency analysis under the control of the CONCUR directive.

CFPP$ VECTOR [s]

CFPP$ NOVECTOR [s]

The VECTOR directive enables vectorization analysis for innermost DO-Loops over the scope (s parameter) specified. At the beginning of a file sent to compiling system, the default is VECTOR FILE. The NOVECTOR directive disables vectorization analysis over the scope (s parameter) specified. The NOVECTOR directive is activated only when NOCONCUR is in control, and is ignored otherwise. Note that the NOVECTOR directive is employed only by the dependence analyser phase, and therefore blocks only phase 1 dependence analysis. That is, CFPP$ NOVECTOR does not imply CDIR$ NOVECTOR. CDIR$

NOVECTOR, however, implies both CFPP$ NONCUR LOOP and CFPP$ NOVECTOR LOOP.

CFPP$ SKIP [s]

The SKIP directive disables both concurrency and vectorization analysis. SKIP is a shorthand for consecutive NOCONCUR and NOVECTOR directives. The principal use of the directive is turn off phase 1 (dependence analyser) and analysis in portions of program that do not contribute to any significant run-time, thereby saving some compile time.

10.4.3   Functions of the translator

The primary function of the translator phase is to rewrite the Fortran-code-with-directives into pure Fortran for use by the code generation phase. Directives (Whether written by the dependence analyser phase or the human programmer) are expanded into a series of special function calls and compiler intrinsics that together implement the requested parallel processing functionality. A primary consideration in this rewriting exercise is to enforce the scoping requirements detailed in the directives. (See the next section for a discussion of individual directives and data scoping parameters.) Every variable in each parallel segment of code has a scope of either private or shared, as declared on the directive. There is only one copy of each shared variable, and it is available to all processors that contribute to the computation. There are potentially many copies or private variables, one per contributing processor.

10.4.4   Parallel processing directives (to the translator)

Translator directives begin with CMIC$ in columns 1-6 and run from columns 7-72. Directives can be continued by using CMIC$* in columns 1-6 on continuation statement(s), where * can be any non-blank, non-zero character. That is, directives follow the Fortran continuation rules. Parameters on directives (for example, private) may be repeated as needed, and need not be ordered. Uppercase and lowercase may be used freely in the directive text. Optional parameters to individual directives are delimited by brackets[]. A full list of the directives and their optional parameters follows with a discussion of each.

CMIC$ PARALLEL *[if(expr)] [shared(var[....])] [private(var[....])]*

CMIC$ END PARALLEL

CMIC$ DO ALL *[if(expr)] [shared(var[....])] [private(var[....])] [savelast] [single] [chunksize(n)] [numchunks(m)] [guided] [vector]*

CMIC$ DO PARALLEL *[single] [chunksize(n)] [numchunks(m)] [guided] [vector]*

CMIC$ END DO

CMIC$ GUARD [n]

CMIC$ END GUARD [n]

CMIC$ CASE

CMIC$ END CASE

CMIC$ SOFT EXIT

CMIC$ CONTINUE

CMIC$ PARALLEL [if(expr)] [shared(var[....])] [private(var[....])]

CMIC$ END PARALLEL

The PARALLEL-END PARALLEL directive pair delimits a parallel region, which provides a technique for modifying some variables' scope to allow correct multiprocessing to occur. Parallel regions provide a powerful mechanism with which the knowledgeable programmer can increase the efficiency of parallel computations by reducing the cost of parallel startup and spreading this cost over multiple parallel exploitation opportunities. Parallel regions are combinations of redundant code blocks and partitioned code blocks (for example, DO PARALLEL, or CASE, described below). The PARALLEL directive indicates where multiple processors enter execution, which may be different from where they demonstrate a direct benefit (partitioned code block). The following paragraphs explain the optional parameters:

if-When specified, a run-time test is performed to choose between uniprocessing and multiprocessing. When not specified, multiprocessing is chosen.

expr - The logical expression that determines (at run-time) whether multiprocessing will occur. When expr is True, multiprocessing is enabled.

shared - The variable(s) listed here will have GLOBAL scope. That is, they are accessible to the master and the slave tasks. The shared clause identifies those variables that by default are not GLOBAL, but for the purposes of parallel exploitation, need to be. By default, GLOBAL variables are those that appear in a COMMON block, the argument list, or in a DATA or SAVE statement, and all others are LOCAL.

private - The variable(s) listed here will have LOCAL scope. That is, each task (master and slaves) will have its own private copy of these variables. The private clause identifies those variables that by default are GLOBAL, but for the purposes of parallel exploitation, need to be LOCAL. By default, GLOBAL variables are those that appear in a COMMON block, the argument list, or in a DATA or SAVE statement, and all others are LOCAL.

>   CMIC$ DO ALL *[if(expr)] [shared(var[....])] [private(var[....])] [savelast]*
>   *[single] [chunksize(n)] [numchunks(m)] [guided] [vector]*

>   CMIC$ DO PARALLEL *[single] [chunksize(n)] [numchunks(m)] [guided]*
>   *[vector]*

The DO ALL and DO PARALLEL directives indicate that the DO-Loop that begins on the next line will be executed in parallel by multiple processors. No directive is used to end a DO ALL or DO PARALLEL loop. The DO ALL [parameters] directive is a special shorthand for the following three directives (note that no END PARALLEL directive is needed when DO ALL is used):

>   CMIC$ PARALLEL [parameters]

>   CMIC$ DO PARALLEL [parameter]

>   :

>   CMIC$ END PARALLEL

That is, the DO ALL initiates a parallel region whose only code is a DO-Loop with independent iterations. Note that when using DO ALL, the loop index variable is private. The following paragraphs explain the optional parameters:

savelast - This directive specifies that private variables' values (from the final iteration of a DO ALL) will persist in the master task after execution of the iterations of the DO ALL. By default, private variables are not guaranteed to retain the last iteration values. Note that savelast can only be used with DO ALL, and that if the full iteration set is not completed (for example, due to a SOFT EXIT), the values of the savelast variables are indeterminate.

The rest of the parameters (single, chunksize, numchunks, guided, vector) specify the work distribution policy for the iterations of the parallel DO-Loop. By default, the iterations are handed out one at a time (that is, single is the default). Only one of the following five work distribution algorithms can be chosen for a given DO-Loop:

single - Parcel out iterations to available processors one at a time.

chunksize(n) - Break the iteration space into chunks of size n, where n is an expression (for best performance, n should be an integer constant). Chunksize(64) is an analog of microtasking's LONGVECTOR directive.

numchunks(m) - Break the iteration space into "m" chunks of equal size (with a possible smaller residual chunk).

guided - Use Guided Self Scheduling [2] to partition the iteration space. This mechanism does a good job at minimizing synchronization overhead while providing decent dynamic load balancing.

vector - The scheduling algorithm is used only in the case of stripmining an innermost vectorized loop. It implies guided chunks down to a minimum strip of 64.

The following examples illustrate some typical uses of parallel regions and DO PARALLEL directive:

```
CMIC$ PARALLEL
      X = 3.14159265
      Y = ZZ/3.1333345
      Z = SQRT(A + Y)
CMIC$ DO PARALLEL
```

```
            DO 400 I = 1,IMAX
               :Code using X,Y,Z
        400 CONTINUE
        CMIC$ END PARALLEL
```

Example 10.1 Redundant initialization

In Example 10.1, each processor redundantly calculates X,Y and Z for its own use. In general this is much faster than having one processor (the master) calculate the values and then broadcasting them to other processors.

```
        CMIC$ PARALLEL
        CMIC$ DO PARALLEL
            DO 200 I = 1,IMAX
                   :
        200 CONTINUE
        CMIC$ DO PARALLEL
            DO 400 J = 1,IMAX
  :
        400 CONTINUE
        CMIC$ END PARALLEL
```

Example 10.2 Multiple Partitioned blocks

In Example 10.2, the parallel startup time is amortized over two DO-Loops. Note that the startup cost may be comparable to the cost of a subroutine call.

```
        CMIC$ PARALLEL
            DO 600 I = 1,JMAX
                   :
        CMIC$ DO PARALLEL
            DO 200 J = 1,IMAX
                   :
        200 CONTINUE
        CMIC$ DO PARALLEL
            DO 400 K = 1,KMAX
                   :
        400 CONTINUE
        600 CONTINUE
        CMIC$ END PARALLEL
```

Example 10.3 Multiple Partitioned blocks

In Example 10.3, no parallelism in the DO 600 loop could be found, but by using a parallel region, the startup time is amortized over IMAX*2 parallel loops.

```
        SUM = 0.0
CMIC$ PARALLEL PRIVATE(XSUM)
        XSUM = 0.0
          :
CMIC$ DO PARALLEL
        DO 200 J = 1,JMAX
          :
        XSUM = XSUM + (A(J)*B(J))
          :
        200 CONTINUE
CMIC$ GUARD
        SUM = SUM + XSUM
CMIC$ END GUARD
CMIC$ END DO
CMIC$ END PARALLEL
```

Example 10.4 Reduction Computation

In Example 10.4, the sum reduction computation on SUM is performed at full concurrent/vector speed. Each arriving processor has its own private copy of XSUM, which is added to the global SUM under protection of the GUARD (discussed below). The END DO directive forces late-arriving processors (those which do not get any iterations of the DO 200 Loop) to jump around the summation into SUM and wait for it to be complete before continuing.

```
        CMIC$ GUARD [n]
        CMIC$ END GUARD [n]
```

The GUARD-END GUARD directive pair delimits a critical region, and provides the necessary synchronization to protect (or guard) the code inside the critical region. A critical region is a code block which is to be executed by only one processor at a time, although all processors in the parallel region execute it. The optional parameter n is an expression that serves as a mutual exclusion flag (using the low-order 6-bits of the value). That is, GUARD 1 and GUARD 2 can be concurrently active, but two GUARD 7s cannot. For optional performance, n should be an integer constant, and the general expression capability is provided only for the unusual case that the critical region number must be passed to a lower level routine. When no n is provided, the critical region blocks only other instances of itself, but no other critical regions. Critical regions may appear anywhere in a program. That is, they are not limited only to parallel regions.

```
CMIC$ CASE
CMIC$ END CASE
```

The CASE directive serves as a separator between adjacent code blocks that are concurrently executable. The CASE directive may appear only in a parallel region. The END CASE directive serves as the terminator for a group of one or more parallel CASEs. In the following example, subroutines ABC, DEF and XYZ are concurrently executable.

```
CMIC$ CASE
    CALL ABC
CMIC$ CASE
    CALL DEF
CMIC$ CASE
    CALL XYZ
CMIC$ END CASE
```

The work in all of ABC, DEF and XYZ completes before execution continues with the code below the END CASE. A special form of the CASE-END CASE directive pair is to use it to force only a single processor to execute a code block in a parallel region, as in the following example.

```
CMIC$ PARALLEL
        :
CMIC$ CASE
    CALL XYZ
CMIC$ END CASE
        :
CMIC$ DO PARALLEL
    DO 200 I = 1,IMAX
        :
    200 CONTINUE
CMIC$ END PARALLEL
```

In the above example, only one processor calls XYZ.

CMIC$ SOFT EXIT

The SOFT EXIT directive indicates that the GOTO statement on the next line branches outside the currently executing partitioned code block or parallel region.

CMIC$ CONTINUE

The CONTINUE directive indicates that the external called on the next line has been specially prepared by the programmer for execution in parallel. The dependence analyser will not generate this directive, nor can it prepare the called subprogram for this special form of processing. This is an important optimization technique for some programs.

10.4.5 Unique features of autotasking

Autotasking offers several features that allow more parallelism to be found and exploited. The three-phase compiling system gives programmers a great deal of freedom in selecting the forms of parallel processing most efficient for individual types of computation. Users also find great range in the forms of directives that can direct the dependence analyser and the translator, and they are encouraged to combine their own knowledge of the problem domain with the dependence analyser's output to create faster-running programs. The concept of a parallel region allows the computational overhead of processor startup to be minimized and amortized over multiple exploitable sections of code. Parallel regions also allow the efficient parallel exploitation of many forms of reduction computations. The savelast parameter on the DO ALL construct allows parallel loops that must carry scalar (or array) elements from the last iteration out of the loop body to be executed correctly and efficiently in parallel. The in-line expansion feature of the dependence analyser is performed before parallelism analysis is performed, leading to many cases of outer parallel loops surrounding inner (in-lined) loops. The SOFT EXIT construct allows loops that contain a jump to outside their range to be safely processed in parallel. The CONTINUE construct permits an important cross-subroutine optimization to occur under user direction. The introduction of the five forms of parallel loop iteration partitioning (single, chunksize, numchunks, guided and vector) add a new dimension to tuning particular DO-Loops. Guided and vector are particularly useful for a variety of programs.

10.4.6   Some results using autotasking

This section shows a series of results using Autotasking on a variety of production codes and benchmarks. As expected, some codes contain very little or no parallelism, some contain a modest amount, and some are almost entirely parallel. It is hard to determine what proportion of codes in any particular problem domain fall into each of the three categories, but it is clear that there are many codes of each type. Independent of the amount of parallelism in a given program, users can almost always benefit from the messages generated by the dependence analyser that describe why vectorization and/or concurrentization have been inhibited.

CPUs	Time (secs)
1	424.8
2	239.3
3	176.7
4	146.0

Case 10.1 Magnetohydrodynamics Code (Cray X-MP/48)

The program in Case 10.1 is a large Magnetohydrodynamics code. When working out the maximum theoretical speedups possible for a code with this level of parallelism (just under 90%), we see that the implementation of Autotasking produces speedups very close to the maximum speedups possible. This is an example of the very low overhead cost associated with synchronization in Autotasking.

CPUs	Microtasking Time(secs)	Autotasking Time (secs)
1	258.311	250.219
2	131.582	157.210
3	92.751	124.939
4	73.638	109.824
5	55.516	97.847
6	53.712	93.981
7	51.927	89.466
8	50.861	87.003

Case 10.2a Microtasking vs. Autotasking, Cray Y-MP/832

Case 10.2a is representative of many programs that have been microtasked, then Autotasked (the microtasking directives were removed for the Autotasked run).The programmer took about two weeks to do the microtasking; the Autotasking system took about 210 milliseconds. It is very difficult for an automatic system to compete with human programmers. As in many cases like this, the human programmer microtasked a series of DO-Loops that contained external calls. The programmer checked the called routines and found it was safe to execute them in parallel. The Autotasking system does not look beyond subroutine boundaries, so was forced to make the safe judgment. It judged that the external call was not safe to execute in parallel, so it marked the loops as non-parallelizable because of the external calls. Programmers confronted with this situation can utilize the CFPP$ CNCALL directive to the dependence analyser to indicate that an external call in the next loop should be considered safe for parallel execution.

CPUs	Microtasking Time (secs)	Autotasking Time (secs)
1	166.122	171.724
2	86.113	87.651
3	59.753	59.601
4	46.819	45.603
5	40.364	37.440
6	34.145	32.026
7	33.999	28.268
8	28.863	25.628

Case 10.2b Microtasking vs.Autotasking, Cray Y-MP/832

Case 10.2b, which compares microtasking and Autotasking, occurs much less frequently. As in Case 10.2a, the time required was about two weeks for microtasking of Case 10.2b versus 190 milliseconds for Autotasking. In this case however, Autotasking found several areas for parallel execution not found by the programmer. In particular, some concurrentizable reductions were found (there is no mechanism in microtasking for this construct) and exploited.

	Cray Y-MP		Cray-2	
CPUs	Actual	Theoretical	Actual	Theoretical
2	1.891	1.893	1.868	1.890
3	2.674	2.695	2.609	2.687
4	3.355	3.419	3.278	3.434
8	5.459	5.727	-	-

Case 10.3a Speedups: LU Decomposition (500x500)

	Cray Y-MP		Cray-2	
CPUs	Actual	Theoretical	Actual	Theoretical
2	1.930	1.941	1.907	1.933
3	2.788	2.828	2.717	2.805
4	3.611	3.665	3.429	3.622
8	6.262	6.595	-	-

Case 10.3b Speedups: LU Decomposition (1000x1000)

Cases 10.3a and 10.3b illustrate speedups over single-CPU versions of large LU-Decomposition computations for an 8-CPU Cray Y-MP system and a 4-CPU Cray-2 system. Although these machines are similar in many respects, their different memory speeds and vector start-up times combine to produce slightly different maximum theoretical speedups. This is a good example of why it is not a good idea to compare speedups between machines. This is especially important when considering machines with very different characteristics.

Kernel Number	Megaflops: Unitasking	Megaflops: Autotasking	Megaflops: Autotasking Plus Mods
1	275.4	1556	1685
2	74.2	70.2	446.0
3	89.9	122.5	285.8
4	149.5	236.7	236.7
5	118.4	950.9	1036.7
6	135.1	169.4	1132.8
7	52.9	50.2	432.5

Case 10.4 NASA Computational Kernels, Cray Y-MP/832

Case 10.4 is a series of computational kernels from NASA/Ames that are representative of a large portion of their workload. Column 2 represents their unitasking Megaflop rates on a Cray Y-MP. In Column 3, these same kernels have been Autotasked, showing a wide range of performance improvements. One of our benchmarkers was allowed to make a specified number of changes, and ran the codes again to get the results shown in column 4. Again we see that the experienced programmer can often make a significant difference in overall performance. In these cases, the benchmarker used information about inhibitors to parallelism put out by the dependence analyser, and added his own experience and knowledge about the problem domains to generate faster run-times. These NASA kernels seem representative of what one can expect from Autotasking, and Autotasking augmented by a knowledgeable programmer. Sometimes the automatic system can find little or no parallelism, and other times it is very good at finding and exploiting parallelism. Usually the programmer can improve the performance of a code, often by knowing information like tripcounts for important DO-Loops, looking beyond subroutine boundaries, and algorithm rewriting.

| Before Autotasking | 242 Megaflops |
| After Autotasking | 1.9 + Gigaflops |

Case 10.5 Utrecht Benchmark, Cray Y-MP/832

This program implements a Black and Red Elliptical Differential Equation Solver. This benchmark, brought in by the University of Utrecht in Holland, is well above 99% parallel. These results were generated completely automatically. It is a shame that not all codes are as parallel as this one.

10.5 SUMMARY

This paper has discussed software for parallel processing available on Cray supercomputer systems. The three generations of Multitasking software (macrotasking, microtasking and Autotasking) have been described, showing how they evolved from the needs of the scientific and engineering applications computing community and from the strengths of their predecessors. All three generations provide some special services not available from the others, and all three will be supported by Cray in the future. Macrotasking, microtasking, and

Autotasking are part of a single integrated parallel processing package, and can be used in any combination in a single program.

Particular attention has been paid in this paper to Autotasking, with discussions of its internal features and some results with production programs.

REFERENCES

1   Callahan, D. , Dongarra, J. and Levine, D. (1988) Vectorizing compilers: A test suite and results. *Proc. Supercomputing '88.*

2   Polychronopouls, C. and Kuck, D. (1987) Guided Self Scheduling: A Practical Scheduling Scheme for Parallel Supercomputers. *IEEE Trans. Computers,* December 1987.

11 Parallel extraction techniques and loosely coupled target systems

P. van Santen* and S. Robinson**

* Department of Computer Science, Brunel University, Uxbridge, UK

** Informatics Division, Rutherford Appleton Laboratory, Didcot, UK

11.1 INTRODUCTION

Faster hardware components and circuits, coupled with advances in machine organization, have lead to faster and faster processing systems but it has long been recognized that program execution speedup is reaching its limit on single processor computers [9], [5], [58]. The obvious direction in which to proceed in order to achieve greater speedup is to use more than one processor for a given computation.

It has been shown [53], [12], that, given a parallel processing system with p processing units and f, the fraction of a program that can utilise those processors, then the speedup Sp obtained for that program satisfies

$$S_p \le \frac{p}{f + (1-f)p}$$

(11.1)

thus

$$f \ge \left[\frac{S_p - 1}{S_p} \right] \left[\frac{p}{p-1} \right]$$

(11.2)

and

$$p \geq \frac{fS_p}{1-(1-f)S_p}$$

(11.3)

From (11.3) a school of thought has arisen doubting the usefulness of employing very large numbers of processors for computation. Amdahl [5] argues that the majority of programs have an average of more than 10% serial code and hence that their speedup is bounded above by 10.

In practice, Amdahl's argument has been disputed. Polychronopoulos and Banerjee [53] have reported the results of experiments that were carried out to measure f, the fraction of parallel code, in LINPACK (a numerical package for solving systems of linear equations). LINPACK is claimed to be typical of those packages that are not very amenable to restructuring for parallel processing but results of the experiments show that, for the first 37 out of the 49 subroutines studied, the average fraction of parallel code, f, exceeded 0.9783 and that only 18% of the whole sample have f 0.8. From this, Polychronopoulos and Banerjee argue that it is often the case that thousands of processors can be used efficiently in real applications.

Many different machine organisations have been proposed for multiprocessor systems. However, all pose the same problem in relation to the software intended to run on them: either new parallel languages need to be designed or existing sequential languages modified. But what of the existing libraries of software written in purely sequential languages? Manual rewriting or modification seems improbable.

The transputer [16]. [66] is a VLSI microcomputer incorporating processor, local memory and intercomputer serial data links on a single chip. It was developed to serve as a node computer in a regularly connected, loosely coupled network of autonomous, and nominally identical, concurrent processing elements. Communication between adjacent transputers is be synchronous message-passing (i.e. the sending process sends a message for the receiving process then waits for an acknowledgement).

The general reluctance to redesign and rewrite existing code, and a lack of familiarity with transputer technology. Occan and suitable multi-process program design methodologies, currently presents a significant barrier to the widespread general use of transputer systems in engineering environments in industry and academia.

At the present, transputer development environments support Occam II, that offers a multi-transputer, multi-process solution path to a software problem and Fortran, Pascal, and C systems that most immediately offer a single transputer, single process solution path to unmodified source code. Therefore, for 'dusty-deck' code, the potential throughout improvements offered by multi-transputer configurations are not immediately available.

There are several solutions to this problem. The first, currently being addressed by the SERC/DTI initiative on the Engineering Applications of Transputers [1], is to promote awareness of the potential of the transputer and associated technology. Part of this activity involves the encouragement of transputer familiarity through courses, workshops and equipment loans.

A second solution is the provision of some standard tools to make the migration of existing high level language source to transputer configurations as simple as possible [28]. One such tool set, "parallel extracting" compilers for the more commonly used, dusty-deck high level languages, promises a most attractive solution to the migration problem.

The aim of our study was to investigate the feasibility of one of these compilers for the development of a concurrency extracting Fortran compiler targeted at loosely coupled multi-transputer hosts. In this respect candidate approaches to concurrency extraction, concurrent code generation, program execution, scheduling and architecture configuration are reviewed and, in some cases, assessed using a static analysis of dusty-deck Fortran and explored using small experiments on transputer technology.

11.2 EARLIER WORK ON PARALLELISM EXTRACTION

The major part of earlier research into "parallelism extraction" has centred in the area of tightly-coupled multi-processor shared memory systems.

These supercomputers use parallelism to provide users with increased computational power, are programmed in some high level language, commonly Fortran, and all vendors provide Fortran Compilers that detect parallelism and generate parallel code to take advantage of their particular machine's architecture

[31], [63], [31]. Besides vendor-supplied compilers, a number of experimental and third-party source to source restructurers have been developed, included Parafrase [40], KAP [19], PFC [4], and VAST [11]. The techniques involved, mainly utilising data dependence and control flow analysis, include loop vectorisation, loop concurrentisation, induction analysis, interprocedural analysis, scalar expansion, loop interchanging, fission by name, loop fission and loop collapsing, strip mining etc as detailed in [52]. Most are seen as concentrating on loops (in the case of Fortran, DO loops) as the main source of parallelism.

Cvetanovic [17] identifies the following parameters that are expected to have the most influence on the performance of any multiprocessor system:-

1. inherent parallelism in the application problem (and the methods used for detection),

2. the methods used for decomposing a problem into tasks,

3. allocation of tasks to processors,

4. grain size of the tasks,

5. the possibility of overlapping communication with processing,

6. data-access mode - whether data items are accessed from a common global memory or first copied to local memories

7. the interconnection structure, and

8. the speed of processors, memories and the interconnection network.

The loosely-coupled architecture provided by transputer configurations (multi-processor, local private memory, synchronous communication) does not immediately lend itself to all of the parallelism extraction techniques employed by the systems mentioned above, due, in particular, to its variance in relation to point (6) of Cvetanovic's list. The inter-processor and inter-process communication problems introduced by the locality of memory (and thereby, the data address space of the running program) need to be addressed differently in any devised techniques for parallelism extraction with transputer target. Some initial work has been reported for such an architecture [21] but the model used ignores any communication costs.

From this it can be seen that the success of any chosen approach would depend on the frequency of the structures that permit extraction (Cvetanovic point (1)), the typical patterns of access to the address space and the typical bandwidth and frequency of inter-process/processor communication.

Exactly what is "typical" in Fortran source needs to be assessed and, therefore, one part of the most promising approach at this stage appears to be an empirical analysis ([60], [61], [22]) of existing Fortran sources. Through this empirical analysis we might quantify any given (or preferred) approach to parallelism extraction. If it can be shown that there exist commonly occurring facets in Fortran source that would lend themselves to a static detection leading to a parallel implementation (in our ideal candidate, by both data and object code distribution across various transputer configurations with narrow bandwidth inter-processor communication), then a compiler that would automatically identify these facets when they occur and arrange their parallel execution on a configured transputer system (perhaps through a connection list of the type provided by the Inmost "Configured-Info" utility) could be seen as feasible.

Further, to assess, in practice, how damaging' the locality of memory is to the existing parallel extraction techniques, experiments that quantify Cvetanovic's other points in relation to transputer targets can be see as desirable.

11.3 PARALLELISM EXTRACTION.

The majority of literature concerning the extraction of parallelism from sequential code is targeted at shared memory (tightly / moderately coupled) multi-processor systems. The main study report investigates several approaches to parallelism extraction including Berstein, Evans and Williams' data dependence analysis [9] and [21], the hyperplane and coordinate methods [42], Parafrase (e.g. [36]), PFC [4], and Percolation Scheduling [48]. None of these approaches differ radically from each other and most concentrate of the extraction of parallelism from loops. The general approach to transforming a sequential program into one to be executed in parallel involves data dependency tests, source restructuring to minimise dependencies (Parafrase, PFC and Percolation Scheduling perform transformations which change the data dependencies in order to increase potential parallelism) and then the partitioning of the program into blocks according to those data dependencies remaining.

The choice of which set of data dependence definitions and tests, and which partitioning scheme that a new parallelising compiler might use should reflect the transputer target.

Due to Percolation Scheduling's approach being limited to a fine grain level of analysis and the relatively high interprocessor communication costs of the transputer, a direct utilisation of this approach is not favoured.

Further, perceiving of Bernstein, Evans and Williams' approach as preliminary to the data dependence tests used in both Parafrase and PFC, we are left the latter two approaches as candidate approaches for parallelism detection for transputer target.

Both Parafrase and PFC use versions of the gcd test and the Banerjee inequality for dependence testing, and both report good results for automatic parallelism detection. In the light of a comparison of these two approaches, performed as part of the study, we do not consider it unreasonable to assume that the two methods produce the same resulting transformed program. Only the details of the detection process vary. In choosing a preferred detection method consider:

1. Firstly, the Coordinate method requires that the loop be rewritten into a fixed form before the parallelisation algorithm may be applied. PFC uses a recursive algorithm aimed at exploiting the recursive nature of the nesting of loops, thus no initial transformations are required. However, for PFC to exploit the maximum parallelism in a loop it will often be necessary to first attempt to remove anti-and output-dependencies (by employing such techniques as recurrence breaking and loop interchange). This is done implicitly within the Coordinate algorithm during the rewriting of the loop.

2. Because the removal of anti-and output dependencies takes place outside the PFC loop rewriting algorithm, the algorithm cannot be guaranteed to generate maximum parallelisation for the loop (although it does generate maximum parallelisation consistent with the data dependencies of the loop as written). How much parallelism is exploited is dependent on the techniques used for recognising the applicability of such techniques as recurrence breaking and loop interchanging. The Coordinate method too will not guarantee maximum parallelisation; the choice of which loops to vectorise determines how much parallelism is exploited. Both methods can be used to exhaustively list the possible rewritings if required.

3. It would appear that the only real advantage one method has over the other is that the PFC method (as well as being more rigorously documented than the Coordinate method) is based on the more familiar notions of flow, anti- and output dependencies and associated dependence graph. The Coordinate method is based on an idea of dependence seemingly only considered by the research team associated with the Coordinate method. This slight advantage gained by the PFC method tends to give it an element of flexibility lacking in the Coordinate method.

The gcd and Banerjee relations used in the PFC approach appear in the literature in two forms, each a result of the initial assumptions of the form of the DO loop control variable is assumed to be 1. However, in the original Banerjee form, the Banerjee relation given assumes the initial value of the DO loop control variable is 0, whilst in the Kennedy and Allen form [4], the initial value is assumed to be 1. In order that future studies, as well as this study, could assess a more generic form of these tests, both the gcd test and Banerjee relations were derived from first principles assuming that the form of the DO statement is DO $i = S_i$, U_i, T_i. These are available in the main study report [69].

The data dependency analysis of DO loops using the gcd and Banerjee relations appears to be suitable for concurrent task identification with transputer target. The limited empirical analysis reported in section 3 suggests that:

1. the source facets employed in this detection approach are frequent (for example, in about 80% of cases the DO loop initial value and step expressions are compile time known constants, 55% of array accesses within DO loops employ linear functions of DO loop control variables as subscript expressions)

2. the source facets limiting the approach, or increasing the cost of application, appear infrequent (for example, only 8% of functions and less than 1% of subroutines employ EQUIVALENCE, over 50% of segments do not include COMMON areas, only 2% of statements in DO loops are I/O statements, only 10% of GOTOs in DO loops actually exit the loop.

3. the resulting granularity size from a whole DO loop or nest of DO loops appears to be quite large and appropriate to overlap with address space communication costs (for example, around 60% of DO loops have 3 or more statements as their body, around 50% of which are assignments).

Results from experiments exploring the effects of partitioning the iterations of aloop across a simple (non buffered) transputer chain with a worst case data address space distribution (single ported memory server) show some speed-up over serial execution, but only for a sufficiently large single iteration execution time. Generally, efficiency of the whole chain is low.

Results from a further experiment, where buffering in the slaves is employed to increase the overlap of communication and computation, show an improvement, both in speedup and efficiency, over the first experiment but only when the product 'number of partitions * single loop iteration execution time' is near its optimal size. Buffering the slaves overlaps some communication and computation effectively lowering the overhead associated with communication between processors (note that this decrease in overhead must be significantly greater than the overhead imposed by the buffering for an improvement over the non-buffered case).

A third experiment was carried out using the above model (both with and without buffering) to get an indication of the performance of guided self scheduling (GSS) on this model. GSS is a technique for the dynamic scheduling of parallel loops. Given a bound k, the minimum partition size, the partitions are each created be the master in such a way that the remaining unpartitioned iterations may be partitioned into large enough partitions to keep p-1 slaves busy. For small k, the results again show some speedup over serial execution. However, the first two experiments with fixed partition size tended to give better times than the GSS experiment although a more even distribution of the workload across processors was achieved.

11.4 ARCHITECTURAL CONSIDERATIONS

The lack of published work in this area has, we feel, had a detrimental effect on our progress, in that basic processor and communication data, which we initially assumed would be available to the community at large, did not turn up in our literature search, and basic ground-work experiments had, therefore, to be done first, limiting the time available for more detailed experimentation.

The results from experiments assessing communication costs are disappointing in that we have been unable to conclusively determine the communication overhead and further experimentation will be necessary. However some curious problems have been identified:

1. Non-reproducible link timing results between different sets of transputers.

2. Non-reproducible link timing results between power cycles.

3. Seemingly identical processors do not execute the same process, involving inter-processor communication, in identical amounts of time.

4. For any given link between two transputers, the transfer rate in one direction cannot be guaranteed to be the same as the transfer rate in the opposite direction.

5. The timings of the block transfer communications indicate higher communication rates, 15 MHz for the T414 using 10 Mbit/sec links, than published.

Some possible explanation for these non-determinisms have been ruled out. Experiments repeated using different transputers rule out the possibility of faulty equipment. We have shown that differing physical lengths of external link has no bearing on the communication times. The routine scheduling that occurs at low priority has also been discounted.

Simple experiments conducted to evaluate the minimum processing overhead involved in the block communication process indicate that this is low, in the order of one processor cycle per word, for this type of transfer. However the results are not conclusive and require further work.

One conclusion that can be drawn is that if synchronization is required between any two processes executing on different transputers then this will have to be regulated by software.

11.5 CONCLUSIONS AND FURTHER WORK

We feel, based on our experience, that there is a need for further detailed performance evaluation of the transputer, its interprocessor communication bandwidth and optimized process distribution strategies. This will facilitate the performance prediction and the technology transfer of transputers.

Further work in this area is continuing and the evaluation of parallel extraction techniques is being extended. Specific areas of investigation which have been identified are:

1. It would be desirable, though non-trivial, to develop a dynamic (run-time) Fortran 77 empirical analyser. This would allow a more detailed analysis of the 'typical' data access activity of running Fortran 77 programs, followed by an assessment of the dynamic distribution of program data space.

2. The distributed DO loop experiments completed only assess the 'worst case' memory server model. These experiments need to be extended and applied to other (for example, COMMON-block server) models. Other candidate topologies need to be assessed.

3. The granularity aspects, such as task grain size, the trade-off between task distribution and data space communication and the locality of address space within segments, need to be more fully explored.

4. Run-time reconfiguration needs to be explored. The movement of memory servers by reconfiguration may reduce the data space transmission distance and thereby reduce communication overheads.

5. The option of statically or dynamically configuring a transputer network to specifically 'match' a given program needs exploration.

11.6 ACKNOWLEDGEMENTS

The authors would like to thank the SERC/DTI Transputer initiative for grant N2a 8R 0746 under which this work was carried out. We would also like to acknowledge the considerable contribution made by Diane Willcock and David Johnston in the literature survey, experimentation and analysis of the Fortran programs.

REFERENCES

To facilitate the reader the full reference list of our main report has been included.

1. *Engineering Applications of Transputers,* Working Party Report, Computing Facilities Committee, October 1986.

2. *IMS T800 Architecture,* (1986) INMOS Technical Note 6.

3. *Transputer Reference Manual,* INMOST 72 TRN 006 03, October 1986.

4. Allen, J.R. and Kennedy, K., (1982) PFS: A program to convert fortran to parallel form, *Proc. IBM Conf. on Parallel Computers and Scientific Computations.*

5. Amdahl, G.M., (1967) Validity of the single processor approach to achieving large scale computing capabilities,. *Proc.AFIPS Comp. Conf.*, 30,pp.483-485.

5a. Anantharaman, T.S., (1987) *Algorithms for Parallel Execution of Programs with Memory Aliasing,* Carnegie Mellon University , CMU-cs-87-109.

6. Atkin, P., (1987) *Performance Maximisation, INMOS Technical Note 17.*

7. Babb, R.G. and Ragsdale, W.C., (1986) A large-grain data flow scheduler for parallel processing on CYBERPLUS,. *Proc.1986 INT. Conf. on Parallel Processing,* pp. 844-848, IEEE Comp.Soc. Press.

8. Banerjee, U., Chen,S., Kuck, D., and Towle, R., (1979) Time and parallel processor bounds for fortran-like loops,. *IEEE Trans. Comp.*, C-28, pp.660-670.

9. Bernstein, A.J., (1966) Analysis of prgrams for parallel processing *IEEE Trans. Elec. Comp.,* EC-15, pp. 757-763.

10. Bokhari, S.H., (1979) On the mapping problem," *Proc. 1979 Int. Conf. on Parallel Processing,* pp. 239-248, IEEE Comp. Soc. Press, 1979.

11. Brode, B., (1981) Precompilation of fortran programs to facilitate array processing. *Computer,* 14, pp. 46-51.

12. Bucher, I.Y., (1983) The computational speed of supercomputers. *Proc. ACM Sigmetrics Conf. Meas. and Modeling, pp. 151-165.*

13. Buehrer, R., and Ekoanadham, K., (1987) Incorporating data flow ideas into von neumann processors for parallel execution, *IEEE Trans. Comp..* c-36, pp. 1515-1522.

14. Burke, M. and Cytron, R., (1986) Interprocedural dependence analysis and parallelization. *ACM SIGPLAN Not.,* 21, pp. 162-175.

15. Chu, W.W., Holloway, L.J., Lan, M., and Efe, K., (1980) Task allocation in distributed data processing. *Computer,* 13, pp. 57-69.

16. Coles, R.W., (1984) The transputer, a component for the fifth generation. *Practical Electronics,* pp. 26-31.

17. Cvetanovic, Z., (1987) The effects of problem partitioning, allocation and granularity on the performance of multiple-processor systems. *IEEE Trans. Comp.,* 36, pp. 421-432.

18. Cytron, R., (1986) Doacross: beyond vectorisation for multiprocessors. *Proc. 1986 Int. Conf. on Parallel Processing, pp. 836-844, IEEE Comp. Soc. Press.*

19. Davies, J., Huson, C., Macke, T., Leasure, B., and Wolfe, M., (1986) The KAP/S-1: an advanced source-to-source vectoriser for the S-1 Mark IIa supercomputer. *Proc. 1986 Int. Conf. on Parallel Processing,* pp. 833-835, IEEE Comp. Soc. Press.

20. Del Corso, D., Corno, F., and Danielle, A., (1987) Selecting the interconnection structure for multiprocessor systems. *Proc. VLSI and Computers: COMPEURO'87,*pp. 787-790.

21. Evans, D.J. and Williams, S.A., (1979) Analysis and detection of parallel processable code. *The Computer J.,* 23, pp. 66-72.

22. Faidhi, J.A.W and Robinson, S.K., (1987) Programmer experience level indicators through source empirical analysis, *The Computer J.,* 30, pp. 52-62.

23. Ferrante, J., Ottenstein, K.J., and Warren, J.D., (1987) The program dependence graph and its use in optimization. *ACM Trans. on Prog. Lang. and Syst., 9, pp. 319-349.*

24. Flynn, M.J.H. and Hennessy, J.L., (1980) Parallelism and representation problems in distributed systems. *IEEE Trans. Comp.,* 29, pp. 1080-1086.

25. Gokhale, M.B., (1986) Macro vs micro dataflow: a programming example. *Proc. 1986 Int. Conf. on Parallel Processing,* pp. 849-852, IEEE Comp. Soc. Press.

26. Gonzalez, M.J. Jr and Ramamoorthy, C.V., (1972) Parallel task execution in a decentralised system. *IEEE Trans. Comp.,* 21, pp. 1310-1322.

27. Harp, J.G., Roberts, J.B.G., and Ward, J.S., (1985) Signal processing with transputer arrays (TRAPs). *Computer Physics Comm.,* 37, pp. 77-86.

28. Hey, A.J.G., (1987) Software migration aids for transputer systems. *SERC/DTI Transputer Initiative Proposal.*

29. Hu, T.C., (1961) Parallel sequencing and assembly line problems. *Operations Research,* 9, pp. 841-848.

30. Jagannathan, R. and Ashcroft, E.A., (1984) Eazyflow: a hybrid model for parallel processing. *Proc. 1984 Int. Conf. on Parallel Processing,* pp. 514-523, IEEE Comp. Soc. Press.

31. Kamiya, S. *et cl. (1983) Practical vectorisation techniques for the facom VP. Inf. Proc. '83,* pp. 389-394, North Holland.

32. Kasahara, H. and Narita, S., (1984) Practical multiprocessor scheduling algorithms for efficient parallel processing. *IEEE Trans. Comp.,* 33, pp. 1023-1029.

33. Klappholz, D., Liao, Y., Wang, D., Brodsky, A. and Omondi, A., (1985) Toward a hybrid dataflow/control flow MIMD architecture. *Proc. 1985 Int. Conf. on Parallel Processing,* pp. 10-15, IEEE Comp. Soc. Press.

34. Kruskal, C.P. and Cytron, R., (1984) The Cedar Machine and its Restructuring Fortran Compiler. *Proc. NATO Advanced Study Inst. on Control Flow and Data Flow: concents of Distributed Programming,* pp. 305-311.

35. Kruskal, C.P. and Weiss, A., (1985) Allocating independent subtasks on parallel processors. *IEEE Trans, Software Eng,* 11, pp. 1001-1016.

36. Kuck, D.J., (1979) Parallel processing of ordinary programs. *Advances in Computers,* 15, pp. 119-179.

37. Kuck, D.J., (1977) A survey of parallel machine organisation and programming. *Computing Surveys,* 9, pp. 29-59.

38. Kuck, D.J., Muraoka, Y. and Chen S., (1972) On the number of operations simultaneously executable in fortran-like programs and their resulting speedup. *IEEE Trans. Comp.,* 21, pp. 1293-1310.

39. Kuck, D.J. and Padua, D.A., (1979) High-speed multiprocessors and their compilers. *Proc. 1979 Int. Conf. on Parallel Processing,* pp. 405-406, IEEE Comp. Soc. Press.

40. Kuck, D.J. and others, (1984) The structure of an advanced retargetable vectoriser. in *Tutorial on Supercomputers: Designs and Applications,* pp. 163-178, IEEE Press, New York.

41. Lake, T.W. *Use of the Dataflow Model of Computation for Transputer Systems,* unpublished.

42. Lamport, L. (1974) The parallel execution of DO loops. *Commun. ACM,* 17, pp. 83-93.

43. Lauwereins, R. and Peperstraete, J.A. (1985) Influence of the computation-communication ration on the efficiency of argument flow multiprocessor architectures. *Mini & Microcomputers and their Applications, Proc. ISMM Int. Symp.,* pp. 128-131.

44. Lee, G., Kruskal, C.P. and Kuck, D.J., (1985) An empirical study of automatic restructuring of nonnumerical programs for parallel processors. *IEEE Trans. Comp.,* 34, pp. 927-933.

45. Manacher, G.K., (1967) Production and stabilization of real-time task schedules. *J. ACM,* 14, pp. 439-465.

46. Midkiff, S.P. and Padua, D.A., (1986) Compiler generated synchronisation for DO Loops. *Proc. 1986 Int. Conf. on Parallel Processing, pp. 544-551, IEEE Comp. Soc. Press.*

47. Nichols, K.M. and Messerchmitt, D.G., (1987) Traffic-specific interconnection networks for multicomputers. *IEEE Trans. Comp.* 36, pp. 1183-1196.

48. Nicolau, A., (1986) *A Fine-grain Parallelizing Compiler,* TR 86-792.

49. Odijk, E.A.M. and van Twist, R.A.H., (1987) Networks for parallel computers. *Proc. VLSI and Computers: COMPEURO'87,* pp. 779-782.

50. Omondi, A. and Klappholz, D., (1984) Data driven computation on process-based MIMD machines. *Proc. 1984 Int. Conf. on Parallel Processing,* pp. 535-538, IEEE Comp. Soc. Press.

51. Padua, D., Kuck, D. and Lawrie, D., (1980) High-speed multiprocessors and compilation techniques. *IEEE Trans. Comp.,* 29, pp. 763-776.

52. Padua, D.A and Wolfe, M.J., (1986) Advanced compiler optimisations for supercomputers. *Commun. ACM,* 29, pp. 1184-1201.

53. Polychronopoulos, C.D. and Banerjee, U., (1987) Processor allocation for horizontal and vertical parallelism and related speedup bounds. *IEEE Trans.Comp.,* 36, pp. 410-420.

54. Polychronopoulos, C.D. and Kuck, D.J., (1987) Guided self-scheduling for parallel supercomputers. *IEEE Trans. Comp.,* 36, pp. 1412-1439.

55. Polychronopoulos, C.D., Kuck, D.J. and Padua, D.A., (1986) Execution of parallel loops on parallel processor systems. *Proc. 1986 Int. Conf. on Parallel Processing,* pp. 519-527, IEEE Comp. Soc. Press.

56. Presberg, D.L. and Johnson, N.W., (1975) The paralyzer: IVTRAN's parallelism analyzer and synchesizer. *ACM SIGPLAN Not.,* 10, pp. 9-16.

57. Ramamoorthy, C.V., Chandy, K.M. and Gonzalez, M.J., (1985) Optimal scheduling strategies in a multiprocessor system. *IEEE Trans. Comp.,* 21, pp. 137-146.

58. Ramamoorthy, C.V. and Gonzalez, M.J., (1969) A survey of techniques for recognising parallel processable streams in computer programs. *AFIPS,* 35, pp. 1-15.

59. Reed, D.A., (1984) The performance of multimicrocomputer networks supporting dynamic workloads. *IEEE Trans. Comp.,* 33, pp. 1045-1048.

60. Robinson, S.K., (1976) *The Study and Application of the Static and Dynamic Evaluation of Source Programs.* Ph.D. Thesis, Brunel University.

61. Robinson, S.K. and Torsun, I.S., (1976) An empirical analysis of fortran programs. *The Computer Journal,* 19, pp. 56-62.

62. Sarkar, V. and Hennessy, J., (1986) Compile-time partitioning and scheduling of parallel programs. *ACM SIGPLAN Not.,* 21.

63. Scarborough R.G. and Kolsky, H.G., (1986) A vectorising fortran compiler. *IBM J. Res & Dev,* 30, pp. 163-171.

64. Tang, P. and Yew, P., (1986) Processor self-scheduling for multiple-nested parallel loops. proc. 1986 int. conf. on parallel processing, pp. 528-535, IEEE Comp. Soc. Press.

65. Thomasian, A. and Bay, P.F., (1986) Analytic queueing network models for parallel processing of task systems. *IEEE Trans. Comp,* 35, pp. 1045-1054.

66. Van Santen, P.J. Robinson, P.J., Feasibility study report parallel extracting fortran compiler. SERC/DTI Transputer Initiative, Contract N2A 8R 0746.

67. Whitby-Strevens, C., (1985) The transputer. *12th Annual Int. Symp. on Computer Architecture,* pp. 292-300.

68. Wolfe, M., (1986) Advanced loop interchanging. *Proc. 1986 Int. Conf. on Parallel Processing,* PP. 536-543, IEEE Comp. Soc. Press.

69. Yasumara, M., Tanaka, Y., Kanada, Y. and Aoyama, A., (1984) Compiling algorithms and techniques for S-810 vector processor. *Proc. 1984 Int. Conf. on Parallel Processing,* pp. 285-290, IEEE Comp. Soc. Press.

Part Four

Tools

12 What tools are required for vector and parallel processing?

A. van der Steen

Academic Computer Centre Utrecht

12.1 INTRODUCTION

The existence of of vector- and parallel systems has made life much more interesting for the application programmer but not much easier. Where for conventional scalar systems there was a relatively stable bulk of basic (or even not so basic) algorithms that were applicable and known to be efficient in certain fields (numerical, database management, etc.) the situation has grown more complex for vector- and parallel systems. Algorithms that were considered out of fashion or unsuitable have to be reconsidered and entirely new algorithms have to be judged on their effectiveness for these new machines. However, this judgement is more complicated than for scalar machines and certain tools are indispensable or at least highly desired for the evaluation of software that is written for vector- and parallel systems. In the following sections we will review some tools that are available from vendors and/or research institutions and we will offer some recommendations concerning improvements that could be made to existing tools and suggest some that do not yet exist.

We will first address vector computers in section 12.2. These systems are known best and there is not much difference in available tools for these systems. Parallel systems are just becoming of age and because there is a much greater possibility of variation in running an algorithm on a parallel machine the software tools for exploiting and optimizing the parallelism shows a corresponding variation. Because there are certain issues that affect shared memory machines but not distributed memory machines and *vice versa* the first category is treated separately in section 12.3 while the last type of machines is addressed in section 12.4. In section 12.5 we will make some concluding remarks.

12.2   VECTOR COMPUTERS

Vector computers are the most wide-spread and well-understood parallel systems. Also, the type of parallelism is limited to simultaneously operating on elements of a vector which makes the process of optimizing the program for execution time more tractable. For vector machines one can distinguish three main tools that help to optimize programs: vectorizing compilers, tools for the tuning of programs, and debuggers. The last class of tools are not fundamentally different from their scalar counterparts and we will not say much about them. In the following subsections we will review these tools that can aid such optimization and we make some remarks about their usefulness and their availability.

12.2.1   Vectorizing compilers

Although often hardly seen as such, vectorizing compilers are the most important tools that are available for vector computers. This may seem a trivial remark but the quality of the compiler has an enormous impact on the performance of the machine as may be seen from Fig. 12.1. These performance differences were entirely due to a better code/dependency analysis and to better code generation, no hardware modifications were applied. We will not go into the matter of comparing the quality of vector compilers here (comparative studies may be found in [2, 10]). We will rather concentrate on desirable features for vector compilers.

	FORT 77/HAP V02-30	FORT77/HAP V21-0E
	Mflop/s	Mflop/s
1. Hydro excerpt	156.3	304.8
2. MLR dot prod.	259.1	276.7
3. Dot product	216.9	341.7
4. Banded lin. eq.	66.7	66.8
5. Tridiag. elim. (above diag.)	2.4	23.6
6. Tridiag. elim. (below diag.)	3.2	26.2
7. Equation of state	290.9	293.5
8. PDE integration	8.8	116.8
9. Integr. predictor	263.2	271.1
10. Diff. predictor	67.1	68.0
11. First sum	9.9	16.8
12. First difference	110.8	113.2
13. 2-D part. pusher	5.1	6.1
14. 1-D part. pusher	8.5	12.5
Average	104.9	137.9
Harm. mean	10.6	30.4

Figure 12.1 Performance of the first 14 Livermore Loops on the Hitachi S810/20 using two different compiler versions.

The figure shows considerable differences especially for loops that do not vectorize readily. In particular for these loops the user should know what transformations have been performed to be able to (partly) vectorize them. This may enable him to avoid some constructs and to use others that are more fit for vectorization. To this end preferably two listing versions should be available. The first one (the type 1 listing) should show the orginial code to which on a statement by statement bases is indicated which statements are scalar, which are partly vectorized, and which are fully vectorized. The second listing (the type 2 listing) should show the transformed code with a reference to the original code lines to facilitate the tracing of the original code lines. Nowadays many vendors provide the first type of listing: Cray, IBM, Hitachi, and Fujitsu (and therefore also Amdahl and Siemens) to name a few. The second type of listing is mostly provided by vendors that use a separate preprocessor stage like Unisys for its ISP and Gould for its NPL series. However, the transformed listing is given in all cases without reference to the original code which makes it sometimes hard to identify the actual changes in the program text. This is particularly true where so-called vector notation (as proposed for Fortran 8X) is employed instead of the conventional loop notation to indicate that certain statements are vectorized. Figure 12.2 shows a type 1 listing of a program fragment as produced by the FORT77/HAP compiler of Hitachi. Scalar- and vector statements are flagged within loops while at the end of a program module messages about the loops are given.

9200		DO 20 L = 7, 107, 50
9300 S		LW = L
9400		DO 10 J = 30, 870, 5
9500 V		X(L-1) = X(L-1) - X(LW)*Y(J)
9600 V		LW = LW + 1
9700	10	CONTINUE
9800 S		X(L-1) = Y(5)*X(L-1)
9900	20	CONTINUE

Figure 12.2 Type 1 listing with flagging of scalar (S) and vector statements(V).

These messages include the estimated iteration count (if possible) and the reason why a certain loop is not vectorized. For instance, in the case of Fig.12.2 the message is:

DO 20 NOT VECTORIZED. ISN = 9200 (this is the statement number)
ITERATION COUNT ESTIMATED AS 3.
UNVECTORIZABLE DUE TO UNRESOLVABLE ARRAY
DEPENDENCE. NAME = X, ISN = 9500,9800

This is the way of giving messages that is to be preferred. Some vendors intersperse the program text with messages which clutters up the code and makes reading difficult.

Figure 12.3 shows a type 2 listing from the preprocessor used for the Gould NPL series.

DO 15 I = IL, IU

      PX(I) = X(I) - A(I-1,2)*PX(I-1) - A(I-NX,3)*PX(I-NX)

15 CONTINUE

is transformed in:

TX(:IU-IL+1) = X(IL:IU) - A(IL-NX:IU-NX,3)*PX(IL-NX:IU-NX)

Figure 12.3 Lower part is type 2 listing of DO 15 loop in upper part.

As can be seen from the figure the DO 15 loop has been transformed to a single line in vector notation. In addition, a new auxiliary vector TX has been introduced to be used in the surrounding loops. It will be clear that for larger programs it is highly desirable to indicate in the type 2 listing which statements of the type 1 listing correspond to the transformed program fragments. Also, the introduction of auxiliary variables should be clearly indicated.

Another compiler feature can make life more pleasant for the programmer: the listing of each program module (type 1) should be followed by a summary of all loops indicating their begin and end in terms of statement numbers, the iteration count, their nesting level, whether or not they are vectorized, and, if not, a very brief indication of the reason (dependent, too short, etc.). This feature is for instance provided for a number of vectorizing compilers made by Pacific Sierra Research Inc. It often gives the results of a first vectorization round at a glance which is nice when further hand optimization must occur.

Automatic vectorization has become more and more sophisticated in the past few years, however, the need to do some hand optimization will always be present. The way this is usually done is by placing compiler directives in the program text in the form of special comment lines. In this way special knowledge that is impossible for the compiler to derive is provided and thus may force loops to vectorise or to refrain from vectorizing. This way of transferring extra information to a compiler is quite simple and elegant and is to be preferred to special calls in the program text which render the program unportable. Although the comment directive practice is widely spread and its operation on any vector machine is almost identical, the format of the directives mostly differ from machine to machine. In Figure 12.4 we show some forms of a directive that forces vectorization in case of a possible (but non-existent) dependency.

Directive	Machine
CVD$ NODEPCHK	Alliant, Gould
C$DIR NO_RECURRENCE	Convex
CDIR$ IVDEP	Cray
*VOCL LOOP, NOVREC	Fujitsu (Amdahl, Siemens)
*VOPTION VEC	Hitachi
C < keyword > IGNORE RECRDEPS	IBM
*VDIR NODEP	NEC

Figure 12.4 Different forms of a no-dependency directive on various machines.

Figure 12.4 shows that Alliant and Gould use the same directive. This stems from the fact that for both vendors Pacific Sierra Research Inc. helped to develop the vectorizing software. A nice feature of the Pacific Sierra strain is that after CVD$ a range parameter can be given which can have the value L for loop, R for routine, or G for global (meaning the entire file). The default range is L and can be omitted as is done in Fig. 12.4. The Fujitsu compiler has a comparable feature, however, specifying the range is mandatory here. For the IBM machines the keyword that triggers the processing of a directive can be chosen at will via the @PROCESS DIRECTIVE (< keyword >) statement. Although nice as it is, this freedom to choose a keyword to ones own liking would not be necessary if could be agreed on a standard form for the comment directives. At the moment one has to go through the annoying process of inserting the same directives again when one runs programs on another machine. There are two conceivable objections to using the same directives on all machines. The first is that there are directives that are not meaningful for all machines. But by ignoring those directives that do not apply to a certain machine (and giving a corresponding message!) one can easily overcome this objection. The other one is real machine dependency. For example, a directive that forces scalar execution of a loop on one machine to prevent excessive vectorization overhead may be omitted on systems with a very short vector start-up time. This will however be a small minority of all the cases where directives were introduced and one should modify them anyway.

12.2.2 Tuning tools for vectorization

The achievements of vectorizing compilers have increased impressively in the last few years. Yet, there will always be programs that need further optimization. Therefore many supercomputer vendors and also some independent software developers provide tools that should help in the optimization. In this subsection we review some of these tools and we comment on desirable features for such tools.

It depends on the circumstances whether one wants to spend much time in optimizing ones programs. When very large existing program packages must be optimized one may choose for a batch-like approach and run them through preprocessor programs like VAST-2 or KAP (a comparison between these products can be found in [9]). These kind of programs will transform the input into programs that should be more fit for vector processing on the target machine. Just like the compilers VAST or KAP cannot capture all possible optimizations and they can be seen as an add-on to the compilers. As the compilers in general have become increasingly sophisticated the need for these kind of packages will probably become less urgent. For machines that employ many special library calls to accelerate execution, like CDC's Cyber 205 Q8 calls, a package like VAST comes in handy because it inserts many such calls automatically (thus making the program non-portable).

When one decides to do more than just automatic optimization the sensible approach is to run a program through a profiling program of some sort and to concentrate on the parts that are most compute intensive. Most vendors provide profiling programs but not all are of the same quality. Cray, Control Data, and Unisys have utilities that are very much alike and are called SPY (Cray, Control Data) and PEER (Unisys) respectively (we do not consider the Cray tools FLOWTRACE and PERFMON here of which especially the last is very machine specific). Figure 12.5 shows a piece of output of PEER for an arbitrary subroutine called MAP.

```
LF*TPF(1) MAP
MAP$1
000000-000037      1210   |*
000040-000077      1537   |*
000100-000137     20399   |*****
000140-000177     34660   |********
000200-000237    100770   |*******************
000240-000277    258183   |*********************************************
000300-000337     39225   |*********
000340-000361      2324   |*

                 ---------
                 458308 Samples ( 70.0%)
```

Figure 12.5 Output of the Unisys profiling utility PEER.

The 70% in parenthesis indicates that subroutine MAP takes 70% of the total time of the execution from the program it belongs to. This is important information as it shows that by optimizing MAP the total execution time will be affected significantly. The output for Cray- and Control Data machines with SPY will be roughly similar. One of the most characteristic features is that the statements are divided into bins, blocks of statements, and a histogram is produced based on sampling in what bin PEER was at the time of sampling. Dependent on the sampling frequency a fairly accurate picture of the distribution can be produced with very little measuring overhead. There are however some objections to this method. The division in bins can be awkward which sometimes can give a somewhat distorted histogram. Furthermore, it can be tedious to relate the bins to the statements in the original listing. One can remove this last drawback by treating every statement as a bin. This last approach is followed by IBM. The histogram is produced on a statement-by-statement basis.

Many minisupercomputer vendors also have profiling programs. As Unix is now almost generally used as the operating system for these machines, the profiling utilities tend to be very similar. For instance, both Alliant and Convex have a **gprof** utility that reports about the time spent in routines and gives statistics about the number of calls and the percentage of the total execution time for each routine. The **lprof** utility gives information on a line-by-line basis and informs about the frequency of execution of every statement and the percentage of time for each statement within a routine. The ease of identifying the most compute intensive parts is higher than for the SPY-like utilities and should therefore be preferred. A possible drawback is the measuring overhead that is generally higher than for SPY-like utilities and which may distort the outcomes if the clock resolution is not high enough.

We think however that profiling programs can still be more informative. The main objective of profiling is of course to reduce the run time of a program and therefore it should be worthwhile when one was informed what the benefit of the vectorization of a certain program fragment was over the scalar execution. In this way one can see whether optimization efforts are effective and where one should turn for the highest benefits. This can be achieved by indicating for every statement what the scalar costs and what the vector costs would be. From these figures also the total effect of vectorization can be computed by means of Amdahl's Law. The Vectune/Fortune tools that are distributed by Fujitsu for its VP series of vector machines do just that. In fact more is done as the true rate of IF statements is estimated and one can indicate via a directive the type of vectorization of if- then and else parts according to the TRUE rate. A noteworthy fact is that no actual run of the program is required. A list of the relative costs of operations (scalar and vector) is maintained and by interpreting the statements the cost for each statement can be inferred. In a pseudo-run also the iteration count of loops, the number of calls to subroutines, and the true rate of if statements become known. Experiments have shown [8] that this way of estimating the costs is quite accurate and effective. Because no real run is required (although a pseudo-run also can take quite some time) such a profiling tool is essentially machine independent and does not need to be run on the vector computer at all. It is therefore surprising that no other vendors have adopted this style of profiling. The Fujitsu tools are split up in a part called Vectune that does the pseudo-run and Fortune that presents the results and may report in batch mode or be used interactively to improve the code.

Apart from the Japanese vendors that all support an interactive vectoriser no interactive vectorizing tools are available from vendors yet. Pacific Sierra Reseach Inc. markets its Forge package that allows interactive optimization for Cray systems. The user is lead through the program and suggestions are done by Forge to improve the vectorization rate depending on the compiler version and the target machine specified. Although it would be hard work to optimize codes of several hundred thousands of lines this way, it could be used for vital subroutines. Also, the educational effect of this way of interactively vectorizing a code should not be underestimated. At this moment Forge seems to be only available for Cray systems. Although this is certainly the largest part of all large vector systems, it is by no means the only one and such a tool would be attractive for other systems too. Is should be noted that again the actual vector machine is not required because no real run of the code is performed.

12.2.3   Other tools for vector machines

As already stated, debuggers are important tools but they are not fundamentally different from those for scalar machines (at least for pure vector machines). The only extra requirement is that they should be able to point out the element(s) participating in a vector operation that cause a run-time error. Furthermore, they should be capable of the usual things: displaying and setting variables, setting and removing breakpoints, etc. We would like to advocate here another utility that may seem outmoded but in fact in many cases actually works faster than an interactive debugger. Control Data has long distributed a utility that would provide a symbolic dump of a program that reflected the status of the program at the time it crashed. With a printed listing, a hint about the offending statement, and the values of the variables at the time of the error one often can locate an error much faster in this way than by interactive debugging, especially for large and time consuming programs.

Although probably not recognized by most people as tools, nowadays many vendors have available a large body of highly optimized Fortran routines. They mostly belong to wide-spread packages like BLAS, LINPACK, EISPACK, etc., and when called, will perform much better than when the corresponding Fortran text is actually inserted. This is mainly true for the non-Japanese machines. For the Japanese machines often comparable libraries are available but with modules with different names and parameter sequences. It would be desirable that they should agree upon the names and calling sequences for a common body of basic subroutines to further enhance portability of codes.

12.3   SHARED MEMORY PARALLEL MACHINES

Nowadays, a large number of shared memory parallel machines is installed. As there is probably not a best achitecture (at least when application areas and the costs are taken into account) the variety of architectures is large and, with it, the models for employing the parallelism of the machines. This, in turn, leads to various ways of supporting the users with tools to use the machines effectively. We will shortly review some of these tools.

12.3.1   Compilers and libraries for parallel processing

Again, and even more so than for pure vector machines, the compilers can be considered as important tools to use the machines in the most effective way. Unlike vectorization which is a relatively easy to single out, parallel processing can come in many variations. Often a distinction is made between fine-grained and coarse-grained parallelism. The latter means that tasks are defined of a considerable size often comprizing several subprograms. These tasks are independent and they may be run in parallel. By contrast, fine-grained parallelism refers to small tasks often containing a single loop or a few statements. Because there is no standard way for expressing parallelism in the current higher programming languages (except in Ada, Modula, and Occam) vendors have found different ways to express parallelism on their particular machines.

For some machines automatic parallelization is available. Alliant was the first one of the vendors to offer this feature as the architecture of the Alliant FX-series makes it quite natural for certain cases. The compiler divides loops with a nesting level of two (or the inner two of higher nested loops) over the available processors by performing particular instances of the outer loop (being a complete inner loop) on different processors in parallel. The inner loop may or may not be vectorizable and is executed accordingly. For this type of parallelism no alterations to the code have to be made on the Alliant. Also long single loops may be broken up in parts and executed concurrently on the available processors. The occurence of reduction variables in the loops as, for instance, in the calculation of sums and innerproduct are also handled correctly without intervention of the programmer. For more complicated types of parallelism one either has to insert comment directives in the same style as for vectorization or one has to actually alter the program.

In the last year other vendors also provide some form of automatic parallelization. Cray has introduced its Autotasking which works simply as an option to the CFT77 compiler. When called in this way a preprocessor generates microtasking-like comment directives that are inserted in the original text and that bring about concurrent processing on the processors that are currently available. Again, doubly nested loops and long single loops are the obvious candidates and the automatic parallelization is (almost) confined to these cases. A listing of the preprocessor output can be obtained to see the generated transformations. This is instructive to the user and allows further modification by inserting or altering directives by hand. An example of a less obvious transformation executed by the Cray Autotasking software is given in Fig. 12.6. Note that the original program fragment does not contain a loop formulation but only a conditional GO TO that is controlled by the value of KK.

```
      350 AK = A(KK)
          A(KK) = C2*AK - S2*B(KK)
          B(KK) = S2*AK + C2*B(KK)
          KK = KK + KSPAN
          IF( KK .LE. NT) GO TO 350
          AK = S1*S2
          S2 = S1*C2 + C1*S2
          C2 = C1*C2 - AK
          KK = KK - NT + KSPAN
          IF(KK .LE. KSPNN) GO TO 350
```
is turned into:
```
      350 CONTINUE
          J1S = KK
          KK = J1S
CMIC$ DO ALL VECTOR IF ((MAX(NT,J1S)-J1S + KSPNN)/KSPNN .GT.
      1333) SHARED(
CMIC$1 NT, KSPNN, C2, S2, A, B) PRIVATE(KK, AK) SAVELAST
CDIR$ IVDEP
      DO 77009 KK = 1, (MAX(NT,J1S)-J1S + KSPNN)/KSPNN
          AK = A(J1S + (KK-1)*KSPNN)
          A(J1S + (KK-1)*KSPNN) = C2*AK - S2*B(J1S + (KK-1)*KSPNN)
          B(J1S + (KK-1)*KSPNN) = S2*AK + C2*B(J1S + (KK-1)*KSPNN)
77009 CONTINUE
          KK  = (MAX(NT,J1S)-J1S + KSPNN)/KSPNN*KSPNN + J1S
          AK  = S1*S2
          S2  = S1*C2 + C1*S2
          C2  = C1*C2 - AK
          KK  = KK - NT + KSPAN
          IF(KK .LE. KSPNN) GO TO 350
```

Figure 12.6 Example of a non-trivial transformation as performed by the Autotasking software of Cray.

Convex and IBM are other vendors that have introduced automatic parallelization. The Convex C2 series has up to four processors and by using the -ep x option one can specify at compile time what is to be the expected number x of processors that the program will run on. The code that is generated will be optimal for the amount of processors specified in the sense that the distribution of looplengths will be tuned to the number of processors. Again, the automatic parallelization is limited to double and single loops. Similarly, IBM has a parallel Fortran compiler which allows automatic parallelization of single and double loops.

As soon as more complicated program structures occur, one has to insert directives to induce parallel execution. For instance, when a subroutine or function call appears in a loop this loop cannot be parallelized because possible data dependencies cannot be checked. On the Alliant machine one can force vectorization/parallelization here by the directive CVD$ CNCALL and by prefixing the header of the relevant subroutine or function with RECURSIVE. For the Convex systems the directive is C$DIR FORCE_PARALLEL while the subroutine or function should be compiled separately with the -re (= reentrant) option. The Convex implementation is to be preferred here as no change to the original program text has to be made while for the Alliant the (admittedly very slight) changes to the subroutine/function header lines should be made.

Concurrency that appears outside loops cannot (yet) be spotted by automatic parallelization software and one has to indicate parallel tasks by hand and in very diverse ways. This is obviously a major problem because it tends to destroy the portability of codes from one parallel machine to another. One simply has to look at the study of Karp and Babb [7] to conclude that the ways of addressing parallelism (at least in Fortran) are still widely different. Of course one could turn for instance to Ada, but this is not yet widely accepted and the rendez-vous mechanism of Ada is not very well suited for fine-grained parallelism. There have been interesting attempts to formulate a vehicle for machine-independent parallelism. One of them is the SCHEDULE package [4] which was developed at the Argonne National Laboratory and runs on several shared-memory parallel machines, including the Alliant FX/80, the Sequent Balance, and the Encore Multimax. The programmer explicitly defines the dependency relationships between subroutines in a program and thus specifies which routines may run concurrently. Because the programming model is subroutine-based it is primarily fit for coarse-grained processes. A nice additional feature of SCHEDULE is its graphical interface to a workstation which enables the monitoring of the parallel execution and so may suggest a possible restucturing for a better load balancing of processes. Another product that is available on several machines for instance on the Encore Multimax, is called the Force [6]. A number of macros, affecting declaration and (parallel) execution can be put into the program text and will be expanded by the Force package to the appropriate parallel code on the target machine. The Force allows for macrotasking- and microtasking-like constructs (to use the Cray terms) and thus will work on coarse-grained as well as on fine-grained parallel code.

The implementation of the Force, SCHEDULE, and the various parallel Fortran dialects that are currently around underline the necessity of standardization. The ANSI group X3J3 that is in the process defining the Fortran 8X standard has decided not to define any primitives for parallel processing in Fortran but a consortium of institutions and vendors have combined forces in the Parallel Computing Forum to define standards for parallel Fortran and they have come up with a first version in August 1988 [11]. The definition is made exclusively for shared-memory parallel machines as the requirements for distributed-memory parallel machines are quite different. Almost all major vendors are represented in the Parallel Computing Forum but, as yet, none of the proposals of [11] have been implemented in any of the compilers of these vendors. When this proposal is accepted widely and has an influence on the next Fortran standard it should be implemented and supported as soon and as widely as possible.

Meanwhile the user requirements for compilers and listings do not fundamentally differ from those for vectorizing compilers. Where automatic parallelization has taken place this should be clearly marked on a statement by statement basis in a type 1 listing. Preferably, a type 2 listing that shows the transformations that has been performed on a program with a direct reference to the orginal program text should also be available. The educational effect of such a listing can hardly be overestimated. Moreover, it can be the basis for a second parallelization effort. For parallel systems a tool that can graphically display the activity of the system would be very desirable as it can help in load balancing of parallel tasks. As far as known to the author such a facility is only available for the SCHEDULE package and on the BBN Butterfly and GP1000 systems.

12.3.2   Other parallelization tools for shared memory machines

As already remarked, parallelization of programs is much more difficult than vectorization and it is to expected that it will never can be automated to the same extent as vectorization. At the moment integrated tools are developed to assist in the interactive parallelization of programs. One of them is the Faust system, a workstation environment (Sun, Apollo, Pixar) for the Cedar machine developed at the Center of Supercomputing Research and Development at the University of Illinois at Urbana-Champaign [3]. Faust will be an integrated system including editors, debuggers, profilers, and a consultant expert system that helps in vectorization/parallelization and even goes one step beyond by advising suitable algorithms to be used in the solving of a particular problem. For the moment Fortran and C are the target languages. Also vendors are beginning to move into this field. Both Convex and Alliant claim to be in the finishing stage of developing interactive parallelization software but as yet no details are available.

As for debugging, a symbolic interactive debugger that can accurately present the status of a program in all processors at any given time is absolutely mandatory. A complication is here that in a multi-user environment errors that are originating from a faulty dependency analysis often are not reproducible but a debugger should be seen as a necessary rather than a sufficient tool. Profiling is also more difficult for shared-memory parallel processors as the behaviour of a program in time is vastly more informative then a simple summary of the time spent in loops or subroutines. This is particularly true where in some systems the number of processors available to a program varies from time to time (as for instance for the Cray and the Convex). Therefore some graphical device that can show the status and distribution of the processes in time is highly important. As some processes may be so short as not to be noticeable when shown in real time, there should be a possibility of a slowed-down replay. Printed versions that give the status of the program in time at specified time intervals should give a more quantitative idea of the behaviour of the program.

For vector machines, and for parallel machines libraries of optimized modules exist for several machines. Alliant and Cray are two of the vendors that have a considerable body of routines that are optimal for their machines and which are often much faster than what can be achieved by even fairly well parallelized Fortran code (see, e.g., [13]). Again, it would be desirable when vendors could decide on a common body of basic (and even less basic) subprograms that would be available to the users with standardized names and calling sequences.

12.4   DISTRIBUTED MEMORY PARALLEL MACHINES

In the last few years even more distributed memory machines have been introduced than any other type of machine (PCs excluded). The difference between these machines is perhaps less than sometimes is suggested. In fact, less than five main types of machines are worth distinguishing. One of these is the hypercube type of machines of which the iPSC and Ncube are representatives. The nodes in such a machine may of course again be vector processors as is the case in the iPSC/VX. A second type consists of the massively parallel computers like the Connection Machine and the AMT DAP. As these machines are SIMD systems, they are a bit special and therefore the requirement for tools for such systems are different too. A third type which is especially popular in the UK is formed by the many systems that are based on the transputer. A fourth type is also available but has only one representative presently; the Suprenum machine.

We will again review some of the available tools and try to formulate the properties of tools that are required or at least desirable.

12.4.1   Compilers and configuration tools

For the hypercube-style systems of which the iPSC and the Ncube are the main representatives, Fortran and C compilers are available. Moreover, on the iPSC Lisp as well as Prolog are available. One must now define explicit data transfer commands for each of the languages as necessary passing of data is to be done by the programmer. At this stage there is no standardization whatsoever for these commands. Note, that the passing of data will be inherently different from that of transputer-based systems as the topology for a hypercube system is fixed while this is not necessarily the case for a transputer system. In the latter case one will need (for the moment) something like a configuration file as used in Helios to describe the connection topology. The same is true for the Suprenum system where one must specify the configuration of processors, busses, and interconnections. This is done in Modula style as is shown in Fig. 12.7 (see also for instance [12, 14]).

```
TYPE
      Cpu1    = CPU          MIPS   =  2.0; TSLICE = 0.05 END (* cpu *) ;
      Bus1    = BUS          MBITS  =  30.0; END (* bus *) ;
      Bus2    = BUS          MBITS  =  300.0; END (* bus *) ;
      Icb1    = BUS          MBITS  =  24.0; END (* inter-cluster-bus *) ;
      Icb2    = BUS MBITS           =  512.0; END (* inter-cluster-bus *) ;
      Clu1    = CLUSTER      Cpuj [8] : Cpu1;
                             Busj  : Bus1; END (* cluster *) ;
      Clu2    = CLUSTER      Cpuk [8] : Cpu1;
                             Busk  : Bus2; END (* cluster *) ;
      Hst1    = HOST         Cpul [1] : Cpu1;
                             Busl : Bus1; END (* host *) ;
      Hst2    = HOST         Cpum [1] : Cpu1;
                             Busm  : Bus2; END (* host *) ;
      SYS1    = LATTICE (* system configuration 1 *)
               #       #        Icb1 Icb1  ;
               #       #        Hst1  #  ;
               Icb1    #        Clu1 Clu1 ;
               Icb1    #        Clu1 Clu1 ;
            END (* lattice *) ;
      SYS2 = LATTICE (* system configuration 2 *)
               #       #        Icb2 Icb2 ;
               #       #        Hst2  #  ;
               Icb2    #        Clu2 Clu2 ;
               Icb2    #        Clu2 Clu2 ;
      END (* other lattice *) ;
END.
```

Figure 12.7 Example of definition of configurations on the Suprenum.

By contrast, the Connection Machine and the AMT DAP have fixed connections which makes it possible to transport data by shifting a plane (both in the DAP and the CM-2 Connection Machine) or to communicate by using process numbers (CM-2). These examples are sufficient to show that the machine structure as yet has a profound effect on the language extensions.

Even when it is possible to build a shell that hides the distribution of the data and the processor topology completely from the programmer (and this will surely still take a few years) it remains to be seen whether this is desirable in all cases. So, one will need two sets of routing primitives. One for systems in which the processor topology is fixed. In these systems the processor (or process) number should somehow be included in the routing primitives as this determines its relative position regarding the other processors (or processes). As for the systems that allow a variable topology, one must somehow define the interconnections of the input/output ports and the primitives for this type of systems must refer to the input/output ports involved. It would be desirable to pull the description of the processor configuration into the programming languages and standardize this description. This could for instance be done by isolating it in a module somewhat like the Interface in Fortran 8x or the package in Ada.

12.4.2   Libraries and debuggers

For the Suprenum an interactive tool, Superb, is available that offers help in the parallelization of Fortran programs [1]. Fortran 77 programs are fed through a frontend part of Superb that performs a number of standardising transformations. This enables the so-called "core" to do a further analysis and indicates a possible choice of data-partition and other transformations from an existing catalogue. After the necessary decisions have been made the resulting transformed program is written by the back-end part of Superb. The transformations are restricted to grid-type computations (comparable to the inner-outer loop parallelization that has been mentioned in the previous section). Because this type of parallelism is very common, many applications may benefit from this tool. Comparable tools for other distributed memory systems would certainly be desirable.

Optimized libraries were seen to be very important in vector- and shared memory parallel machines. This is even more true for distributed memory machines. Not only the fastest possible algorithms should be executed in each node, one also has to assure the highest possible usage of all nodes by careful load balancing. In addition, the data transfer between nodes should be kept as low as possible. There is a large body of literature (see for instance [5]) that describes algorithms for distributed memory machines from which programmers may benefit. Vendors have recognized the need for libraries and, for instance, Intel makes available commonly used software like LINPACK, EISPACK and FFT's. For transputer systems as an example the libraries from Topexpress might be mentioned (but there will doubtlessly be many more).

For the massively parallel machines like the DAP and the CM-2 the requirements concerning numerical libraries are essentially the same but as yet the usual packages as mentioned above are not (yet) present. For the DAP, however, a considerable amount of numerical software is available that performs many of the common algorithms in a highly optimized way. For the CM-2 only low-level routines like SUM, DOTPRODUCT, and MAX are available at present. The same is true at present for the Suprenum.

Most distributed memory systems appear in a much more complicated form to the user than the earlier mentioned categories of machines. He should often be aware of the connection topology of the machine and he must know about the interprocess communication. This makes it particularly important to have debuggers at hand that not only can show the status of each node in a program but can also check the status of the messages that have been sent (an example is the iPSC debugger which enables one to find lost messages). In distributed memory machines the sending and receiving of messages are the means of synchronising the concurrent processes and thus are the main cause of deadlocks and other subtle programming errors. Although it would be perhaps utopic to expect that a standard debugging interface could be realised for all distributed memory machines, it would certainly be useful to define the minimal necessary information that should be provided by a debugger (and preferably in a standard form). This information should of course include the current processor configuration, the processes running at the nodes, process identification labels, and the message structure (meaning the dependency of messages of processes and other messages).

12.5 CONCLUDING REMARKS

Having surveyed existing and desirable tools to facilitate the task of parallel programming we now will make some concluding remarks and summarize the observations made in the earlier sections.

We have concentrated mostly on Fortran and numerical programming as these areas have been at the forefront of application development on almost all parallel machines. It is to be expected that many other fields will follow. Actually the development of many of them is in full progress, e.g., in the AI field. We may expect that within a few years tools will be available that are more user friendly than we are accustomed to now. Many of them will be based on knowledge systems and will have a sophisticated graphical interface both for representing the results as well as for visualizing the parallel processes that constitute the application at hand.

As parallel processing begins to mature it is not unreasonable to expect and to require some standardization in the tools that should assist in the task of developing efficient parallel programs. Just like the effort of the Parallel Computing Forum has yielded proposals for the Fortran language standard for shared memory machines, similar proposals could be done for other languages and for parallel tools in general. As we summarize the material of the previous sections we try to list some of the requirements that should be included in such standardization actions. Some of them will be almost trivial while others will require considerable effort.

- The listings of vectorizing and parallelizing compilers should indicate on a statement-by-statement basis which statements are vectorized and/or parallelized in a type 1 listing.

- Listings that show the program transformations performed by the compiler (type 2 listing) should correlate with the original program text.

- Summaries of the vectorization and/or parallelization of loops should be given at the end of each program module.

- Vectorization and/or parallelization directives should be standardised.

- Vectorization and/or parallelization messages and suggestions should be given below the program text and not interspersed with the text.

- A profiler should be able to predict the vectorization and/or parallelization effect for a program and its constituent modules by means of a pseudo-run (at least for shared memory machines). For distributed memory machines the communication time and the possible overlap of communication and other processing should be taken into account.

- Standardized interactive parallelization tools that can run on machines or workstations which are not necessarily connected to the target machine should be available.

- A graphical and interactive tool to monitor the progress of a parallel program to facilitate a better load balancing for coarse grained parallelism should be available.

- The Parallel Fortran proposals from the Parallel Computing Forum (or an adaptation thereof) should be used as soon and as widely as possible and a definition of standard communication primitives for distributed memory machines, both for a fixed and a user definable topology should be decided upon.

- System configuration definitions, preferably within the programming languages themselves should be formulated.

- A minimal body of important numerical algorithms should be defined and implemented optimally on the various kinds of parallel systems.

- Debuggers of distributed parallel systems should provide information about the current configuration, the process and the message structure.

Doubtlessly more topics could be added that need standardization. We have tried to identify here what at least should be done to make parallel processing more generally accepted as a natural way of data processing instead of being considered as perhaps a necessary but undesirable deviation of the normal way of computing.

REFERENCES

1   Bast, H-J. Gerndt, M. and Thole, C-A. (1988) SUPERB — The Suprenum parallelizer. *Supercomputer,* 6, 2, pp51−57.

2   Callahan, D. Dongarra, J. and Levine, D. (1988) *Vectorizing Compilers: A Test Suite and Results,* Argonne National Laboratory, Technical Memorandum 109.

3   Center for Supercomputing Research and Development, *Research Review 1986 and 1987,* University of Illinois at Urbana-Champaign, 1987, 1988.

4   Dongarra, J.J. and Sorensen, D.C. (1986) *SCHEDULE: Tools for Developing and Analyzing Parallel Fortran Programs,* Argonne National Laboratory, Technical Memorandum 86.

5   Fox, G. *et al.* (1988) *Solving problems on Concurrent Processors,* Prentice-Hall Inc., Englewood Cliffs.

6   Jordan, H.F. (1986) Structuring parallel algorithms in a MIMD, shared memory environment. *Parallel Computing,* pp93–110.

7   Karp, A.H. and Babb II, R.G. (1988)A Comparison of 12 Parallel Fortran Dialects, *IEEE Software,* pp52–67.

8   van Kats, J.M. LLurba, R, and van der Steen, A.J. (1986) *Result of a Benchmark Test on a Siemens VP-200 with Comparisons to Other Supercomputers,* Academic Computing Centre Utrecht, Technical Report 19.

9   Luecke, G. *et al.* (1988) A comparative study of KAP and VAST-2: two automatic vector preprocessors with Fortran 8x output. *Supercomputer,* 5, 6, pp15–25.

10 Nobayashi, H. (1989) A comparison study of automatically vectorizing Fortran compilers. *Vector Register,* 2, 4, pp 3–8.

11 Parallel Computing Forum, *PCF Fortran: Language Definition,* version 1, August 1988.

12 Solchenbach, K. (1989) Suprenum-Fortran -- an MIMD/SIMD language. *Supercomputer,* 6., 2, pp25–30.

13 van der Steen, A.J. and van der Pas, R.J. (1989) *A Family Portrait: Benchmark tests on a Cray Y-MP and a Cray-2S,* Academic Computing Centre Utrecht, Technical Report 30.

14 Thomas, B. and Peinze, K. (1989) Suprenum comfort of parallel programming. *Supercomputer,* 6, 2, pp51–57.

13 Tools to aid in the design, implementation, and understanding of algorithms for parallel processors*

J. Dongarra, D. Sorensen and O. Brewer

Mathematics and Computer Science Division, Argonne National Laboratory

13.1 INTRODUCTION

The emergence of a wide variety of commercially available parallel computers has created a software dilemma. Will it be possible to design general-purpose software that is both efficient and portable across a wide variety off these new parallel computers? Moreover, will it be possible to provide programming environments that will be sophisticated enough to make explicit parallel programming a viable means to exploit the performance of these new machines? For many computational problems, the design, implementation, and understanding of efficient parallel algorithms can be a formidable challenge. Efficient parallel programs are more difficult to write and understand that efficient sequential programs, because the behaviour of parallel programs is nondeterministic. They are, in general, less portable than serial codes, because their structure may depend critically on specific architectural features of the underlying hardware (such as the way in which data sharing, memory access, synchronization, and process creation are handled).

---

*This work was supported by the Applied Mathematical Sciences subprogram of the Office of Energy Research, US Department of Energy, under Contract no. W-31 109-Eng-38.

We have implemented two tools that aid in the development of parallel algorithms that are portable across a range of high- performance computers. The first tool, Schedule, aids in implementing and analysing programs within a large-grain control flow model of computation. The underlying concept is based on a natural graphical interpretation of parallel computation that is useful in designing and implementing parallel algorithms. This graphical interpretation may be used to automate the generation of a parallel program through a facility called Build. Schedule also provides a means for postprocessing performance analysis through an animated visualization of the flow of a parallel program's execution. This animation is accomplished through the Trace facility. The second tool provides a graphical display of memory access patterns in algorithms. Such patterns can be important in understanding memory bottlenecks in compute-intensive algorithms.

Section 13.2 discusses some of the motivation behind the tools. Section 13.3 describes the SCHEDULE package in detail, the implementation of SCHEDULE, and the SCHEDULE postprocessing environment. Section 13.4 describes MAP, used in the analysis of memory access to programs. Section 13.5 gives information about how to obtain the new tools. Finally, Section 13.6 summarizes our efforts and discusses further research that will aid in understanding parallel algorithms.

13.2 MOTIVATION

13.2.1   Graphical representation

In developing software, the initial definitions and specifications are often done graphically with such things as flow charts or dependency graphs. A human can visualize the overall structure of the problem far more easily from these geographical representations than from words and numbers. Unfortunately, of course, the computer cannot. These charts and graphs must eventually be translated to a computer language in order to write a computer program. With a modern workstation environment one can envision going far beyond the notion of a simple flow chart. The automatic generation of text from a visual specification is within reach. Moreover, a postanalysis of performance is facilitated through such a representation.

With the use of a graphics interface, implemented on a workstation for example, a user can develop the parallel program as a computational graph, where the nodes in the graph represent the computation to be performed and the arcs represent the dependencies between the computations. From this graphical representation, a lower-level executable portable program can be generated, which when executed will perform the computations specified by the graph in an order consistent with the dependencies specified. This programming environment allows for a high-level description of the parallel algorithm and, when the high-level description is translated into a common programming language, permits portable program execution.

The environment presents the algorithm developer with an abstract model of computation that can bind effectively to a wide variety of existing shared-memory multiprocessors. Specific machine intrinsics may be confined to the internal workings of such a tool in order to provide a common user interface to these parallel processors. Thus the new environment removes the problems created for the algorithm developers through the different programming models and execution environments embodied in each of the individual multiprocessors.

Another problem facing the developers of algorithms and software for parallel computers is the analysis of the performance of the resulting programs. Often performance bugs are far more difficult to detect and overcome than the synchronization and data dependency bugs normally associated with parallel programs. We have developed a fairly sophisticated postprocessing performance analysis tool associated with the graphics programming interface just described. This tool is quite useful in understanding the flow of execution and processor utilization within a parallel program. However, more detail is often required in order to obtain a useful analysis of performance. In most of the advanced-computer architectures that implement shared memory, some sort of memory hierarchy is involved. The interaction of memory access with this hierarchy is crucial to the performance of a program. To aid in understanding this phenomenon, we have developed another tool which provides a visualization of the memory access patterns of a parallel program.

13.2.2   Related work

The notion of visual aids to programming is certainly not new. Indeed, the entire August 1985 issue of *IEEE Computer* was devoted to this topic, and several of the articles appearing in that issue are germane to this article. A number of efforts are under way to provide parallel programming tools [7, 19, 1, 3 6]. Our research has been influenced primarily by the work of Babb[2], Browne[5], and Lusk and

Overbeck[18]. Our major objective has been to provide a common interface that will allow researchers to exploit existing hardware in the near term. However, we are convinced through our experience with this package that the underlying ideas are sound and worthy of further development. We believe that the ultimate solution to software problems associated with parallel programming lies with new programming languages or perhaps with a particular extension to existing languages. However, regardless of programming language developments, visual aids in programming and performance analysis are sure to have a significant role in future environments for software development.

13.3 SCHEDULE

The Schedule package provides an environment for the portable implementation of explicitly parallel algorithms in a Fortran setting. Once implemented using Schedule, the user's source code is identical for each target machine the application is run on. The package is designed to allow existing Fortran subroutines to be called through Schedule, without modification, thereby permitting users access to a wide body of existing library software in a parallel setting.

The underlying idea in Schedule is that many parallel computations may be represented in a large-grain control flow form and that this is a useful way to think about and construct parallel programs. A parallel program is derived by breaking up a problem into units of computation and execution dependencies between them. These dependencies represent assertions made by the user about the order in which units of computation may execute. Of course, the actual order of execution cannot be known in advance and is likely to differ every time the program is run. The graph only assures that a unit of computation that is dependent on the results of some others will not execute until they are completed. This concept is similar to the large-grain dataflow ideas [2.5]. Indeed, the graph must respect data dependencies, but the computation is not driven by dataflow firing rules. Moreover, while data items are implicitly carried along arcs, one does not explicitly associate a data item with an arc. This approach greatly reduces the complexity o the graphical representation.

When designing a parallel algorithm using Schedule, one is required to describe the parallel structure of the program through a graphical representation of the units of computation and execution dependencies between them. A unit of computation is simply a subroutine name together with a list of shared parameters to be passed to the subroutine at the time of execution. Shared data structures must be declared in the main program or placed in a named common block to assure that they are valid and accessible to the units of computation during execution. These notions are then implemented in a Fortran program written in terms of subroutine calls to Schedule. A pair of Schedule subroutine calls is associated with each node in the graph. One call records a specification of the unit of computation represented by the node; the other records the execution dependencies associated with the node that are necessary to coordinate the parallel execution. The user must take the responsibility of ensuring that the execution dependencies specified are valid. These concepts are perhaps more easily grasped through an example, but we shall postpone this for a moment.

13.3.1 Build: constructing a program from a graph

Once a control flow graph has been constructed, a Schedule program can be written to represent the graph mentioned earlier. However, the specification of data dependencies comprise an extremely tedious and error prone part of constructing a Schedule program. Since this information is based on an underlying graphical representation that is more readily understood and conveyed visually, it makes sense to attempt to construct these specifications graphically, perhaps at a workstation.

For static dependency graphs, the translation is fairly straightforward and easily automated, allowing the computer to generate the necessary code from the graphical description of the problem. We have developed a mouse-driven graphics input tool called Build (see Fig. 13.1) for use at a workstation that will enable a user to interactively draw a dependency graph on a workstation screen, specify the user-applied subroutines for each node in the graph, and have the workstation generate the Fortran code with the necessary calls to the Schedule library. This code can then be compiled, linked with the user-supplied subroutines and the Schedule library, and run on the target parallel processor.

The graphics display of Build has two parts: the user control interface and the drawing surface. A dependency graph can be constructed, displayed, and manipulated on the drawing surface with the user control interface and certain mouse button sequences. The definition of the graph can be saved and later retrieved. At any time in the construction of the dependency graph, the Fortran code with the appropriate Schedule calls that represent that graph can be generated. This program must be usually edited to supply additional information and to fill in correct calling sequences in place of dummy parameters. However, the user does not need to supply any text associated with the specification of data dependencies. This is all done automatically from the graph.

To use this tool, one clicks on a mouse to create the nodes that will be in the dependency graph. Clicking another button draws the arcs that represent control dependencies between nodes. After constructing the dependency graph in this manner, the user associates his subroutine names and parameter lists with each node via an on-screen menu.

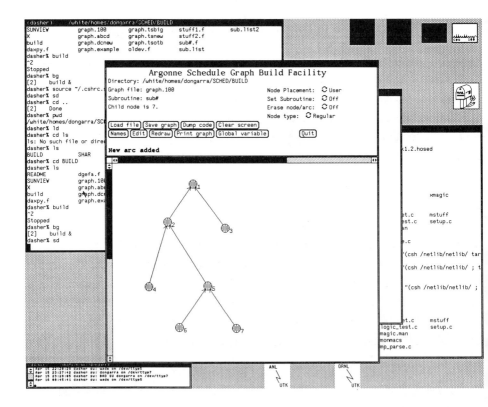

Figure 13.1   Example of Build facility.

With a final mouse click, a Fortran program representing the dependency graph is generated automatically. Additional editing is required to associate the correct calling sequence with each unit of computation. However, the tedius textual information that is needed to describe the dependencies implied by the edges of the graph will not require any modification.

13.3.2 Schedule: A parallel programming interface

A Schedule program may be written by hand or generated through the Build facility just described. The nature of a Schedule program will be described with a rather generic psuedocode. Detailed programming examples may be found in [14]. here is a brief indication of the structure of a Schedule program.

```
subroutine paralg( < parms > )
declare global variables

declare local variables
external subname

do 100 j = 1 ,nunitis
         .
         .
         .
jobtag  = the identifier of this unit of computation
icango  = number of nodes jobtag depends on
ncheks  = number of nodes which depend on jobtag
list    = list of identifiers of these ncheks dependents

call dep(jobtag, icango, ncheks, list)
call putq(jobtag, subname, arms)
         .
         .
         .
100 continue
    return
    end
```

This subroutine is invoked from a main program by the statement

```
call sched(nprocs,paralg,arms).
```

The main subroutine either has declared the shared data or has placed it in named common. The subroutine paralg merely records the units of computation and the data dependencies. Once this has been done, control is released by paralg and some generic work routines begin execution of the recorded units of computation while obeying the dependencies specified by the graph. This mechanism is described below in more detail.

The example shown above provides for static scheduling of parallel processes. By this we mean that the number of processes and the dependencies between them is known in advance. In many situations, however, the computational graph will not be known in advance; hence, we will need the ability for one process to start or spawn another depending on a computation that has taken place up to a given point in the spawning process. This feature, which we call dynamic spawning, is provided by the Schedule package via routines similar to those for static scheduling.

The call to the Schedule routines dep and putq, respectively, places process dependencies and process descriptors on a queue. A unique identifier jobtag is associated with each node of the dependency graph either by the user or by referencing a Schedule subroutine. This identifier is a positive integer. Internally it represents a pointer to a process. The items needed to specify a data dependency are non-negative integers icango and ncheks and an integer array list. The integer icango specifies the number of processes that the process jobtag depends on. The integer ncheks specifies the number of processes that depend on the process jobtag. Thus icango is set to the number of incoming arcs, and ncheks is set to the number of outgoing arcs at the node indexed by jobtag. The list is an integer array whose first ncheks entries contain the identifiers (i.e., jobtag s) of the processes that depend on the process jobtag.

icango = 2
ncheks = 3

icango = 2

ncheks = 3

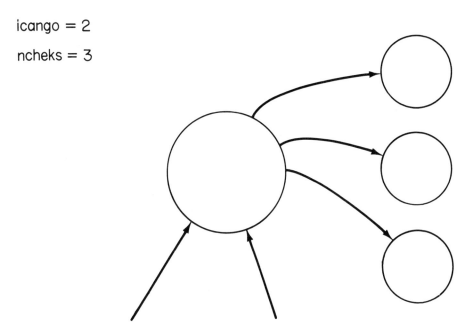

Figure 13.2 A node in a dependency graph.

In Fig. 13.2 a typical node of a data dependency graph is shown. this node has two incoming arcs and three outgoing arcs. As shown to the left of the node, one would set *icango* = 2, *ncheks* = 3, and the first three entries of list to the identifiers of the processes pointed to by the outgoing arcs.

The initial call to sched(nprocs,subname,<parms>) results in nprocs virtual processors called work to begin executing on nprocs separate physical processors. Typically nprocs should be set to a value that is less than or equal to the number of physical processors available on the given system. These work routines access a ready queue of jobtags for schedulable processes (those whose data dependencies have been satisfied). After a **work** routing has been successful in obtaining the jobtag of a schedulable process, it makes the subroutine call associated with that jobtag during the call to putq. When this subroutine executes a return, control is returned to work, and a Schedule routine chekin is called which decrements the icango counter of each of the ncheks process that depend on process jobtag. If any of these icango values has been decremented to zero, the identifier of that process is placed on the ready queue immediately.

We depict this mechanism in Fig. 13.3. The array labeled **parmq** holds a process descriptor for each jobtag. A process descriptor consists of data dependency information and a subroutine name, together with a list of addresses of parameters that will satisfy the calling sequence for that subroutine. This information is placed on **parmq** through the two calls

CALL   DEP(jobtag,icango,ncheks,list)
CALL   PUTQ(jobtag,subname, < parms >)

When making these two calls the user has assured that a call to subname with the argument list < parms > is valid in a data dependency sense whenever the counter icango has been decremented to the value zero. When a work routine has finished a call to **chekin,** it gets the jobtag of the next available schedulable process off the ready and then assumes the identify of the appropriate subroutine by making a call to subname with the argument list < parms > .

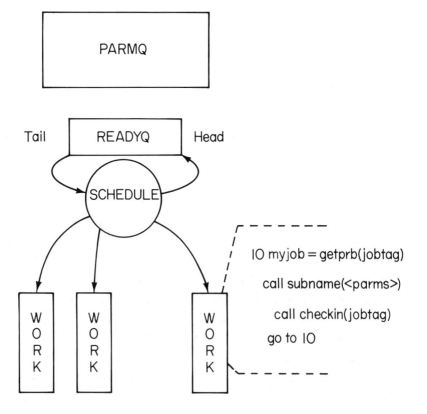

Figure 13.3 The Schedule mechanism.

This figure is slightly misleading. The readyq is actually distributed in an attempt to avoid contention for locks as much as possible. Thus, each work routine has a readyq associated with it. That queue is polled first. If no work is found, the remaining queues are polled round robin until taskdone is posted or new work is found. In earlier versions of the package these queues were fixed-size arrays. A version using circular queues and a more sophisticated allocation mechanism has been developed that avoids any restrictions on the number of nodes allowed in a graph [16]. Examples consisting of several thousand units of computation have been executed under this version.

A certain amount of overhead is associated with the mechanism just described. However, it is not excessive as long as the units of computation in the graph involve a reasonable amount of work. A recent study by Diaz and Lee [9] shows that the overhead resulting from the Schedule mechanism described above is negligible. Sublinear speedup occurs in their study only when there are inherent serial sections forced by the nature of the graph.

13.3.3 Trace: graphical performance analysis of Schedule programs

Once a Schedule program has been written and executed, we have found it is useful to observe an animation of the run-time behaviour of the program. From this animation it is possible to visualize the parallel parts in execution as they occurred while the application was running. This visualization helps to understand what performance issues arose during execution and what bottlenecks might have developed. Programming errors associated with synchronization may also be detected. Since the control dependency graph has such a natural graphical interpretation, it was possible to construct a postprocessing tool to trace and animate the flow of execution. We call this the Trace facility.

To use the graphics Trace facility, the user constructs a Schedule program as previously described, the difference being that the user links to the Schedule graphics library rather than to the regular library. The Schedule program is then executed on the parallel processor of interest. While executing, it produces an output file of trace events. The information in the file is a trace of the user specification of the computational graph and the execution of the graph by the computer. The trace file records the definition of the graph along with the execution and completion of the subroutine. When execution has completed, this file is then moved to a workstation where a program to display graphically the information in the trace file has been installed. The current implementation of the graphics facility funs on a Sun workstation under Suntools. Fig. 13.4 shows an example of a computational graph as it would appear on the screen before the replay of execution is started.

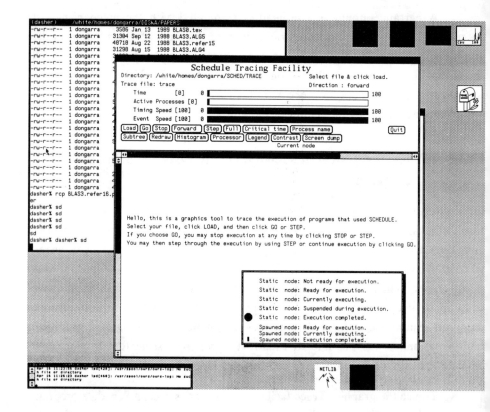

Figure 13.4 Information on the workstation screen.

A number of buttons and slide bars help in controlling the information to be viewed. To load a trace file, one first selects the desired trace file and then clicks on the Load button; the control dependency graph is then displayed on the screen. The arcs represent the control dependencies between subroutines. There are five states for a static node in the graph: clear, lined, hashed, circled, and black. The clear nodes represent subroutines waiting to have their control dependencies satisfied before starting execution. The lined nodes represent subroutines whose control dependencies are satisfied, but whose execution has not started. The hatched nodes represent subroutines that are currently executing. The circled nodes represent subroutines whose execution has been temporarily suspended because they have dynamically spawned other processes. The black nodes represent subroutines that have finished execution. The rectangular nodes represent processes that have been spawned dynamically. The numbers associated with each node in the graph represent the tag that the user has assigned to each process. The nodes in the dependency graph will change their state as the trace proceeds.

The viewing of events can be stopped or restarted by clicking on the Stop or the Go button at any time. Execution begins at the bottom of the graph and works its way to the top, with the top node the last item to execute. The Full button is used on conjunction with the Redraw button to expand what is displayed on the canvas by a factor of four.

The **Critical time** button is used after execution has completed. It displays the time required to execute the various paths in the graph and can be used to display the critical path of execution (i.e., the path that is taking the most time to execute). The critical path determines the running time of the entire application.

The **Subtree** button is used to display a subtree of the graph. To use this feature, one places the mouse cursor on a node. The node number clicked on will be displayed in bottom right line of the top panel. To see the subtree, one clicks the Subtree button. This step can be repeated to zoom in on a particular party of the graph.

The **Step** button is used to single-step through the execution of the trace file. A way to use this is by loading a trace file, starting execution, and stopping execution at the desired point. Then the **Step** button is used to single-step through the execution. The activity can be resumed at normal speeds by clicking the **Go** button. The **Forward** button is used to display the execution either forward or backward in time.

The **Histogram** button will display a histogram of the events run versus the number of processors active.

These tools can influence the design of an algorithm by providing insight into how the program behaves when run in parallel. An example of their use is in the solution of a triangular linear system partitioned by blocks. As the program executed on an Alliant FX/8, an output file was produced which recorded the units of computation as they were defined and executed. The file was then shipped to a Sun workstation where a graphics program interpreted this output, constructed the graph, and played back the execution sequence that was run on the Alliant. In the graph shown in Fig. 13.5, the black nodes show processes that have completed execution, the hatched nodes show executing processes, and the white nodes show processes waiting to execute.

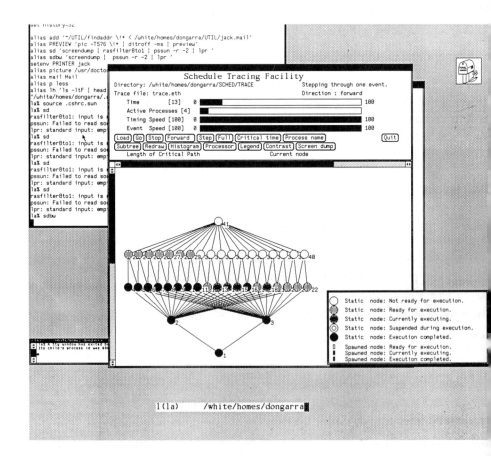

Figure 13.5 Computational graph replay.

In addition to discovering mistakes in the specification of the graph, this representation is useful in exposing more subtle aspects of the executing program. During execution the bar graph labelled active processes at the top tracks the number of processes actually executing. The bar labelled timing speed can be adjusted to speed up or slow down the replay. The events will occur in time proportional to execution time. This gives a much better indication of serial bottlenecks and load balancing problems within an executing program. Once load balance anomalies have been discovered, they can be corrected by revising the execution dependencies to force certain processes to complete before others.

13.4 MEMORY ACCESS PATTERN PROGRAM

The second tool we discuss, the Memory Access Pattern (MAP) program, is helpful in understanding how an algorithm uses memory hierarchy. On modern high-performance computers, memory is organized in a hierarchy according to access time. This hierarchy takes the form of main memory, cache, local memory, and vector registers. The basic objective of this organization is to attempt to match the imbalance between the fast processing speed of the floating-point units and the slow latency time of main memory. In order to be successful, algorithms must effectively utilize the memory hierarchy of the underlying computer architecture on which they are implemented.

The key is to avoid unnecessary memory references. In most computers, data flows from memory into and out of registers and from registers into and out of functional units, which perform the given instructions on the data. Algorithm performance can be dominated by the amount of memory traffic rather than by the number of floating-point operations involved. This situation provides considerable motivation to restructure existing algorithms and to devise new algorithms that minimize date movement.

For computers with memory hierarchy or for true parallel processing computers, it is often preferable to partition the matrices into blocks and to perform the computation by matrix-matrix operations on the blocks. This approach provides for full reuse of data while the block is held in cache or local memory. It avoids excessive movement of data to and from memory and gives a surface-to-volume effect for the ratio of arithmetic operations to data movement, i.e. $O(n^3)$ arithmetic operations to $O(n^2)$ data movement. In addition, on architectures that provide for parallel processing, parallelism can be exploited in two ways: (1) operations on distinct blocks may be performed in parallel; and (2) within the operations on each block, scalar or vector operations may be performed in parallel.

The performance of these block algorithms depends on the dimensions chosen for the blocks. It is important to select the blocking strategy for each of our target machines, and then develop a mechanism whereby the routines can determine good block dimensions automatically.

Since most memory accesses for data in scientific programs are for matrix elements, which are usually stored in two-dimensional arrays (column-major in Fortran), knowing the order of array references is important in determining the amount of memory traffic. We would like to take an arbitrary linear algebra program, have its matrices mapped to a graphics screen, and have a matrix element flash on the screen whenever its corresponding array element was accessed in memory. This type of tool would provide insight into the algorithm's behaviour and would enable the programmer to compare the memory access patterns of different algorithms.

13.4.1   Implementation of MAP

The MAP tools are intended to provide an animated view of the memory activity during execution. These tools allow us to play back a program's execution to study how an algorithm uses memory, and to experiment with different memory hierarchy schemes and observe their effects on the program's flow of data.

There are two basic aspects to accomplishing our goals: preprocessor instrumentation, which is accomplished by the Memory Access Pattern Instrumentation (MAPI) program, and postprocessor display graphics, which is accomplished by the Memory Access Pattern Animation (MAPA) program. The MAPI preprocessor analyses an arbitrary Fortran program and, for each reference to a matrix element, generates a Fortran statement that calls a MAPI routine that records the reference to the matrix element. This works for any Fortran program. However, many programs dealing with matrices reference the Basic Linear Algebra Subprograms. To accommodate the Level 1, 2, or 3 BLAS [17,11,10]. MAPI will translate those calls into calls to MAPI routines that understand the BLAS operations and record the appropriate array references. The replaced routine will record the memory access to be made, as well as the number of floating-point operations to be performed, and then call the Level 1, 2, or 3 BLAS originally intended. This allows us to reduce the size of the trace file by recording the range of values referenced per trace line, rather than a trace line per matrix element. The output of MAPI is a Fortran module that, when compiled and linked with a MAPI library, executes, the original code and produces a trace file. This trace file is used as input to MAPA in order to display the memory accesses on the arrays in the Fortran code.

13.4.2   Execution of the instrumented program

When the instrumented program executes, it generates a readable ASCII file that contains an encoded description of how the arrays in the program have been referenced. There are basically three types of trace lines generated: array definition, read access, and write access. If a call to one of the BLAS has been made, the trace file may contain the information about a row or column access or both. The name of the BLAS is recorded, and during playback the name of the BLAS executed will be displayed. In addition, the events are time stamped, allowing the MAPA program to merge information with other trace files and have the relative order of operations preserved. We also record the amount of floating-point work that has taken place for a given memory reference. Fig. 13.6 displays the output of MAPA for a view of LU decomposition.

13.4.3   Cache modelling

The MAP tools also have a feature to allow statistical analysis and data collection of various cache systems. The cache consists of a simple, single cache memory. The basic cache policy is consecutive linear placement with immediate write-back. The cache placement and replacement algorithms work with pages of cache memory. The size of a cache page is flexible, but is required to be a power of two ranging from 1 to 65536.

Six cache replacement mechanisms have been implemented. These are Least Recently Used (LRU), Least Frequently Used (LFU), First-In-First-Out (FIFO), Clock, Last-In-First-Out (LIFO), and Random. The LRU mechanism chooses the page in cache that was used the longest time ago. The LFU mechanism chooses the page that has been used the fewest number of times since it was loaded into the cache. The FIFO mechanism simply keeps track of which order pages were loaded into cache and replaces pages in the same order. The Clock mechanism is an approximation to LRU using FIFO, but as pages are used, a usage bit is set so the page will be skipped over as the FIFO queue is traversed. The LIFO mechanism is similar to the FIFO except that instead of replacing the pages in the order they were loaded, the pages are replaced in reverse order. The Random mechanism simply generates a random page number and replaces that page. When the cache is full and a new page from main memory needs to be loaded into the cache, the current cache replacement mechanism chooses the page in cache to be replaced.

When the MAPA tool executes, an additional box displaying cache activity is shown on the screen. When a cache hit is detected, the corresponding element turns yellow (on a colour Sun monitor). When a cache miss is detected, the elements in cache that will be written over turn red.

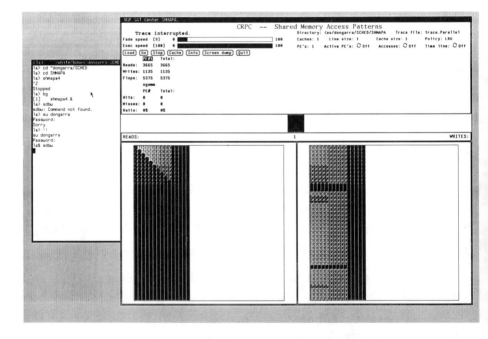

Figure 13.6 MAPA output for LU decomposition.

13.4.4 MAPA: The control panel

The MAPA program maps the arrays to the graphics screen and highlights the elements of the arrays when they are accessed. The program can display up to four different arrays at one time. The top row displays the read accesses to the arrays, and the bottom displays the writes.

The panel subwindow (see Fig. 13.7) is MAPA's main user control interface and contains several features:

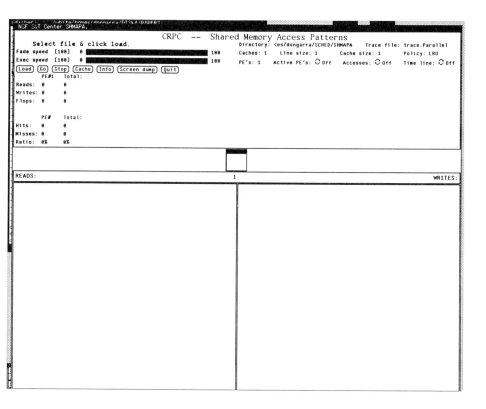

Figure 13.7 MAPA control panel.

The **Directory** button allows the user to step through various directories to locate the desired trace file. The **Update speed** slider controls the length of time the memory reference is held on the screen before fading away. The **Execution speed** slider controls the speed at which events are processed when GO has been chosen. The speed control slider expresses the event display speed as a percentage of the fastest possible speed. The **Load** button initializes and resets MAPA for another trace file. The Go button processes events from the trace file consecutively without stopping. The Stop button stops the tracing of events. The **Quit** button exits the MAPA tool.

13.4.5   Execution of MAPA

The canvas subwindow occupies the lower two-thirds of the window. Graphics information is displayed here. The canvas is divided into two rows of four squares. The first row now displays the load activities, and the second row displays the store activity.

Each of the four columns of squares across the canvas can be used to display an array. When the trace file is started, a load of a matrix element is denoted by a blackening of an area of the block used to represent the array. As time evolves and if no further reference is made to that specific matrix element, the area will gradually lighten until, at some time after the original access, it will return to its original colour. If a subsequent reference to that element is made, the area representing the element will again darken. In this way a user can observe the locality of reference the program is able to achieve. The same situation is true for store operations. As a store is made, the area representing the element affected darkens, and after time the area will return to its original color. If the BLAS have been used, the whole area affected by the operation is changed at once.

13.4.6   Example

We are involved in the design and implementation of a transportable linear algebra library in Fortran 77, called LAPACK[4]. The library is intended to provide a uniform set of subroutines to solve the most common linear algebra problems and to run efficiently on a wide range of high-performance computers. We have been experimenting with three different organizations for the algorithm to factor a matrix in preparation to solving a system of linear equations via Gaussian elimination. Each method performs the same number of floating-point operations; the algorithms differ only in the way in which the data is accessed. The three methods are block jki (a left-looking algorithm), block Crout, and block rank update (a right-looking algorithm). See [13, 8] for more details.

When MAPA displays the trace file produced by merging the trace files from the execution of the instrumented versions of the three different programs, we obtain the picture shown in Fig. 13.8.

Table 13.1 was generated on a matrix of order 100 and a blocksize 64. As can be seen, in this case algorithm 1 (block jki) has fewer store operations overall and slightly more load operations. We would expect this algorithm to perform better than algorithm 3 (block rank update) and marginally faster than algorithm 2 (block Crout).

Table 13.1   100 x 100 matrix blocksize 64

		LUI	LU2	LU3
Random	LOADS	102530	108515	99965
	STORES	33180	37455	90180
Diag.	LOADS	84100	90085	81535
Dominant	STORES	14750	19025	71750

The row marked Diag. Dominant reflects the fact that the matrix is diagonally dominant; thus, no pivoting is performed during the factorization, resulting in fewer memory references. (For these results, we assumed that the data would be held in the memory hierarchy once it was fetched for the operation, that is, fetched once for each block operation.)

From this information one can conclude that the algorithm corresponding to LU3 may be less efficient than either LU1 or LU2 as a result of more store operations.

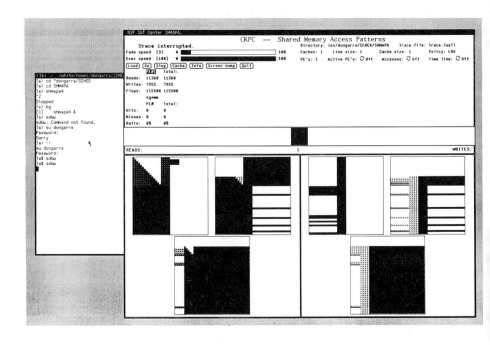

Figure 13.8 Display of Fortran execution of a matrix of order 40, blocksize 5.

13.5 AVAILABILITY OF OUR TOOLS

The software described in this report is available electronically via netlib [12]. To retrieve a copy, one should send electronic mail to netlib@mcs.anl.gov. In the mail message, one should type

> send index from anl-tools
> send build from anl-tools
> send map from anl-tools

Unix shar files will be sent back. To build the parts, one need only ship the mail file (after removing the mail header) into an empty directory and type make.

Versions of the Schedule package are now running successfully on the Vax 11/780, Alliant FX/8, Sequent Balance 21000, Encore Multimax, Cray-2, Cray X-MAP, Cray Y-MP, IBM 3090, and Flex 32 computers. An earlier version of the package ran on the Denelcor HEP computer. The Schedule internals had to be modified for each of these machines. These modifications were minor in some cases, but extremely difficult in others. The graphics tools Build and Trace are also available in X-Windows. They have been used extensively on Sun workstations but should port to any workstation supporting X-Windows.

13.6 CONCLUSIONS AND FURTHER WORK

We have discussed two tools that aid in the development of parallel algorithms. Both tools rely heavily on the use of post-execution graphical displays to help the programmer understand the behaviour of a parallel algorithm. These tools allow users to view trace files generated by executing parallel algorithms. Using such tools provides insight into algorithm behaviour and potential bottlenecks. A number of parallel programs have been developed using Schedule. These applications are reported in some detail in [15].

We note, however, that many research issues remain. One issue is how the ideas presented here extend to distributed memory environments; we are collaborating with J. C. Browne in this regard. It is also unclear how these ideas carry over to SIMD computer architectures.

REFERENCES

1   Ahuja, S.Carriero, N. and Gelernter,D. (1986) Linda and Friends. *IEEE Computer.*

2   Babb, R. G. (1984) Parallel processing with large grain data flow techniques. *IEEE Computer,* 17, 7, pp.55-61.

3   Bershad, B. N. Lazowska, E. D. and Levy, H. M. (1987) *PRESTO: A System for Object-Oriented Parallel Programming,* TR 87-09-01, Department of Computer Science, University of Washington.

4   Bischof, C.Demmel, J. Dongarra, J. Du Croz, J. Greenbaum, A. Hammarling,S and Sorensen. D. (1988) *LAPACK Working Note No.5; Provisional Contents,* Argonne National Laboratory Report, ANL-88-38.

5   Browne, J. C. (1986) Framework for formulation and analysis of parallel computation structures, *Parallel Computing,* 3, pp. 1-9.

6   Browne, J. C. Azam, M. andSobek, S. (1988) *Architectural and Language Independent Parallel Programming: A Feasibility Demonstration,* Tech. Report, Department of Computer Science, University of Texas, Austin.

7   Carle, A.Cooper K. Hood, R. Kennedy, K. Torczon,L. and Warren, S. (1987) A pratical environment for fortran programming, *IEEE Computer,* 20, 11, pp. 75-89.

8   Demmel, J. Dongarra, J. Du Croz, J. Greenbaum, A. Hammarling, S. and Sorensen, D. (1987) *Prospectus for the Development of a Linear Algebra Library for High- Performance Computers*, Argonne National Laboratory Report, ANL-MCS-TM-97.

9   Diaz, J. C. (1986) Calculating the block preconditioner on parallel multivector processors. *Proc. of the Workshop on Applied Computing in the Energy Field,* Stillwater, Oklahoma.

10 Dongarra,J. J. Du Croz, J. Duff, I. and Hammarling, S. (1988a) *A Set of Level 3 Basic Linear Algebra Subprograms,* Argonne National Laboratory Report, ANL-P1-0888.

11 Dongarra, J. J.Du Croz, J. Hammarling,S. and Hanson, R. (1988b) An extended set of Fortran basic linear algebra subprograms. *ACM Trans. Math. Software,* 14, 1, pp. 1-17.

12 DongarraJ. J. and Grosse, E. (1987) Distribution of mathematical software via electronic mail. *Comm. of the ACM.*

13 Dongarra, J. J. Gustavson, F. and Karp, A. (1984) Implementing linear algebra algorithms for dense matrices on a vector pipeline machine. *SIAM Review,* 26, 1, pp. 91-112.

14 Dongarra, J. J. and Sorensen, D. (1987a) Schedule: Tools for developing and analyzing parallel fortran programs. in *the Characteristics of Parallel Agorithms,* (ed. L. Jamieson, D. Gannon and R. Douglass,) MIT Press, pp. 363-394.

15 Dongarra, J. J. and Sorensen, D. C. (1987) A portable environment for developing parallel fortran programs. *Parallel Computing,* 5, 1, pp. 175-186.

16 Hanson, F. B. and Sorensen,D. C. (1988) *The Schedule Parallel Programming Package with recycling Job Queues and Iterated Dependency Graphs,* Argonne National Laboratory Preprint 22-1188.

17 Lawson, C. Hanson, R. Kincaid, D. and Krogh, F. (1979) Basic linear algebra subprograms for Fortran usage. *ACM Transactions on Math. Soft.,* 5, pp. 308-323.

18 Lusk, E. and Overbeek, R. (1983) *Implementation of Monitors with Macros: A Programming Aid for the HEP and Other Parallel Processors,* Argonne National Laboratory Report, ANL-83-97.

19 Snyder, L. (1984) Parallel programming and the Poker Programming Environment. *IEEE Computer,* 17, 7, pp. 27-36.

14 The ParTool project: development of a parallel programming environment*

M. van Steen and H. Sips

TNO Institute of Applied Computer Science, The Netherlands

14.1 INTRODUCTION

The ParTool project is an on-going Dutch research effort aimed at the creation of a parallel processing development environment. ParTool (Parallel Tools) enables development of parallel programs which will satisfy two, somewhat contradicting requirements. First, the environment supports the development of programs that efficiently use the resources of a given target parallel machine. Second, these programs will be well-engineered, meaning that modularity, well-structuredness, and above all, portability over a wide range of parallel architectures, are incorporated. These two requirements are met by following a layered approach toward software design, allowing hardware architectural features to influence design in a controlled and maintainable fashion.

This paper contains a description of the ParTool project. In section 14.2 some basic problems which motivated the initiation of the project are discussed. In section 14.3 the objectives of ParTool are briefly presented, followed in section 14.4 by an overview of the envisaged architecture. In section 14.5 the software design process as supported by ParTool is presented. The current status of the project is discussed in section 14.6.

---

* This research is sponsored by the Dutch funding agency SPIN

14.2 THE NEED FOR HIGH-PERFORMANCE SYSTEMS

Many applications in the scientific and engineering fields have always required powerful computing systems. This demand for high-performance systems not only stems from requirements based on human and operational factors, but also from requirements related to time-critical data processing.

For example, in the field of engineering design, high-speed systems are often needed to achieve satisfactory turn-around times of design applications for finite element analysis, computational fluid dynamics, etc. Other example applications are found in the field of energy resource exploration (seismic data processing, reservoir modelling), and fields in which visualization plays a prominent role. In addition, many applications have critical parts which are often subject to hard timing constraints. A typical example is formed by software used for nuclear reactor safety. In order to provide online analysis of reactor conditions, automatic control for normal and abnormal operations, etc., guaranteed (fast) response and analysis times are crucial. Currently, only supercomputers can provide the necessary computing power for such applications.

So far, substantial effort has been directed toward technological improvements of sequential computers, leading to the current generation of supercomputers. Unfortunately, the investments required to further increase the performance of sequential systems are enormous, and it can be expected that these will inhibit substantial improvements from being made in the near future.

The enormous costs related to current supercomputers have led to the development of parallel processing technologies as an alternative to further increase computing power. Not only do parallel processors allow a relatively straightforward enhancement of sequential processing techniques, the shifting technology and economics of computing has brought them to the forefront of commercial innovation. Instead of building machines with a small number of highly- engineered processors using the fastest and most expensive component technologies, machines are currently built that have a large number of processors based on low-cost, mass-produced, industry standard microprocessors.

Although this alternative approach to achieve high-speed computing systems is economically extremely attractive, application of parallel processing techniques is subject to a number of characteristics that make the issue of developing efficient programs much more complicated to deal with than in the sequential case.

For example, a developer of parallel software is confronted with a model of computation in which elements such as processor-memory pairing and interconnection topology have a significant influence on software design decisions. Without taking the architecture of a parallel processor into account, development of applications that meet the required performance criteria will not be possible [Karp 87]. Another characteristic is that the architecture of parallel processors is still changing, and it cannot be expected that a single architecture will eventually emerge from all current developments. Consequently, in designing parallel programs, a developer is confronted with a software portability problem. Although this problem is also inherent to sequential software development, it becomes even more difficult to deal with in the parallel case.

It is currently recognized that development of parallel software is not only extremely intricate, it is also becoming the bottleneck for successful introduction of massively parallel architectures [Schatz 89].

14.3 PARTOOL : COMBINING EFFICIENCY AND PORTABILITY OF PARALLEL PROGRAMS

In order to deal with the intricacies of developing parallel software that is both efficient and portable over a wide range of parallel architectures, the use of automated programming support tools is essential. Moreover, as parallel software development involves many different kinds of problems, the specific support tools should be easy to combine so as to cover the complete software development process. Building and integrating such tools into a parallel programming environment is the main goal of the ParTool project, a recently initiated joint effort of Dutch research institutes, universities, and industry. Tool integration takes place at two levels. At the higher-end, a user-interface layer provides an application developer a consistent view of the environment, while at the lower-end tools communicate through a common object management system. It will be possible to enhance the functionality of the environment by adding new parallel development tools as they come available.

Parallel programming is often characterized by a high degree of experimentation and prototyping in order to obtain the required efficiency on a given target machine [Schwan 88]. In order to support this experimental approach towards parallel software development, the ParTool environment incorporates instrumentation tools that allow for preliminary evaluation of parallel programs. In addition, special attention is paid to building and integrating tools in a such a way that they allow for flexible prototyping.

At first instance, the project concentrates on target applications of a technical-scientific nature, and will provide tools for application development for MIMD machines, including shared memory as well as distributed-memory architectures. It is not envisaged to generate application code in a specific machine language, but rather in some widely used high-level language such as Fortran or C. The ParTool system itself will be embedded in a workstation-based environment, presumably one which is based on the Unix operating system.

14.4 ARCHITECTURE OF THE PARTOOL ENVIRONMENT

In order to support experimentation and prototyping of parallel software development, the ParTool environment is centered around an object base as shown in Fig. 14.1. The object base contains application designs, algorithm descriptions, libraries, architectural models, etc. It is not envisaged to build the object base as part of the project, but rather to use an existing system such as for example the PCTE [Boudier 89]. Several subsystems, each consisting of a collection of tools, will be developed. In Fig. 14.1, some relevant subsystems are shown as vertical-oriented, rounded rectangles.

An application modelling and analysis subsystem will enable a developer to concentrate on designing the global structure of an application, as well as modelling its overall behaviour. Using this subsystem programs result which are organized as a tree-structured collection of modules. Application of data flow techniques such as used in the field of software engineering (see e.g. [Babb 87] or [Ward 86]) provide insight in the dynamics of the parallel program, including its input/output behaviour. Modelling applications will proceed through graphical interaction. In addition, a program design language for textual representations of models will be used for documentation purposes, and for generation of skeleton code in a standard target language such as Fortran or C.

Another major subsystem is built around an algorithm specification language called Booster. This high-level language allows for the specification of algorithms in such a way that as much parallelism is preserved as possible. Booster is centered around a single array-like data structure, called a shape. Shapes extend the array concept by allowing the description of more complex geometric structures other than rectangular ones. In addition, the indexing-mechanism inherent to arrays has been replaced by so-called views. Views are used to access parts of a shape (i.e. select a subset of a shape), to access a combination of several shapes, but also to access for example a permutation of the data of a shape without affecting its original structure. A detailed description of Booster can be found in [Paalvast 89].

The model of computation introduced by Booster allows for the description of algorithms in a machine-independent manner, thus guaranteeing portability among different parallel architectures. Parallelism itself is introduced by data- and code-decomposition techniques applied to the programs written in Booster. The decomposition techniques are supported by a separate collection of tools, as shown in Fig. 14.1. In the process of decomposing an algorithm, hardware architectural features are taken into account so as to obtain an efficient implementation of the algorithm described. As in the case of application modelling, a decomposed algorithm is eventually translated into a standard high-level programming language.

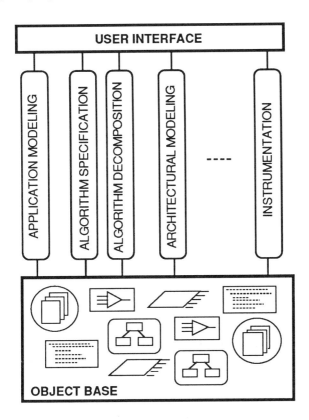

Figure 14.1.

In order to experiment with designs with respect to a given parallel machine, it is necessary that information on different architectures is available. To this aim, a subsystem is included for modelling a wide range of parallel machines. From these models characteristics can be retrieved by the application modelling system, as well as the algorithm decomposition system, so that a design can be tuned toward a given architecture. The definition of this subsystem is currently in a preliminary stage.

Finally, an important subsystem is formed by various instrumentation tools. As we see it now, this subsystem will include simulators for application and architectural models, algorithm animators, and analysis tools for performance evaluation.

Apart from building the above mentioned subsystems, the ParTool project also concentrates on a number of objects which are stored in the central object base. In particular, effort is paid to the development of algorithms for scheduling a computation graph on a given processor model. Also, a linear algebra library will be developed where main emphasis lies on portability of its objects.

14.5 THE PARTOOL SOFTWARE DESIGN PROCESS

The ParTool environment encourages an application developer to follow a layered approach toward parallel software design. This approach is visualized in Fig. 14.2. At the highest layer, global design takes place through the application modelling layer. This layer is followed by the algorithm specification and decomposition layers. As soon as the design process has proceeded to this point, the application developer can concentrate on the problem of finding an optimal schedule for the computation graph which resulted from decomposing the various algorithms of the application. Hereafter, code is generated in some high-level target language.

Note that compilers and run-time systems will not be developed within the ParTool project. It is our strong feeling that it is impossible to make generic and efficient compilers for a wide variety of parallel processors. The manufacturer of the parallel processor must provide the compilers for their machines, together with a set of communication primitives. The fact that powerful compilers are supplied by manufactures as part of their standard software support package, justifies our decision to leave compiler development out of the ParTool project.

The layers mentioned above reflect a design process that will generally proceed in a highly iterative way. Note that although the layers suggest a top-down approach towards software development, a different approach can be easily followed as well. For example, when adapting existing applications, a developer may start with describing the computation intensive kernels in Booster (i.e. start at the algorithm specification layer), and proceed with integrating these descriptions at the application modelling layer.

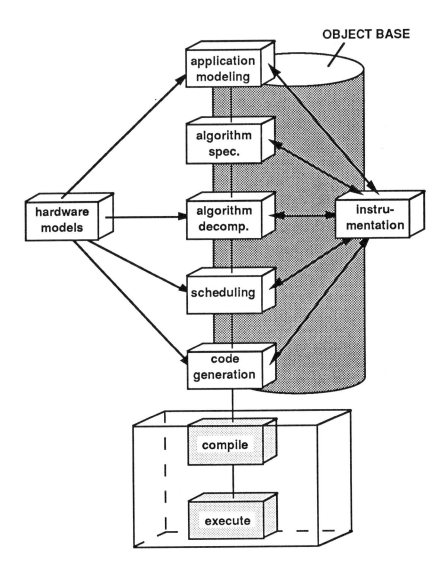

Figure 14.2.

Each layer is directly coupled to the object base thus allowing exchange of data at every level of design. At all layers, except for algorithm specifications, design decisions can be influenced by hardware architectural features. In addition, instrumentation will be available at every layer.

14.6 STATUS OF THE PROJECT

The ParTool project has officially started, and will continue until the end of 1992. The project members are the TNO Institute of Applied Computer Science, Philips Corporate CAD Centre, Delft University of Technology, University of Utrecht, and Centre for Mathematics and Computer Science. The total research effort comprises approximately 50 full-time equivalents. ParTool is subsidized by SPIN, a Dutch funding agency for computer science research.

REFERENCES

1. Babb II, R.G. and DiNucci, D.C. (1987) Design and implementation of parallel programs with large-grain data flow, *The Characteristics of Parallel Algorithms.* eds L.H. Jamieson, D.B. Gannon, R.J. Douglass, MIT Press, Cambridge, Mass.

2. Boudier, G. Gallo, F. Minot, R. and Thomas, I. (1989) An overview of PCTE and PCTE+. *SIGPLAN Notices,* 24, 2, pp. 248-257.

3. Karp, A.H. (1987) Programming for parallelism. *Computer,* pp. 43-57.

4. Paalvast, E.M.R.M. (nyp) *The Booster Language,* Internal report TNO Institute of Applied Computer Science, no. 89 ITI B18.

5. Schatz, W. (1989) Programming is the problem. *Datamation,* pp. 57-61.

6. Schwan, K. Ramnath, R. Vasudevan, S. and Ogle, D. (1988) A language and system for the construction and tuning of parallel programs. *IEEE Trans. on Soft. Eng.* 14, 4, pp.455-471.

7. Ward, P.T. (1986) The transformation schema: An extension of the data flow diagram to represent control and timing. *IEEE Trans. on Soft. Eng.* SE-12, 2, pp. 198-210.

15 The Intel iPSC/2 concurrent file system

D. Moody

Intel Scientific Computers Swindon, UK

1 THE IPSC/2 CONCURRENT SUPERCOMPUTER

Before describing the Concurrent Input-Output system (CIO) it is important to understand the features of the iPSC/2 computational system. The iPSC/2 is a distributed memory MIMD system based on 80386/80387 processors (nodes) each with 1-16Mbytes of memory. The numeric performance of each node may be enhanced by the addition of a scalar extension (SX) and/or a vector extension (VX) such that each node may perform at up to 20Mflops (32-bit precision). Each node has eight Direct-Connect communication links. These are serial connections each supporting usable data rates of 2.8Mbytes/s bidirectionally (ie 5.6Mbytes/s aggregate). Up to seven of these links are used to connect the individual nodes together to form a hypercube. The major feature of the Direct-Connect technology is the ability to dynamically create (and subsequently destroy) a direct path between two non-neighbouring nodes such that the overhead of sending messages over long distances is negligible and intermediate nodes are completely unaffected by messages passing through.

This technology has two significant benefits. Firstly, the programmer generally does not need to be concerned with the topological layout of the processors and can assume universal connectivity. Secondly, if a subset of the nodes are each connected to dedicated I/O processors using Direct-Connect, then all nodes may be dynamically connected to these I/O processors when they require I/O services.

Programming the iPSC/2 is simple. Node 0 is connected to a multiuser host system (based on Unix V.3.2) known as the System Resource Manager (SRM).

Programs are developed on the SRM (or a networked workstation) and then loaded into the nodes via Direct-Connect. The Direct-Connect network allows the SRM to establish direct links with any node. Each compute node runs a small executive called NX/2 which provides application processes with communication and I/O services. Running NFS on the SRM allows nodes direct access to files on the local area network as well as files on the SRM. A diagram of a standard computational node is shown in Fig. 15.1.

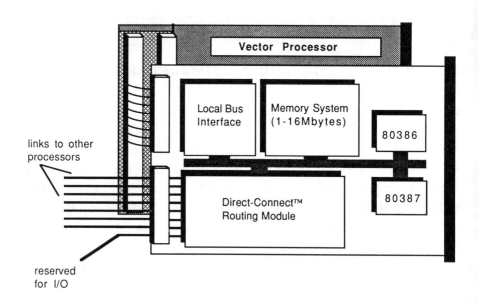

Figure 15.1 Compute node with associated vector processor.

15.2 CONCURRENT INPUT-OUTPUT SYSTEM HARDWARE

CIO is based on multiple I/O processors, known as I/O nodes, each dedicated to handling their own I/O devices. Up to 127 of these I/O nodes may be connected to the compute nodes of the iPSC/2 on a one-to one basis using the Direct-Connect link reserved for I/O shown in Fig. 15.1. A diagram of the I/O node is provided on Fig. 15.2. Clearly, it is very similar to a compute node, but it has only one Direct-Connect link since it communicates with only one compute node. I/O nodes incorporate a SCSI controller and a minimum of 4Mbytes of memory. Optionally a bus adaptor may be connected in the next slot to allow the I/O nodes control of one or more VME or Multibus 2 devices.

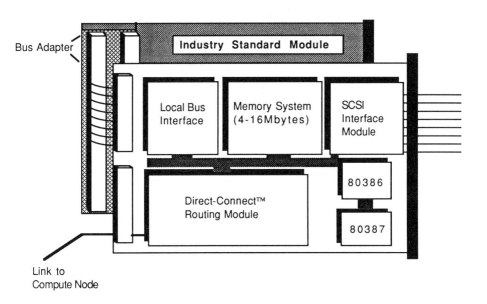

Figure 15.2 I/O node with Multibus II or VME adapter plus SCSI interface.

Although an I/O node is physically connected to a single compute node the Direct-Connect network allows all compute nodes to communicate with each I/O node. A diagram of an iPSC/2 system with eight compute nodes, four I/O nodes and 8Gbytes of disk storage is given in Fig. 15.3.

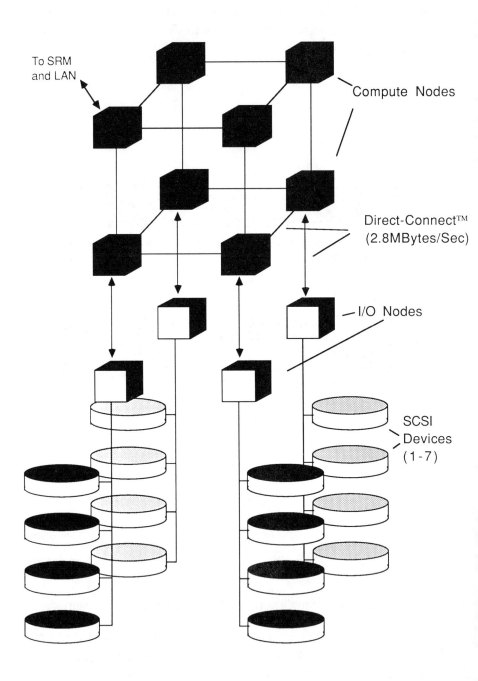

Figure 15.3 Schematic of an iPSC/2 system with eight compute nodes, four I/O nodes and 8Gbytes of disk storage.

The use of separate I/O nodes removes the need for compute nodes to manage I/O devices. In turn this ensures that applications can remain well balanced on the compute nodes since they will not be interrupted by other nodes requesting I/O support. However, where a user has special requirements the functions of compute node and I/O node can be combined in a single node.

15.3 CONCURRENT FILE SYSTEM

CFS is the software which manages all disks connected to the iPSC/2 CIO system, its most important attribute being the ability to make the parallel nature of the I/O system transparent to the application and the user. Unlike the programming of the computationally intensive portion of an application where parallelism is generally expressed explicitly, CFS can handle parallelism implicitly.

The problem of multiple disks on separate computing entities has been investigated in the past with a distributed computing model incorporating distributed file systems. NFS from Sun Microsystems is an example of such a file system. The major problem of this approach when applied to concurrent supercomputers is that any one file is constrained to reside on a single disk. This would clearly cause a bottleneck at the I/O node if data is required concurrently by several compute nodes cooperating in a single application. However, NFS and CFS complement each other extremely well and the integration of NFS into CFS will allow workstation users access to the capacity and performance of the CIO system.

Another alternative for combining many disks is disk-striping. This method does not fit the concurrent supercomputer architecture well as it is best suited to providing high transfer rates over a single fast channel, rather than over several medium speed channels.

CFS manages all disks connected to the system as a single logical entity (up to 889 500Mbytes disk drives may be connected through 127 I/O nodes). The system allocates blocks to a file from all of the disks, a technique known as declustering [2]. The result is that the data required by multiple compute nodes, whether from a single file or multiple files, is likely to be on separate disks and can be transferred simultaneously. The user can create one file as large as the total disk capacity of the system, or hundreds of files across many disks without needing to know the physical location of any file, block or directory.

CFS works with file blocks of 4Kbytes in size. Each disk in the CIO system has a volume number so each file block is uniquely identified by a block number comprising the volume number and the logical block number on that volume. As a write operation is under way the file blocks are automatically distributed over all I/O nodes and disks by CFS. I/O nodes are usually able to receive blocks into a cache memory area of at least 2Mbytes in size, effectively removing delays caused by disk latency. This caching of data is completely transparent to the user.

Multiple compute nodes attempting to access parts of a single file will typically be receiving the data from multiple I/O nodes concurrently, these concurrent channels supporting an aggregate transfer rate of over a hundred Mbytes/s (in proportion to the number of I/O nodes on the system). The application may restrict allocation to a specified set of disks if this form of tuning is beneficial.

CFS supports the same 'stdio' standard I/O library calls as the Unix operating system. Any application on any set of iPSC/2 nodes can create and access a file through Unix style hierarchical directories. All iPSC/2 languages - Fortran, C, Common Lisp, Ada and Strand 88 - support the use of CFS. Users of these languages already performing file access through the iPSC/2 System Resource Manager will find their programs to be completely compatible with the new file system, with no changes required to exploit concurrency. A set of asynchronous read and write calls are provided to allow the overlay of I/O requests and computation within an application.

15.4 FILE STRUCTURE

Each CFS file includes a header block containing a header with information about the file such as its size, modification times and access permissions. In the case of small files the data also resides in the header block, but for larger files the header block contains a list of block numbers for the data blocks. Indirection is used for extremely large files.

Each I/O node runs a copy of the disk process which is responsible for file allocation and file structure modification. Each disk process performs these functions for the files whose file header blocks reside on its disks. The disk process performs disk block allocation using a free block bit map for each disk. Clusters of 32 bits are handed out to processes doing allocation so that files tend to be allocated in contiguous areas on the disk, increasing performance by allowing reading and writing of multiple blocks at once.

15.5 FILE NAMES

Files within CFS are identified by a unique pathname component, usually /cfs, distinguishing them from files on the SRM. The Unix compatible tree structured directory is kept entirely in a single CFS file which is managed by the NAME process running on a single I/O node. Since the directory is managed by a single process there is no problem with coherency due to multiple concurrent accesses, although it is recognized that this process could become a bottleneck in an environment where there are a large number of open and close operations. However, the target environment is where files are opened rarely and read or written often.

15.6 AUXILIARY FUNCTIONS

There are two other processes which perform management functions that relate to the file system - the administration process and the header process. These each reside on one I/O node.

The administration process keeps track of application processes on compute nodes, informing disk processes when an application process terminates so that open files may be closed. This process also assists in the implementation of pipes and in starting up CFS. The header process loads application processes into nodes from executable object files which reside in the host file system or in CFS.

15.7 A SIMPLE EXAMPLE

When a compute node executes an OPEN statement the NAME process on the first I/O node (Fig. 15.4) finds the first file block through the directory. It then causes this block to be transferred to the compute node and to be stored in a CFS file header cache, which is classed read-only. A SEEK statement simply changes a pointer to one of these data blocks in the list. Then, the first READ statement causes a few blocks to be read by the relevant I/O node, the first being returned to the compute node immediately, the remainder being held in the I/O node's cache area. The accesses are then directed round all the disks one by one until the next block is required from the first disk again. This time the data is already in the I/O node cache area (assuming sequential access) so there is no disk latency. The caching algorithm attempts to get eight blocks into cache each time a disk is accessed for each file transfer it is currently handling. 'Look ahead' ensures that the cache is reple nished when half of the blocks have been consumed by the compute node. A typical piece of C code using CIO is shown in Fig. 15.5, each compute node executing the same program.

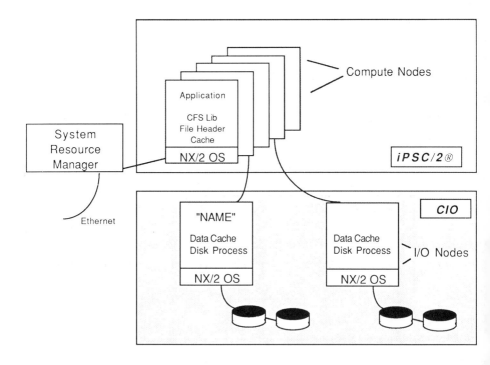

Figure 15.4 Concurrent File System configuration.

C Program for Nodes

```
f=fopen  (fname,"rw");
s=fseek  (f,offset,0);
s=fread  (buf,size,f);

{ computations on buf }
.

.

s=fwrite  (buf,size,f);
fclose  (f);
.

.
```

Figure 15.5 Using C/O and CFS.

15.8 EXTENSIONS INCLUDED IN CFS FOR FORTRAN I/O

Several functions over and above the normal Fortran language I/O constructions have been included in CFS to handle certain occurrences caused by the way Fortran traditionally buffers data. These system calls are byte oriented reads and writes, which can be blocking or non-blocking. Much of the detail of these functions is given in [3]. They are compatible with the equivalent I/O constructions in C and allow C and Fortran programs to share data. Another example of an extension is when each node of the system needs a separate scratch file. If each node runs the same code all nodes would open the same file - clearly not what is required. To make this simple to overcome CFS has the convention that three hash signs appearing in a file name are replaced by three digits representing the node number. For example (in Fortran) if

$$OPEN(10,FILE = '/cfs/scratch\#\#\#')$$

were executed by node 13, the actual file opened would be '/cfs/scratch013'. This allows the same code fragment to be run on different nodes and still create separate scratch files.

15.9 PERFORMANCE

The primary performance goal of CFS is to achieve high data transfer rates between disk storage and parallel applications running in the iPSC/2 compute nodes. Figures 15.6 and 15.7 show some early results measured by reading a large file into several nodes. Fig. 15.6 shows the aggregate data rate achieved as a function of the number of I/O nodes (each I/O node with two disk drives). Good scaling is seen with 4 and 8 compute nodes as I/O nodes are added. Other lines show early saturation because the small number of compute nodes taking part in the test limits the number of I/O requests that can be generated. Fig. 15.7 shows the same data with compute nodes on the horizontal axis. Again scaleability is demonstrated together with a small amount of overloading as the number of compute nodes exceeds the number of I/O nodes.

15.10 CONCLUSIONS

It is possible to obtain high performance and scaleability from parallel I/O system while retaining compatibility and flexibility. This has been independently verified at the University of Virginia [4] using beta versions of hardware and software. Further development is required in the production of suitable database products to take full advantage of the capacity of such systems, but a tool is now available for those applications which do not make use of commercial database products. The next stages in the development of such systems will be the addition of backup facilities, probably by the use of helical scan tape cartridge drives, (backup may then be carried out autonomously by each local I/O node) and the provision of data integrity insurance through the use of redundant disk drives.

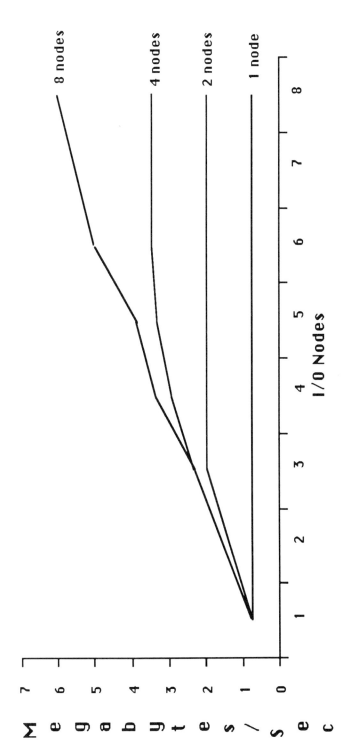

Figure 15.6 Saturation performance as a function of the number of I/O nodes.

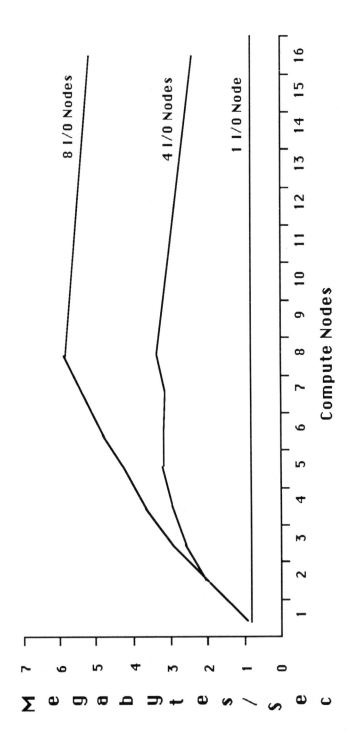

Figure 15.7 Saturation performance as a function of the number of active compute nodes.

REFERENCES

1. Reddy, A.L.N., and Banerjee, P. (1989) Evaluation of multiple disk I/O systems, submitted to *ICPP 1989*.

2. Asbury, R. and Scott, D. (1989) Fortran I/O on the iPSC/2. Is there read after write?. *Proc. of The Fourth Conf. on Hypercube Concurrent Computers and Applications*.

3. Pratt, T.W., French, J.C., Dickens, P.M., and Janet, S.A. Jr. (1989) Comparison of the architecture and performance of two parallel file systems. *Proc. of the Fourth Conf. on Hypercube Concurrent Computers and Applications*.

Part Five

Libraries

16 Library software
for transputer arrays

L. Delves,

University of Liverpool

16.1 INTRODUCTION

Local memory MIMD parallel systems are potentially of great interest because they can provide very high peak Mflop rates at low cost. In the UK, transputer arrays are becoming increasingly common members of this class, and everyone at this meeting will be aware of the explosive interest in their use as highly parallel MIMD computers. In the UK, essentially every University and Polytechnic has one or more transputer-based research project. Edinburgh University has a 400 T800 Meiko system; and smaller arrays are selling very well. It is already evident that transputer arrays provide very cost effective machines for scientific computing. They are not yet however particularly easy to use: single-transputer Fortran is available, but auto-parallelizing compilers are still several years off, so that porting an existing Fortran code is not painless. Parallelism must be expressed explicitly and parallel algorithms coded directly.

If transputer arrays are to become part of the mainstream market for scientific and engineering computing, it is essential to make life easier for the applications programmer who wants to get answers, and is relatively uninterested in parallelism for its own sake. The simplest way to do so effectively, is to provide parallel library software which can be called from an existing serial program; then, at least programs which do their most intensive number-crunching via library calls (a relatively large number of applications fall into this category) can make an invisible use of parallelism, provided that the appropriate parallel routine is available. At Liverpool, we have been working intensively on the production of parallel library software for transputer arrays. I give here a summary of the state of play, and of proposed future work in this area. However, we are not the only group in this field; and I will attempt to summarize other library and library-related software, both serial and parallel, which is now, or soon will be, available on transputers.

16.2   SERIAL LIBRARY SOFTWARE

We begin by looking at single-transputer software - as essential as multiprocessor packages partly because parallelism is not always needed, and partly because the parallel libraries being constructed call upon basic single-processor libraries.

16.2.1   NAG serial Fortran library

This is, in Europe, by far the most widely used numerical library. The Mark 12 Fortran library contains over 750 user-callable routines; it has been implemented for T800 transputers using the Inmos Fortran compiler, under TDS; however, it should be totally compatible with the L Fortran compiler, either under TDS or using the standalone toolkit, and every site should get a copy. The port was funded by Inmos. Meiko users, unfortunately, will have to wait for a Meiko Fortran implementation, since this compiler is not link compatible with L.

We expect to start a Mark 13 implementation, again using the latest Inmos compiler, shortly. These implementations have been straightforward ports, with no special tuning for the T800 architecture. However, the simplest way to tune the NAG library is to provide efficient implementations of the Level 2 BLAS, and for news of such implementations, see below.

16.2.2   Other NAG products

(a)   NAG graphics library

This is a standalone library of graphics routines which provide scientific graphics: 2- and 3- dimensional graphs and plots; axis drawing, scaling and annotation; contour plots; etc. The routines are callable from within a Fortran program, and the library (previously referred to as the NAG Graphics Supplement) is standalone in the sense that it does not require the NAG Fortran LIbrary to be available.

The library does make calls on a low level set of driver routines, to provide portability across different output devices. We have just completed an implementation of the Graphics Library, under 3L Fortran, and assuming the basic Inmos graphics software provided with a B007 transputer graphics card. Given this, or a compatible graphics driver, the library provides full colour high resolution graphics for transputer users.

(b)   GLIM statistical modelling package

We have also just completed a single-transputer implementation of GLIM: the Generalized Linear Modelling package marketed by NAG. This is not library software, since no user programming is needed; but I thought I would mention it here to give the availability a little publicity.

(c)   Genstat general statistic package

Finally, we have just begun a study of Genstat. This is a much larger package than GLIM, and provides general statistical facilities with probably the best developed statistical procedures in this field. A parallel implementation is being discussed; but this work is at an early stage, and no completion dates have been set. Both this, and the GLIM and Graphics ports, have been funded by an SERC/DTI ExtraMural Research contract jointly by NAG Ltd. and the Transputer Initiative.

16.2.3   Other high level single transputer libraries

A second serial high level library for transputers is that written in Occam by Topexpress Ltd. This contains 50+ routines, providing facilities in the most widely used numerical areas. Unlike the NAG library implementation, it is accessible from Occam, and also available directly to Meiko Fortran users since Meiko Fortran allows the linking of occam libraries (as does the latest version of the Inmos standalone toolkit). However, it cannot provide the breadth of facilities that the NAG library offers after 15 years and many hundreds of man years of development.

16.2.4   Low level single transputer libraries

There are also several libraries of low level facilities now on the market. These include, typically, vector-vector and possibly matrix-vector operations, coded as efficiently as possible in assembler. The purpose of these libraries is two-fold. First, they provide building blocks which can be called by the user to carry out inner loops of his program faster than either the Fortran or Occam compilers can achieve; while second, they satisfy the same purpose for builders (such as ourselves) of high level libraries. As an example, the NAG Mark 12 (and later) Fortran library, makes extensive use of call to the Level 2 BLAS (Basic Linear Algebra Submodules); if an optimized set of these is available; most of the linear algebra routines in the library speed up automatically.

(a)   Liverpool low level libraries

We have an ongoing program me providing assembler routines as building blocks for our parallel library; and libraries containing these routines, interfaced respectively to Occam and to 3L Fortran, are now being marketed by NA Software Ltd., with whom the development so far has been carried out. The Mark 1 libraries each contain 70 + routines in single and double precision, implementing:

1. a complete set of Real Level 1 BLAS;

2. a set of Extended BLAS (operations involving more than two vectors).

These routines run typically 2 - 6 times faster than the Fortran equivalents (18 times faster is our record so far), or 1.5 - 3 times faster than the equivalent Occam. They gain their speed by:

1. Maximum use of overlap between the integer and floating point processors.

2. Careful optimisation of the memory fetches and use of onchip memory (the slow speed of external RAM is a limiting factor in most user programs).

3. Extensive unrolling of loops to reduce loop overheads.

4. Recognition of special cases.

We are now in the process of extending these libraries to include:

1. The complex Level 1 BLAS.

2. A complete set of Level 2 BLAS.

3. Assembler versions of some widely used high level routines.

This work has been funded by the SERC Transputer Initiative, and by NA Software Ltd.

(b)   TopExpress Low Level Library

A similar library of assembler routines is marketed by TopExpress Ltd. This library is callable from Occam, Fortran, C or Pascal, and also contains a set of vector-vector operations. Not unnaturally, we have not used this library ourselves; but it appears comparable in scope to our own Mark 1 libraries.

(c)   FLOLIB

Flolib, developed by System Software Factors Ltd., is a particularly interesting example of a package making use of low level runtime library facilities. Flolib is a Fortran program analyser, which performs much the same job as a vectorizing compiler on a vector processor: it analyses and reconstructs loops, replacing them when possible by calls to a library of assembler routines (in the transputer version: provided by us). The current version of Flolib can handle only single loops. It outputs revised Fortran including the library calls, which must then by compiled and linked with the runtime library. However, in practice it proves very effective on many programs; we report here the speedups we have measured, relative to the original Fortran code, for two test problems:

> Program 1: known to be vectorizable. Speedup factor 3.2
>
> Program 2: thought to be unvectorizable. Speedup factor 1.1

These speedups are for complete programs; the second was an already optimized Radar Image processing code which consisted largely of calls to FFT routines. FLOLIB will be further developed within Supernode 2,emerging eventually (it is planned) as a fully automatic parallelising compiler; but I expect to see intermediate versions on the market in the next year which will provide at least semi-automatic parallelization of Fortran codes, via the insertion of calls to a parallel runtime library.

16.3   PARALLEL NUMERICAL LIBRARIES

16.3.1   The Mark 1 Liverpool parallel libraries

Finally, we look at what we think is the most interesting part of our work: parallel libraries. With Transputer Initiative and EEC (Esprit) support, we have been developing numerical library facilities which use the parallelism of the array, but are callable from a serial Fortran subroutine; versions callable from Occam (the base language being used) are also available, and other language versions are planned. We describe briefly here the current state of the work.

(a)   The user interface

It was, as noted above, assumed that the user of the library may have a serial Fortran program from which the library modules will be called. Such a user will have all of his data on a single host processor; he will access the array by making a standard call to a main library routine placed on the master processor, with data passed to this routine via its parameter list, This main routine then passes data on as required, and controls the flow of the calculation. We thus take the user program to be running on a single master transputer (e.g. a B004) linked to the array via a single channel. Library routines are assumed to be called serially from this master transputer, and to make sole use of the array (or part array) on which the library code is placed. This model describes well a user with a serial Fortran program, as well as currently available arrays, which are accessed via a large memory master transputer, typically sitting within the host, and attached via a single link to the array of slaves. It does represent a restriction on the use of the array, and of the library, by an Occam programmer, who in principle might wish to call library routines from one or more slave processes running on any part of the array; this is not possible with the current library structure (unless the slave has access to its own dedicated sub-array -not a realistic hypothesis with current sized arrays).

(b)   Dynamic loader

However, a potentially much greater restriction is imposed by the current static nature of the Occam linker/loader provided by Inmos. This requires that code for all processors to be loaded in a standard form (SC format) prior to program start. A precompiled library routine is a collection of such SCs; two routines can not then co-exist on the array. To overcome this restriction, we have arranged to load library code to slave processors dynamically. The method used to achieve this is described in Delves and Brown (1988). When a library call is made, the effect is that the slave code is sent down a predefined load path to each library transputer, and then started. The master library routine then has access to this code just as if it had been loaded statically. When the library routine is completed, the slave processes terminate and control returns to the main process. Hence, further routines may be loaded and run in the same way.

This mechanism is transparent to the user. It is also transparent to the library routine developer, who can write and debug this code using the normal static environment; conversion to dynamic load form is a mechanistic process which can be carried out when the routine is fully developed.

The dynamic loading mechanism overcomes the major problems when using libraries on transputer arrays. Since the time to load the array with code is independent of problem size, it is also obviously efficient for a large problem; in practice, we find it does not affect timings significantly even for quite small problems.

More details of the mechanism used are given in Brown and Delves (1988).

(c)   Contents of the Mark 1 libraries

The Mark 1 version of the library is available interfaced to both Occam and Fortran; the Fortran version has been produced by recoding the master processes, leaving the slave codes in Occam, and a totally rewritten manual is provided so that the Fortran coder need never have heard the term Occam. So far, implementations for Occam/TDS and for standalone 3L Fortran on PC-hosted arrays, are ready; versions interfaced to fullscale operating systems (Helios, Trollius, Meikos, Idris) will follow shortly, with the order of production dependent on user demand.

The routines produced are portable across differing arrays, but as with all transputer codes, not topology-independent. So far, we have produced codes for linear, and rectangular grid, topologies, both with and without wraparound; and for balanced binary trees. The Mark 1 libraries contain routines for all three topologies. A given array may support one, two, or all of these, and a Library Manager is provided which has knowledge of the array size and topology, and ensures a graceful failure if a routine needing an unavailable facility is called. The libraries contain single and double precision codes for the following problems:

Matrix-Matrix Product
$Ax = b$ (dense, two versions, for single and multiple right hand sides)
$Ax = b$ (Band system)
$Ax = b$ (triangular system, multiple RHS)
$Ax = b$ (general sparse system, two routines)
$Ax = x$ (inverse iteration)
FFT (1-D complex data; three routines)
Sorting
Zeros of a polynomial
Linear programming via the Simplex method

One aim in producing the Mark 1 library has been to explore the design parameters, to see if the constraints needed to keep the user interface simple cripple the efficiency, and to see if we both understand and can utilize the behaviour of large arrays. The timings we have obtained so far (see, e.g. Delves and Brown (1988) refer only to quite small arrays (16 transputers) and we feel strongly the need to extend these to larger arrays. However, they lead us to the following tentative conclusions:

1. The architecture of transputer arrays is sufficiently clean that the fairly simple timing models we have derived reflect quite well the actual behaviour of the codes.

2. Routines with computer:datapassing ratios at least as high as the Level 3 BLAS, can be implemented efficiently within our programming model (all data starts, and results end, on a single node). Arrays with 100 - 1000 transputers should be useable for problem sizes which arise in practice.

16.3.2   The TopExpress parallel library

TopExpress Ltd have also developed, and announced, a parallel library [3]. It appears to be quite comparable to the Mark 1 Liverpool libraries, in both its scope and in its user interface. As with ours, it has been written primarily in Occam, but is available interfaced to Occam, Fortran, or Pascal. So far, we have not been able to make direct comparisons with our own library.

16.3.3   Planned developments

The Mark 1 libraries provide a useful kernel of parallel routines, and demonstrate that easy-to-use facilities can be developed for transputer arrays. Continued development of the libraries has now been ensured by the go ahead of the Esprit2 funded Supernode 2 project. Within this project, we are collaborating with NAG Ltd. to produce both major developments of the numerical library, and a new library of Finite Element software, the latter project being led by my colleague Dick Wait. A total of 42 man years of Esprit funded effort, and a further 10-20 man years of University and other funded effort, will be spent over the next four years (subject to a review after two years) on these topics; and a parallel library of over 100 routines is being aimed at. While it is too early to describe firm plans, the following developments were anticipated within the preliminary Esprit1 funded project, and hence may well be implemented:

(a)   Pre-distributed data

For most problem areas, the overheads associated with distributing the data from the master program are negligible. However, this is not always so (Levels 1 and 2 BLAS, for example), and the facility is available within the Mark1 design to call data distribution routines followed by a sequence of routines which assume the data is already in place. Similarly, it is possible to re-enter a preloaded library routine with new data, without reloading the code, which allows efficient iterated calls of a single routine.

There is a second reason for providing for pre-distributed data: if the user has a very large problem, the data may well not fit within the memory of his masterprocessor, and then there is no alternative but to generate the data out on the slaves.

(b)   Systematic use of low level libraries

It is intended that future routines will make full use of the single transputer assembler libraries; in particular, of the optimized Level 2 BLAS now being written.

(c)   Tracking future architecture/software enhancements

The library will also, it is hoped, take cognisance of future improvements in both transputer hardware and basic software, for example, through routing facilities.

(d)   An Ada version?

Ada will shortly be available in single transputer form; we are currently discussing an Ada version on the library.

(e)   Versions for other parallel systems

We sometimes forget that not every parallel computer is built from transputers. But we have remembered often enough that the basic library design has kept a strong eye on problems of portability to other MIMD architectures. Doing anything about it is dependent on the availability of resources.

16.4 ACKNOWLEDGEMENTS

The work described in this paper was funded from a number of sources, including the EEC, via Esprit Projects P1085 (Supernode 1) and P2447 (Supernode 2); the UK SERC via the Transputer Initiative; Inmos Ltd; NAG Ltd; N.A. Software Ltd; and the University of Liverpool. NAG Ltd is a partner in the ongoing work within Supernode 2. Many colleagues have contributed to the project, and I wish to thank in particular C. Addison, S. Audish, T.B. Boffey, N.G. Brown, R. Buro, D. Clegg, S.T. Downing, R. Hay, G. Howard, T. Oliver, C. Phillips, J. Prasad, G. Pryde, P.Stainton, J. Tierney, R. Wait, R. Wilkinson and C. Willis for their continuing efforts and for many discussions.

REFERENCES

1   Brown, N.G. and Delves, L.M. (1988) *A Dynamic Library Loading Mechanism for Transputer Arrays,* P1085 Working Paper, Liverpool University.

2   Delves, L.M. and Brown, N.G. (1988) A numerical library for transputer arrays, invited paper presented at *IFIP WG2.5 Working Conference on Aspects of Computation on Asynchronous Parallel Processors,* Stanford, USA; proceedings to be published.

3   Information on the TopExpress libraries has been provided by Francis Wray of TopExpress Ltd (private communication).

17 Efficient use of parallel matrix-matrix kernels in linear algebra

on the Alliant FX/80, the Cray-2, the ETA-10P, and the IBM 3090

P. Amestoy, M. Daydé[*], and I. Duff[†]

CERFACS, 42 Av. G. Coriolis, 31057 Toulouse, FRANCE.

17.1 INTRODUCTION

We consider the use of Level 3 BLAS computational kernels (Dongarra, *et al.* 1988) on parallel vector computers with a global shared memory. This class of computer architecture is widely used in the design of today's supercomputers including the Cray-2, the ETA 10P, the IBM 3090, and the Alliant FX/80. The aim of this work is to show that, based on the use of Level 3 BLAS kernels, portable and efficient code can be designed even in a multiprocessing environment. We illustrate this on the solution of sets of linear equations

$$Ax = b \qquad (17.1)$$

both when the matrix A in (17.1) is full and when it is sparse, extending discussions in Daydé and Duff (1988) and Amestoy and Duff (1988), respectively.

After a parallelization study of the Level 3 BLAS kernels we consider the case of full systems of equations and compare the parallelism obtained within the computational kernels with that obtained over the kernels. In section 17.4, we examine the case when A is sparse and analyse the influence of this lower level of parallelism (within Level 3 BLAS) on the global parallelism of the method. Finally, we present some conclusions in section 17.5.

---

[*] also ENSEEIHT-IRIT, 2 rue Camichel 31071 Toulouse, FRANCE.

[†] also CSS Division, Harwell Laboratory, Oxford, UK.

17.2 PARALLELIZATION OF THE LEVEL 3 BLAS ROUTINES

The algorithms described in this paper use two of the Level 3 BLAS subroutines GEMM for multiplying two matrices, and TRSM for solving a set of triangular systems. We use tuned Fortran versions of these or partially or fully assembler-coded versions depending on the availability of assembler-coded kernels in the manufacturer's library.

The Level 3 BLAS routine GEMM realizes the matrix-matrix operation :

$$C \leftarrow \beta\, C + \alpha\, AB,$$

where α and β are scalars, and A, B, and C are matrices. The update of C can be partitioned in block columns of C where the operations on each block column are clearly independent. We thus parallelize GEMM by calling a single processor version of GEMM for each submultiplication. For the submultiplications, we use the assembler-coded version of DGEMM provided by the ESSL Library on the IBM 3090, and a tuned version of SGEMM implemented by invoking the assembler-coded routine MXMA from the SCILIB library on the Cray-2. On the Alliant, we simply report timings of the DGEMM routine from the scientific library which is already parallelized (as are most of the BLAS subroutines). The performance of the parallel versions of GEMM, denoted by GEMMP, are reported in Table 17.1 , where the order of all matrices is equal to 512.

Table 17.1. Performance in Mflops using DGEMM on the ALLIANT FX/80, the CRAY-2, and the IBM 3090

Machine	1 proc. GEMM	several proc. GEMMP	Speed-up
Alliant FX/80 (8 proc.)	11.6	73.2	6.28
Cray-2(4 proc.)	438.0	1435.8	3.28
IBM 3090 (3proc.)	79.5	232.6	2.92

TRSM performs the solution of a triangular system of equations AX = B where A is a triangular matrix, X overwriting B. We obtain parallelism by blocking the computation across the columns of B.

Therefore independent triangular solutions are executed on separate processors. Note that the triangular solution is itself blocked over the columns of A (except on the ETA-10P where it does not help), so that the solution is obtained by successively solving for small triangular systems on the diagonal using TRSM, followed by a matrix-matrix multiplication using the more efficient kernel GEMM. On the Alliant and the IBM, the solver used on the small triangular blocks on the diagonal is a tuned Fortran code (using loop unrolling). On the Cray-2 the diagonal triangular solution uses an assembler-coded rank-two update from the Harwell Subroutine Library. We illustrate the results in Table 17.2, where the order of all matrices is equal to 512.

Table 17.2 Performance in Mflops using TRSM on the Alliant FX/80, the Cray-2, and the IBM 3090

| | 1 proc. | several proc. | |
Machine	TRSM	TRSMP	Speed-up
Alliant FX/80 (8 proc.)	10.4	62.2	5.97
Cray-2(4 proc.)	368.3	926.0	2.51
IBM 3090 (3proc.)	59.7	175.3	2.93

When considering benefits provided by the exploitation of parallelism within the Level 3 BLAS kernels, the performance obtained must be compared with that obtained by parallelizing over calls to Level 3 BLAS. Additional freedom can be obtained by parallelization over BLAS if it is possible to overlap calls to different BLAS (or other) routines. We discuss this further in the context of full and sparse linear algebra.

17.3 USE OF LEVEL 3 BLAS IN FULL LU FACTORIZATION

We consider the solution of the dense system of linear equations AX = B using blocked LU factorization. Although there are several blocks algorithms (see, for example, Daydé and Duff, 1988), in the context of this paper we restrict the discussion to the KJI-SAXPY variant. In the blocked KJI-SAXPY algorithm we factorize the matrix by block columns, and we use a matrix-vector based elimination scheme to reduce each block column in turn. This unblocked factorization calls GEMV and TRSV from the Level 2 BLAS.

We summarize the results of Daydé and Duff (1988) on the Cray-2, the ETA-10P, and the IBM 3090 for this algorithm in Table 17.3.

Table 17.3   Summary of performance in Mflops of KJI-SAXPY on a single processor of three vector supercomputers

Order of matrix	Cray-2	ETA-10P	IBM 3090
100	47.9	17.7	33.3
500	263.6	88.7	54.1
1000	336.8	119.0	62.1

We use the parallel versions of GEMM and TRSM discussed in Section 17.2. The routine is simply replaced by the parallel equivalent. A great merit of this is that we maintain portability even to a parallel environment. More parallelism can be obtained in the blocked LU factorization by overlapping the factorization of block column $k+1$ with updates arising from the k-th step or required by the $k+1$-th step. Table 17.4 show the results of these two forms of parallel implementation on the Cray-2 and the IBM 3090 on 1000-by-1000 systems.

Table 17.4 Performance in Mflops of parallel implementations of KJI-SAXPY on the Cray-2 and the IBM 3090.

	Cray-2 (4 proc.)		IBM 3090 (3 proc.)	
	Mflops	Speed-up	Mflops	Speed-up
Parallel Level 3 BLAS	713.4	2.12	132.3	2.13
Parallel version	743.0	2.20	182.6	2.94

The gains in using a parallelized algorithm are evident, but it is still an open question to know if they outweigh the loss of portability.

Table 17.5 Performance in Mflops of KJI-SAXPY using parallel BLAS on the Alliant FX/80

	1 proc.		8proc.	
N	Mflops		Mflops	Speed-up
1000	10.5		59.9	5.68

The parallelization of the level BLAS 1 and level BLAS 2 kernels can provide a reasonable performance improvement when low cost synchronizations are available. Microtasking on the Alliant is a good example of this. We present in Table 17.5 some preliminary results obtained on the Alliant FX/80 using the parallel versions of GEMM and level 1 BLAS kernels from the Alliant Scientific library, and parallel versions of DTRSM, DGEMV and DTRSV developed in CERFACS that perform better than those currently supplied by the manufacturer.

17.4 FACTORIZATION OF SPARSE MATRICES: MULTIFRONTAL METHOD

We consider the parallel solution of (17.1) when A is a sparse matrix. We assume that the sparsity pattern of the matrix is symmetric. The algorithm is based on a multifrontal approach (Duff and Reid, 1983) where tasks are distributed among processors according to an elimination tree that can be automatically generated from any pivotal strategy. Furthermore, if a multifrontal technique is used for the factorization, then the operations at each node involve Gaussian elimination steps on a full matrix which can be partitioned as

$$\begin{array}{cc} A & B \\ C & D \end{array} \tag{17.2}$$

where pivots can be chosen from A and the computed Schur complement $D - CA^{-1}B$ is passed to the father node.

The structure of the elimination tree is linked to the ordering of the original matrix, and we choose the minimum degree ordering for the present study. We present results on the Calgary olympics colliseum matrix from the Harwell-Boeing test collection (Duff, Grimes, and Lewis, 1987). The order of the matrix is 3562, it has 156610 entries, 412 nodes in the elimination tree, and the factorization requires 70 million of operations.

First we briefly describe vectorization enhancement of the multifrontal code. These changes include techniques used in full elimination and are based on the use of matrix-matrix kernels. For the elimination process we use a row oriented (frontal matrices are stored by rows) adaptation of KJI-SAXPY, termed KIJ-SAXPY. We have also improved the assembly phase to reduce the amount of indirect addressing. The performance obtained using this test matrix is 79.0

Megaflops on a single processor of the Cray-2, and 33.0 Megaflops on a single processor of the ETA-10P. We achieve very high computational rates, obtaining, on large problems, about half of the peak performance of the target machine and a speed-up, dependent on machine, from 7 to 11 with respect to the original code.

Since the degree of parallelism arising from the elimination tree decreases while going towards the root, it is important to introduce an additional level of parallelism at the elimination level within a node. We adopt a block spawning strategy based on the same ideas as in full linear algebra, blocking the computation in the elimination process and using parallel matrix-matrix kernels. We also introduce parameters to control this additional level of parallelism. The management of the tasks is based on a greedy algorithm well adapted to dynamic synchronization and was implemented in the earlier code of Duff (1988). We illustrate the performance of this code on the Alliant FX/80, the Cray-2, the ETA-10P, and the IBM 3090. Tables 17.6, and 17.7 show the importance of the second level of parallelism. We also ran the code successfully on the four processors of the Cray-2 but the speed-ups were disappointing, largely because of memory conflict on that machine. However an unvectorized version of our code did achieve good speed-up on the Cray-2 (3.3 on four processors).

Table 17.6 Performance in Mflops of multifrontal method using block spawning on the Alliant FX/80

	1 proc.	8 proc.	
	Mflops	Mflops	Speed-up
No Block Spawning	3.9	10.0	2.62
Block Spawning	3.9	17.0	4.50

Table 17.7 Performance in Mflops of multifrontal method using block spawning on the IBM 3090E

	1 proc.	3 proc.	
	Mflops	Mflops	Speed-up
No Block Spawning	28.3	61.3	2.17
Block Spawning	28.3	71.3	2.52

17.5 CONCLUSIONS

We have shown that though an optimal implementation of a code for solving linear systems depends on the characteristics of the target computer, a portable and efficient code can be designed using tuned versions of Level 3 BLAS. We have demonstrated how the Level 3 BLAS can be used to exploit parallelism in the solution of both sparse and full linear equations. In the case when A in (17.1) is full, we have seen that the parallel version of LU factorization provides, on the average, only a small performance improvement over the version using only parallel BLAS on both the Cray-2 and the IBM 3090. On the Alliant FX/80, we can efficiently parallelize all the BLAS kernels, including Level 1 BLAS, using microtasking so that we do not expect or obtain a great improvement of the speed-up with a parallel version of the LU factorization on full matrices. We have also noticed that, although the Cray-2 is a very powerful vector machine it has some limitations in its use as a multiprocessor. In the case of sparse matrix factorization we have shown that, using parallel matrix-matrix kernels, we can increase the degree of parallelism of the method by a significant factor.

REFERENCES

1   Amestoy, P.R. and Duff, I.S. (1988) Vectorization of a multifrontal code. Report TR 88/3, CERFACS Report CSS 231, Computer Science and Systems Division, AERE Harwell. *Int. J. Supercomputers Applications* (To appear).

2   Daydé, M. and Duff, I.S. (1988) Use of Level 3 BLAS in LU factorization on the CRAY-2, the ETA 10-P, and the IBM 3090/VF. Report TR 88/1, CERFACS Report CSS 229, Computer Science and Systems Division, AERE Harwell. *Int. J. Supercomputers Applications* (To appear).

3   Dongarra, J.J., Du Croz, J., Greenbaum, A., Hammarling, S., and Sorensen, D.C. (1987) *Prospectus for the Development of a Linear Algebra Library for High-performance Computers.* Report TM 97, Mathematics and Compuiter Science Division, Argonne National Laboratory.

4   Dongarra, J.J., Du Croz, J., Duff, I.S., and Hammarling, S. (1988). A set of Level 3 basic linear algebra subprograms. Report TM 88 (Revision 1), Report AERE R 13297, Computer Science and Systems Division, AERE Harwell. *ACM Trans. Math. Softw.* (To appear).

5   Duff, I.S. (1988) Multiprocessing a sparse matrix code on the Alliant FX/8. Report CSS 210, Computer Science and Systems Division, AERE Harwell. J. *Comput. Appl. Math.* (To appear).

6   Duff, I.S., Grimes, R.G., Lewis, J.G. (1987). Sparse matrix test problems. Report CSS 191, CSS Division, Harwell Laboratory, England. *ACM Trans. Math. Softw.* (To appear).

7   Duff, I.S. and Reid, J.K. (1983). The multifrontal solution of indefinite sparse symmetric linear systems., *ACM Trans. Math. Softw.* 9, pp.302-325.

18 Designing numerical libraries and application tools for highly parallel machines

H. Liddell

Centre for Parallel Computing, Queen Mary College University of London

18.1 INTRODUCTION

The first Distributed Array Processors (an ICL 4096 processor DAP) was delivered to Queen Mary College in 1980 with virtually no existing user-oriented software apart from the DAP Fortran compiler. Since that time one of the major tasks of the DAP Support Unit (now part of the College's Centre for Parallel Computing) has been the development of library software and other applications tools for the three generations of DAP product. This software was developed in response to the requirements of the large UK and international community who have used the national DAP service, a facility which had the effect of stimulating considerable national interest in the application of highly parallel computers to problems in science and engineering.

A major collection of library software is the DAP Subroutine library (Liddell and Bowgen, 1982) which is now marketed as the AMT General Support Library. In addition a number of specialist libraries for specific applications areas have been developed by us and by other groups. These include an image processing library, a signal processing library, the DAP FE library, graphics facilities and other tools. In this paper we will concentrate on the evolution of the libraries and tools developed by our research group at QMC, but reference will be made to other facilities. We conclude by considering future developments and portability issues, a study which forms part of the research being undertaken as part of the Alvey Active Data Model project, ARCH001, which is a collaborative activity with the Universities of Edinburgh, Southampton and Salford, with industrial partners AMT, Marconi and GLH.

The original DAP is due to be replaced in the near future by a 4096 processor AMT DAP 610-32. There are many improvements in this latest version of the system, the most obvious from the user point of view is the data visualization capability and the ability to attach the machine to either a Vax or a Sun host. QMC also has two other AMT DAP 510s attached to Sun workstations, an environment which provides supercomputer power and high performance graphics in one's own office or laboratory. The DAP 500 series (Parkinson, Hunt and MacQueen, 1988 - Fig. 18.1 illustrates the main features of the architecture) are 1024 processor machines, with the single bit processing elements (PEs) arranged as a 32 x 32 array, each with its own memory. The minimum size of the latter is 32K bits per PE, but the architecture supports up to 1 Mbits/PE. The new 610-32 (which is attached to a Vax host) has 64 Kbits per PE giving a total memory size of 32 Mbytes. Other improvements over the earlier ICL DAPs are the improved VLSI technology components, and the cycle speed of 10 MHz which is twice as fast as the original 4096 processor DAP. Data visualization is provided by a fast I/O channel with a transfer rate of 50 Mbytes/s; this can be used to attach a high resolution colour display. Medium speed I/O is obtained through the host connection unit either via the host itself or through the VME bus interface, which can support transfer rates of approximately 4 Mbytes/s.

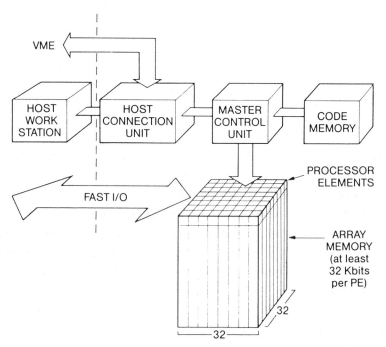

Figure 18.1 DAP 510 schematic.

An important aspect of any multiprocessor system which has to be considered by the algorithm designer is the interprocessor connectivity. The DAP has two systems - connections to nearest neighbours and a bus system for rows and columns which provides rapid data fetch and broadcast facilities. These systems give an excellent communication/computation balance for most applications, with none of the communication bottleneck experienced in some other multiprocessor systems. The DAP is an example of SIMD architecture where all PEs simultaneously execute the same instruction; however, each PE has an activity control register which provides a degree of local autonomy and permits easy simulation of concurrent operations.

Many of the architectural features are reflected in the language Fortran-Plus which is a forerunner of the next Fortran standard - 8X. A program designed to run on the DAP has two major parts. One runs on the host machine and is written in a standard language such as Fortran 77 or C, and handles I/O and user interaction; the other part runs on the DAP and is written in an extension of a standard language designed for use in a parallel environment. Program development facilities and the run-time environment are provided on the host, data is transferred to the DAP using standard subroutines and computation based on the Fortran-Plus code is done on the DAP. Fortran-Plus provides vector and array extensions to Fortran 77, together with other Fortran 8X concepts. Other software includes the application support libraries, a low level assembler, run-time software and a powerful data routing system called Parallel Data Transforms (Flanders and Parkinson, 1988) which provides underlying support for languages, library and application software.

18.2 THE DAP SUBROUTINE LIBRARY

The DAP is a highly parallel computer consisting of more than 1000 processors so its exploitation requires algorithmic techniques which are often very different from those developed for conventional serial computers. Many examples can be quoted - two are matrix multiplication (Gostick, 1979) where an outer product method is employed instead of the usual inner or middle product algorithms, and solution of dense linear equations where either a Gauss Jordan or Hybrid Gauss Jordan/Gauss Elimination technique is used (Parkinson, 1984; Bowgen, Hunt and Liddell, 1983). For larger problems it is often necessary to use a hybrid serial/parallel strategy (Liddell and Parkinson, 1988; Liddell, 1989). Dennis Parkinson's paper, to be found elsewhere in these proceedings, gives examples of the use of a super parallel algorithm strategy for the case where one needs to solve a number of repeats of a given problem or sub-problem simultaneously on a multiprocessor system (Parkinson, 1989). A subroutine library must try to cater for all possible requirements of its users, and in order to solve a particular problem several different strategies may be required in the parallel environment, depending on the size of the problem, the number of processors and the number of sub-problems which can be solved simultaneously, whereas a single algorithm might suffice in a serial computer environment. Thus it is neither appropriate nor efficient to take an existing subroutine library and convert it for use as a massively parallel machine, although there may be strong commercial pressures to do so!

In order to attempt to provide at least a familiar user interface, our approach has been to supply library facilities of equivalent functionality to those, say, in the NAG library. Even so, additional utility routines relating to data organization, mapping etc. are needed which are not relevant for serial computers. A major part of the user interface of any library is the documentation system which reflects the structure of the library itself. The DAP subroutine library documentation style is based on the format used in the NAG library. Each routine is provided with full printed and machine-based documentation for online use; the latter consists of the sections Purpose, Specification, Arguments and Error-indicators. The full documentation includes a sample example of the use of routine. Following NAG, the library is divided into chapters relating to different subject areas which are reflected in the first three characters of the name of each routine, corresponding to the modified SHARE classification code. For example, Chapter 7 : F04 is used for simultaneous linear equations; Chapter 5 : F01 contains routines for matrix operations. However, the naming convention for individual routines differs from NAG because Fortran-Plus (in common with many versions of Fortran 77) names are not limited to six characters. Thus, the three characters modified SHARE classification code is followed by a name indicative of the purpose of the routine - e.g. F01_M_INV, F04_BIGSOLVE, S04_ARC_SIN. The library manual also contains an introductory chapter, a quick reference catalogue and an index of routines.

The collection of algorithms from which routines are selected for inclusion in the library was built up by setting up a trial library facility on the national service DAP into which users were invited to submit routines. Most of the routines were provided by members of the DAP Support Unit at QMC, often in response to specific user requirements. There are approximately 200 routines in the collection, nearly all callable from Fortran-Plus (formerly DAP-Fortran), from which a subset of 93 fully documented and validated routines form the current standard version of the library. This was converted and implemented on the 1024 processor ICL mini-DAP in 1986 as part of an SERC Cooperative Grant proposal and more recently on both the AMT DAP 510 and 610 machines where it is known as the General Support Library (GSLIB), jointly owned by AMT and QMC.

Before being added to the GSLIB library, all routines undergo validation tests, designed and written at QMC, which have been collected together in a validation suite. The library is linked in at the consolidation stage of the compilation process and can be run under Unix or Vax/VMS. Most routines are implemented with 32 bit (4 byte) precision for REAL and INTEGER quantities. Fortran-Plus has valuable precision facilities at the byte rather than the word level, and to implement all routines over the full range of precisions would lead to a large increase in the number of routines. However, additional precision versions of some of the routines are already available and more are planned (eg REAL*6 and possibly REAL*8 for linear algebra). In fact, experience has shown that 6-byte (REAL*6) precision is sufficient for most numerically intensive calculations, in order to give a satisfactory compromise between performance and stability.

18.3 THE DAP FE LIBRARY

Finite element software usually comprises three major sub-program units - the pre-processor, the processor and the post-processor (Greenough, Emson and Smith, 1984). The main FE program consists of a few program statements which call these various subprograms. The overall structure is illustrated in Fig. 18.2.

The pre-processor includes routines for input (or generation) of element data, definition of problem-dependent parameters, boundary condition data and an automatic mesh generator. In an interactive workstation environment it is desirable to include graphics routines to display the mesh and the input data, so that data errors can be eliminated at an early stage (data checking is particularly important in 3D applications). The processor unit includes procedures for evaluating element shape functions, element stiffnesss matrix calculations, assembling the full system of global equations, incorporating boundary conditions and finally, solving the resulting global system of equations. For time-dependent problems, one needs to solve systems of linear ODE's, and for resonance problems one must include methods for solving eigenvalue problems. The post-processor includes routines that will plot profiles of the approximate solution obtained, contours of constant values of the latter, error estimates for each element, or contours of estimates of point-wise errors. Colour graphics can be used to enhance some of the results. Self adapting features must be incorporated in an interactive environment - this involves feedback to the pre-processing and processing stages of the calculation.

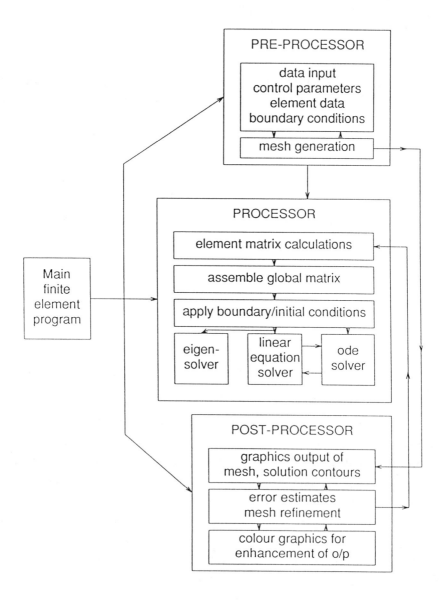

Figure 18.2 Structure of finite element programs.

Work on the DAP Finite Element Library was primarily financed by two related SERC Research grants at QMC (Liddell and Parkinson) and Liverpool (Wait). In order to provide early accessible software tools for the research community it was decided to provide parallel routines of equivalent functionality to those in the NAG/SERC Finite Element Library. Again this is not a matter of straight translation - algorithms must be designed specifically for the highly parallel DAP hardware, but which maintain the generality of the SERC routines in their applicability to many types of problem. A full discussion of the design philosophy is given in Liddell, Parkinson and Wait, (1986). More than 50 Fortran-Plus routines have been developed for the processor phase. These include standard matrix and vector operations, equation solvers, numerical integration, shape functions, stress-strain matrices for the plane strain problem, strain displacement matrices, assembly routines and utility routines. The shape functions include 4-node quadrilateral elements, 8-node quadrilaterals, 3-node triangular elements and 6-node triangular elements. Distributed loading has also been added to provide more flexibility in solid mechanics applications, Boundary conditions for field problems can be of Dirichlet, Neumann or Cauchy type. A number of application (level 1) problems have been developed, including solid mechanics, fluid flow, with Dirichlet boundary conditions or with Dirichlet and Neumann boundary conditions and a time-dependent fluid flow problem. Documentation for all the routines has been written; the format corresponds to the standard for the DAP subroutine library, but the variable names are compatible with those in the NAG/SERC FE library. The library was originally developed on an ICL PERQ + Mini-DAP simulation system, then transferred to the mainframe DAP for use by other groups; and it was also implemented on the ICL mini-DAP and later moved to an AMT DAP 510 attached to a Sun workstation, and to the new AMT DAP 610 provided by the Computer Board to continue the DAP Service.

A good deal of the early work associated with this project involved a study of the various mapping strategies which might be employed in the various phases of the Finite Element calculations. In the element stiffness matrix calculations, this is a completely parallel process as each can be calculated independently and a serial algorithm used vertically within each processing element (a multi-serial approach). However, one of the major tasks computationally is the solution of the global system which is node based rather than element based. Hence a finite element computation on a highly parallel system such as the DAP has a data assignment and global assembly phase that has no direct counterpart in a serial algorithm. During this phase it is necessary for data to be transmitted from one processor to another, this is determined by the element topology data. It is not a fully parallel process but can be done efficiently using a low level utility routine from the DAP subroutine library. The global system matrices which arise in the FE method tend to be banded, symmetric and positive definite and these are stored in the DAP by diagonals using a long vector or linear array form of mapping. The preconditioned Conjugate Gradient method is well suited to the solution of this type of system, but the preconditioning strategies which are suitable for parallel computation are different from those used on serial computers. The analysis of suitable preconditioning strategies has constituted an important part of the algorithmic research associated with the project.

The research on sparse matrix solvers resulted in the development of a number of parallel DAP routines : a conjugate gradient solver, a conjugate gradient routine without assembly of the global matrix, and four preconditioned conjugate gradient solvers; the strategies applied in the latter are diagonal scaling, 1-step point Jacobi, m-step point Jacobi and m-step 4 colour Gauss-Seidel. A comparison of the methods is given in Lai and Liddell, (1987) and (1988a). In general the routines will solve at most 1024 equations (4096 on the DAP 610), but the extension of the methods to larger systems has also been investigated, which involve using multi-nodes per processor. The solvers are based on block Gauss-Seidel preconditioning strategies. A parallel technique for incorporating boundary conditions into the system has also been developed. The method commonly used on serial computers in which one deletes from the global stiffness matrix any entry corresponding to a boundary node is not suited to a parallel environment; instead, direct elimination is applied to the set of element equations and a multi-serial algorithm applied before assembly of the global system. This technique and others are discussed in Lai and Liddell, (1988b).

The main objective of a mesh generation program is to provide high quality, error-free input to finite element or finite difference calculations and to reduce the manual labour associated with defining individual element geometries and element topologies at the pre-processing stage of such calculations. A method was developed to construct a mesh of uniform nodal density by exploiting as far as possible the parallel processing properties of the DAP (Mouhas, 1987). This method is easily applicable, it requires a minimum of user interaction and works for virtually any polygon whether simply or multiply connected. The user selects the desired nodal density and the type of element required (triangles, quadrilaterals etc.); the program then automatically generates a set of nodes in the interior as well as on the boundaries of the specified domain. At the end of the node generation stage a parallel smoothing algorithm was incorporated, in order to improve the quality of the result by ensuring that no two nodes lie too close to each other, thus avoiding steep gradients or badly shaped elements in the final result.

The discretization proceeds in two separate stages: Point generation and element generation. The point generation process employs ideas similar to those of Suhara and Fukuda, (1972) and Cavendish, (1974) with the main difference that the points are generated in parallel using an iterative procedure which incorporates a smoothing technique. Since points on the boundary are generated automatically, no user input is require other than the polygon vertices. The element generation process uses a divide and conquer technique (e.g. Preperata and Hong, 1977; Lee and Schachter, 1980) which is suitable for general SIMD type architectures and completes the construction of the Delauney triangulation in log(N) steps. Points are recursively divided into non-overlapping sets of N/2 and the separate triangulations are constructed and merged in parallel. This may necessitate the introduction of spurious points to ensure that N is an exact power of 2. In the final result, unwanted triangles are removed from the mesh using a parallel version of a point-in-polygon algorithm. The results of this work were presented in Mouhas, (1988). Line drawing algorithms for displaying the mesh on a video monitor were developed, together with shading routines for displaying the solution. The line drawing routine can handle up to 1024 lines in parallel and produce a 1 bit 1024 x 1024 image. The shading routine creates a 4 bit 1024 x 1024 image and produces a linear interpolation in the interior of each element, resulting in a contour display over the solution region.

A brief study of the solution of a simple time-dependent flow problem was undertaken. This was based on the NAG/SERC Finite Element library demonstration problem 4.1, and was implemented on the AMT DAP 510 with Sun host. The DAP section is written in Fortran-Plus, while the host is in C in order to interface with the low-level Sun graphics. The example relates to "consolidation" in soil mechanics.

As part of the Finite Element work demonstration programs were developed on the AMT DAP 510. These programs include automatic mesh generation, solution and graphical output using the DAP data visualization system; early versions were implemented on the mini-DAP. The first demonstration is based on the SERC/NAG (finite element library (level 1) program Seg 3.1, and is a steady state potential flow problem, with potentials described on the boundary. It can be interpreted as the flow of groundwater in an acquifier, with a hole in the centre to represent a solid pipe or tunnel). A slightly modified version showing progress during the interactions was ialso produced; demonstration includes a host program windowing facility with five subwindows - a canvas for handling interactive input by the user, and message, control, logo and active panels (Fig. 18.3). The user interface makes considerable use of menus, mouse, windows and Sun graphics facilites.

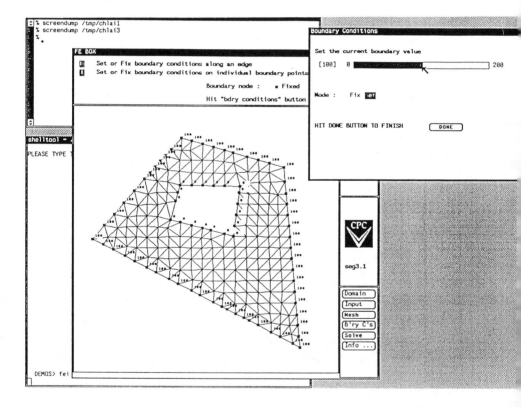

Figure 18.3 Host program display for demonstration.

The time dependent flow problem discussed above was also implemented. As with the first demonstration, extensive use is made of interactive facilities in the host, and automatic mesh generation and colour coded contour map of the solution is displayed on the DAP video. Another demonstration is being developed for a larger problem - a 2D elasticity example based on 8 noded elements where 2 or 3 elements are stored per processor. For these larger problems (involving tens of thousands of nodes) it is sometimes necessary to use higher (6 byte) precision arithmetic. Further details of the demonstrations are discussed in Faidi, Lai and Mouhas, (1988).

18.4 OTHER APPLICATIONS TOOLS

Although early experiences with the mainframe DAP highlighted the importance of being able to demonstrate applications of the machine, this was hampered by the batch-only mode of operation and lack of high speed communication channels between the DAP and any graphical output devices. The provision of a graphics workstation host and the fast video output capability revolutionised the user interface; since these facilities became available from 1986 onwards there has been considerable development of low-level graphics facilities and tools for image and signal processing applications.

Prior to the availability of the mini-DAP system in 1986, members of the research group (Grant Bowgen, David Fincham, John Quinn, Dennis Parkinson) within the QMC DAP Support Unit were studying techniques for creating views of 3D objects using parallel algorithms to create pictures for pixel based display screens. A particular application was the development of a molecular graphics program (Hubbard and Fincham, 1985; Quinn, 1989) which draws molecules in two chemically meaningful ways: space filling drawings allow the shape of molecules to be easily seen and sphere and cylinder pictures which show topographical features. Depth cueing is included by default to allow easy interpretation of molecular shape. The hidden surface problem is solved using a Z buffer algorithm. On the AMT DAP 510 space filling drawings with 500 spheres can be drawn in about 1 second, whilst molecules with 50 atoms are drawn at a few frames per second, allowing an almost smooth rotate - translate - zoom facility.

Another example which is inherently parallel in nature is ray tracing. An important property of the DAP ray tracing program (Hellier, 1989) is that it operates by using a sequential ray tracer in every PE; concurrency is exploited by data parallelism so no special techniques are needed to map the application onto the DAP. The program generates 24-bit RGB images and includes a data compression technique so that it can be displayed using 8-bit pixels at each point in the picture, three 8-bit colour values are computed together with a fourth value which represents the luminance. This information is transformed into a 512 x 512 array of 2 x 2 superpixels using the Parallel Data Transforms (PDTs) described briefly below. A complete scene containing seven objects and 415711 rays is generated in 32 seconds on the AMT 510 (14 secs on the 605).

AMT have developed a low-level graphics library, much of which is based on techniques developed by Bowgen, Quinn and Parkinson. This library can be used to construct images and to cause them to be displayed on the video monitor. Each image is 1024 x 1024 pixels, stored as an 8-bit number. For most routines the user supplies a colour value (in the range 0-255), or an array of colour values, as a parameter. When the picture is output from the hardware framestore to the monitor, the 8-bit pixel value is converted into a colour value via a look-up table held in the display hardware. Each entry in the table specifies three 8-bit values - the R, G and B intensity values. A default table is supplied, which can be changed by the user. The routines in the library, which are callable from Fortran-Plus or APAL (Assembly Language) code, allow the user to nominate a data area within a DAP program to act as a screen buffer, specify a colour look-up table, draw dots, lines and characters into the screen buffer and output the buffer to the screen. There are also debugging aids.

The Image Processing Library (Active Memory Technology, 1988a) is divided into four chapters - image conversion routines, which convert between raster, sheet mapped and crinkle mapped images; image processing primitives, for adding, subtracting and shifting entire images; shifting operations; low-level image processing matrices which perform tasks such as edge detection, convolutions and transforms. A DAP Image Manipulation Package (DIMP) was developed for the ICL 4096 processor DAP by Smith, (1983), which can manipulate arbitrary sized raster images. Intercept Systems Ltd have also developed a general purpose visualization system, DAPIX, (Intercept Systems, 1988) which is designed to exploit the parallelism of the DAP 510 by combining traditional graphics functions with of pixel based image-handling techniques.

The DAP Signal Processing Library, DSPLIB Version 1 (Active Memory Technology, 1988b), contains 196 routines for performing Fast Fourier Transforms (FFTs), windowing, signal generation and signal format conversion; for each function in the library there are 14 subroutines, one for each Fortran-Plus data precision: INTEGER*1 to INTEGER*8 and REAL*3 to REAL*8; version 2 also includes a set of one-dimensional FFTs which use tapered arithmetic in which the precision of the calculation increases as the algorithm proceeds (Active Memory Technology, 1989). All FFT routines in the library operate simultaneously on N independent batches of data where N is 1024 for the DAP 500 and 4096 for the DAP 600 series.

Finally, a very powerful tool for generalized mapping and data routing is provided by the Parallel Data Transforms (Flanders and Parkinson, 1988). This allows data remapping statements to be included in a user's code which are pre-processed and used to remap data in the DAP memory. Different data mappings are represented as mapping vectors which provide a concise one-dimensional representation of a class of mappings of multi-dimensional data onto multi-dimensional arrays of processors. The PDTs are used as underlying tools for many of the routines in the other libraries.

18.5 FUTURE DEVELOPMENTS

Developments of the Fortran-Plus language which are planned (Active Memory Technology, 1989) include an unconstrained version of the language which will handle arrays of any size and shape, and a new compiler which will be kept up-to-date with the developing Fortran 8X standard which is expected to become an ISO standard in 1990. These versions of the language will be based on the Virtual Array Processor (VAP) which is AMT's version of a Virtual System Architecture (VSA); the design and implementation of the VSA is a major goal of the Alvey Active data model project (ARCH 001) which is a collaborative project involving the Universities of Edinburgh, Salford and Southampton, Queen Mary College and industrial partners AMT, GLH and Marconi. It is believed that the existence of a virtual architecture would greatly facilitate the implementation of numeric and symbolic languages and applications across a range of parallel architectures such as the DAP and arrays of transputers.

Application libraries and other tools will have to be modified to be compatible with the new languages being developed; however, there is also a need for compatibility with existing Fortran-Plus programs and for performance reasons the experienced user needs to be able to map his/her problem onto the DAP in the most efficient manner. One of the aims of the Alvey project is to begin to quantify the trade-off between performance cost, ease of software design and portability across a range of parallel architectures.

A program of work which has attempted to provide portability for a range of vector and parallel algorithms employs the BLAS modular approach (Dongarra *et al.* 1988a) in which the use of a set of Basic Linear Algebra Subprograms for problems in linear algebra were suggested. Extended versions, level 2 and level 3 BLAS, were subsequently proposed (Dongarra *et al.* 1988b) which were aimed at matrix-vector and matrix-matrix operations respectively, designed primarily for efficiency across a range of machines including vector processor and multiprocessor systems. The work is being further extended in the US/NAG LAPACK project (Bischof *et al.* 1988) which aims to build a portable parallel MIMD linear algebra library, which is a collection of Fortran 77 routines into which parallelism is introduced by means of the level 3 BLAS and the Schedule mechanism (Dongarra and Sorensen, 1986). The application of the use of BLAS in transputer systems is being investigated by Delves and Brown (1989) and Van den Berghe (1989) has considered a general block structured approach to linear algebra on the DAP which is a similar approach to that used in the BLAS.

There is an urgent need for good applications software which will enable the various parallel computer architectures to be exploited. To date, most experience has been in the development of specific systems targeted at obtaining maximum efficiency from a particular architecture. While this is very important, it is also necessary to develop portable software systems and standards in areas such as graphics, which are aimed at enhancing the usability of parallel, particularly massively parallel SIMD and MIMD computer systems and also mixed MIMD/SIMD architectures, in order to achieve the levels of performance required by many of today and tomorrow's large scale applications.

REFERENCES

1   Active Memory Technology (1988a) *Image Processing Library* (man014).

2   Active Memory Technology (1988b) *Introduction to the DAP Signal Processing Library* DSPLIB.

3   Active Memory Technology (1989) *Fortran for the DAP - Statement of Direction.*

4   Bischof, C. Dongarra, J. Du Croz, J. Greenbaum, A. Hammerling, S. and Sorensen D. (1988), *LAPACK Working Note No. 5 Provisional Contents,* Argonne National Laboratory Report, ANL-88-38.

5   Bowgen, G. Hunt, D. and Liddell, H. (1983) The solution of N linear equations on a P-Processor Parallel Computer, presented at the *SIAM Conference on Parallel Processing for Scientific Computing.*

6   Cavendish, J. (1974) Automatic triangulation of arbitrary planar domains for the Finite Element method. *Int.J.Comp.Inf. Sciences,* 9, 3.

7   Delves, M. and Brown, N. (1989) *The Design of the Supernode Numerical Library,* private communication.

8   Dongarra, J. Du Croz, J. Hammerling, S. and Hanson, R. (1988a) An extended set of FORTRAN basic linear algebra subprograms. *ACM Trans.Math.Soft.,* 14, 1, pp 177.

9   Dongarra, J. Du Croz,J. Duff, I. and Hammerling, S. (1988b) *A Set of Level 3 Basic Linear Algebra Subroutines,* Argonne National Laboratory Report ANL-MCS-P88-1.

10 Dongarra, J. and Sorensen,D. (1986) *SCHEDULE - Tools for Developing and Analyzing Parallel Fortran Programs,* Argonne National Laboratory Report ANL-MCS-TM-816.

11 Faidi,S. Lai,C. H. and Mouhas, C. (1988) *DAP Finite Element Demonstration Programs,* CPC Internal Report 2.39.

12 Flanders,P. andParkinson, D. (1988) Data mapping and routing for highly parallel processor arrays, in *Future Computing,* 1, 1, Oxford University Press.

13 Gostick, R. (1979) Software and algorithms for the distributed array processor. *ICL Technical Journal* 1, pp.116.

14 Greenough, C. Emson, C. and Smith, I. (1984) *The NAG/SERC Finite Element Library ,* Rutherford Appleton Laboratory Report RAL-84-107.

15 Hellier, R. (1989) *Ray Tracing, DAP Applications Notes AN6* (Active Memory Technology).

16 Hubbard, R. and Fincham, D. (1985) An algorithm for generating shaded molecular surface graphics on an array processor. *J. Molecular Graphics* 1, 1.

17   Intercept Systems (1988) *DAPIX - the DAP Visualisation Package.*

18   Lai , C. H. and Liddell, H. (1987) A review of parallel finite element methods on the DAP. *Appl.Math.Modelling,* 11, pp.330-340.

19   Lai, C. H. and Liddell, H. (1988a) Preconditioned conjugate gradient method on the DAP, in *Mathematics of Finite Elements and Applications* VI, Academic Press, pp.145-156.

20   Lai, C. H. and Liddell, H. M. (1988b) Finite elements using long vectors of the DAP. *Parallel Computing* 8, pp.351-361.

21   Lee, D. and Schachter, B. (1980) Two algorithms for constructing a Delauney triangulation. *Int.J.Comp.Inf. Sciences* 9, 3.

22   Liddell, H. and Bowgen, G. (1982) The DAP Subroutine Library, *Comput.Phys.Commun.* 26, p.311.

23   Liddell, H. Parkinson, D. and Wait, R. (1986) A Parallel computational environment for finite element calculations, presented at *1st Int. Conference on Vector and Parallel Computing,* Loen, Norway.

24 Liddell, H.   Parkinson, D. (1988) Mapping large scale computational problems on a highly parallel SIMD computer in Parallel Processing for Scientific Computing, *SIAM,* pp. 277-283.

25   Liddell, H. (1989) Applications of highly parallel processors. Int. Meeting on Parallel Computing, Verona, Italy, Sept. 28-30. *Parallel Computer Applications,* Chapter 6, pp. 269-279.

26   Mouhas, C. (1987) Automatic mesh generation on the DAP. Paper presented at *VAPP III.*

27   Mouhas, C. (1988) Computing the Delauney triangulation on SIMD processor arrays : a divide and conquer approach. Paper presented at *CONPAR 88.*

28   Parkinson, D. (1984) The solution of N linear equations using P processors, *Parallel Computing'83,* (ed. M Felmeier *et al.,*) North Holland.

29   Parkinson, D. (1989) *Super Parallel Algorithms* (this seminar).

30   Preperata, F. and Hong, S. (1977) Convex Hulls of finite sets of points in two or three dimensions. *ACM Comm.,* 20, 2.

31 Quinn, J. (1989) *Note 4: Molecular Graphics, DAP Applications Notes AN4* (Active Memory Technology).

32 Smith, K. (1983) An image manipulation package for the DAP. *Parallel Computing '83,* Free University of Berlin (North Holland).

33 Suhara, J. and Fukuda, J. (1972) Automatic mesh generation for finite element analysis, *Advances in Computational Methods in Structured Mechanics and Design,* UAU Press.

34 van den Berghe, S. (1989) *Note 5: Linear Algebra - LLT Decomposition, DAP Applications Notes AN5* (Active Memory Technology).

Part Six

Languages

19 Software portability for parallel computers using Strand

M. Gittins

Artificial Intelligence Ltd

19.1 INTRODUCTION

Parallel processing offers great potential for reducing processing costs and increasing the power of data processing. The difficulty is that the current software industry is oriented towards writing software for sequential machines. If one starts from concepts, tools and languages appropriate for sequential machines, programming parallel machines is hard. Faced with this issue there are two possible options; either to throw away the existing set of concepts, tools and languages or to muddle through changing the existing sequential set. Throwing away the existing set does not mean that some material cannot be salvaged, but it does mean starting from a different position.

Strand is a langauge that is based on concepts and ideas that relate to parallel execution, rather than sequential; i.e. the operational model that Strand conforms to is not one of sequential processing, it is one of concurrent execution. The nature of Strand includes abstractions that remove the programmer from considerations of the details of the hardware being programmed, or the characteristics of the operating system being used. He or she is therefore free to concentrate on the important issues of programming the task at hand, not worrying about building in the parallelism. Once written, a Strand program can then be run on a wide variety of hardware platforms, usually without modification.

Strand is targeted at medium grained MIMD architectures, for example the Intel iPSC/2, Sequent symmetry or Meiko Computing Surface. Notice that we include both distributed memory and shared memory machines in this set. Strand on fine grained SIMD machines, such as the AMT DAP or connection machine, is a research issue that has not yet been addressed. Distributed systems, for example networks of Sun workstations, are also with the ambit of Strand, treated, in present Strand systems, as a dispersed parallel machine rather than true distributed systems. A sequential system is a special case of a parallel system (N = 1), therefore Strand runs effectively on such a system.

19.2 PORTABILITY ISSUES

(Hardware, operating systems, explicit parallelism)

A wide variety of hardware architectures can now be purchased by the would-be parallel user. It is not clear which architecture will predominate in the future, indeed it is more than likely that new architectures will be developed. The choice of hardware usually determines the operating system (or lack of it) that will be used, and the primitive operations that can be performed, i.e. the types of fork or spawn operation, memory sharing, message passing etc. Programs written in C, Fortran or Cobol will have explicit calls to what ever primitives are available. If the program is moved to another machine the calls will need to be changed to correspond to the new environment. However the real problem is much deeper, the program will be structured to utilize the features of the particular environment. If the new environment has a different set of features, which it typically has, then the program structure will need to be changed.

19.3 STRAND MODEL

The central component of the Strand operational model is a process. A Strand process is a very different creature from a process in the Unix world. A Strand process is short lived, very small, and exists in large numbers, i.e. it is extremely lightwieght. This means that it is quick to create and destroy. In some respects a Strand process is similar to a stack frame. It is of a similar size, it has arguments, and knowns which procedure it corresponds to. However it has no concept of returning, and is not part of any heirarchy such as a stack or tree, there is no parent-child relationship.

A process only exists to reduce, that is to spawn a set of relpacement processes and then terminate. The act of reduction involves selecting a suitable fragment of Strand code, a clause, and spawning the processes called in that clause. It might appear that this means an ever increasing number of processes, however a clause might have no calls within it. Additionally some process calls correspond to primitive operations of the Strand system, called kernels. A kernel is like a build-in routine, and rather than reduce in the normal manner a kernel process performs some particular action, e.g. adding two numbers, or loading a file. All actual manipulation of data is performed by kernels.

A process has arguments which might be variables or data, either simple, atomic data like numbers of strings, or more complex data structures comprising lists and tuples. Processes can share data or variables, i.e. more than one process might refer to the same data or variable, these act as communication channels between processes. A running Strand system is therefore a network of interconnected processes, where the interconnections are the data.

One process might write to a variable, another might read it. A simple clause, foo, might look like:

foo:
> get_num(X),
> print_num(X)

When this clause is used to reduce a process, foo, two new processes are spawned, get_num, which assigns to the variable X, and print_num uses the value assigned to X.

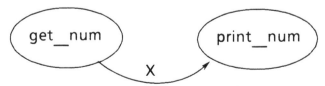

A process may be unable to select a clause to reduce because data is not available. If this is the case the process must wait for the variable to be assigned a value. For each variable a set of processes may be suspended until the variable is assigned. This is a non-busy wait and once the variable is assigned a value the suspended processes will be woken automatically.

In the small example, print_num will suspend until X has been assigned a value. Strand variables are a single assignment. This means that a variable is really an unassigned value. Once a value has been assigned, process arguments such as X refer directly to the data. The concept of a variable being the notation for a memory location is not appropriate in Strand.

Processes may exist on different processors. The example above spawns two processes on the same processor, but further reductions may spawn processes on other processors. Alternatively, simple annotation may spawn processes on other processors. In either case the value assigned to the variable X is available to the print_num process. Therefore the act of assigning to a variable will communicate the value assigned to all processes that require it. This means that assignment takes care of the requirement for communication. Strand has no communication primitives. Also, as the variables are a single assignment, it is an easy way to acheive synchronization by use of variables.

19.4 DESCRIPTION

Strand programs are composed of a set of clauses which have the form

$$H :\text{-} G1, G2, ..., Gm \mid B1, B2, ... Bn. \qquad m,n \geq 0$$

where H is the clause head, :- is the implication operator, the Gs are the clause guard, | is the commit operator and the Bs are the clause body. The period signifies the end of a single clause. A clause head has the form

$$p(A1, A2, ..., An) \qquad (n \geq 0)$$

where p names the clause and A1, ... An are its arguments. Clauses with the same name and number of arguments are grouped to form a process definition. Each clause specifies a rule of process behavior. The head and guard collectively specify a set of preconditions under which a process may execute. A clause whose body is empty specifies that if the preconditions are satisfied then the process terminates. A clause of the form:

$$H :\text{-} G1, G2, ..., Gm \mid B1.$$

specifies that if the preconditions are satisfied then the process changes state to the process B1. A general clause of the form:

$$H :\text{-} G1, G2, ..., Gm \mid B1, B2, ..., Bn.$$

specifies that if the preconditions are satisfied then the process changes state to B1 and simultaneously forks the processes B2, ..., Bn.

The *Strand* language uses static dataflow, simple assignment to variables and a flat process structure. It also places restrictions on matching and assignment operations involving two variables. Strand programs are expressed using the notation presented in section 19.2. Two restrictions are placed on the form of programs.

1. No variable may occur more than once in the head of a clause. (In fact, we can and do define syntactic sugar that permits this; however, this restriction is made here to simplify presentation of Strand semantics).

2. The clause guard contains only predefined test operations.

The clause body contains a collection of predefined and/or programmer defined processes.

A *Strand* computation corresponds to a pool of concurrently executing processes. Each process corresponds to a term of the form

$$p(T1, T2, ..., Tn) \qquad (n \geq 0)$$

which comprises the program state p/n and a data state consisting of the terms T1, T2, ..., Tn. Computation proceeds by repeatedly removing a process from the pool. If the process is an assignment process it is executed immediately; otherwise a reduction attempt is made. A reduction attempt involves selecting a clause from the program, matching the process to the clause head and executing the clause guard. If the preconditions specified by the head and guard are satisfied then the process commits. This causes new instances of the processes defined in the clause body to be added to the process pool.

19.5 THE MATCH ALGORITHM

The match algorithm is shown in Table 19.1. The algorithm is applied left to right textually and depth first in term structures. It returns a set of bindings for variables in the clause, fails or suspend.

Table 19.1 The match algorithm

| | | process T1 | |
clause T2	variable	constant	structure
variable	T2: = T1	T2: = T1	T2: = T1
constant	suspend	if T1 ≠ T2 fail	fail
structure	suspend	fail	match args

Matching two structures involves checking that they are both lists or tuples of the same size and executing the match algorithm on corresponding arguments of the structures. Notice that the table contains no assignments to variables in the process. Another way of saying this is that the matching only reads the data state and does not modify or *side effect* it.

Strand provides a variety of tests which can be used to perform type checking, arithmetic comparison and term comparison. The purpose of these tests is to allow a clause to be chosen on the basis of some local constraints concerning the state of a process. Any number of tests can be written in the clause guard, they are executed from left to right textually after matching is complete. Each test returns either true, fail or suspend. If all tests return true then the guard evaluates to true. If any test evaluates to fail or suspend then the guard evaluates to fail or suspend respectively. Tests generally return suspend if they encounter an unbound variable during evaluation.

19.6 EXAMPLE

A simple example module is shown on the following page. The details of the syntax are discussed in the next section. This module contains two procedures.

The first procedure, cpd, consists of two clauses and calculates compound interest using a naive algorithm. The second procedure, simple-interest, computes the simple interest on a capital sum, Cap.

% Strand program to compute compound interest
```
        -compile(free).
        -exports([cpd/4]).
```

```
cpd(Cap,Rate,Years,Result):
        Years > = 0, Years  <1 |
        simple_interest(Cap,Rate,Years,Result).
cpd(Cap,Rate,Years,Result):
        Years > = 1 |
        Years1 is Years -1 ,
        simple_interest(Cap, Rate,1, NewCap),
        cpd(NewCap,Rate,Years1,Result).
```

% an internal routine to calculate simple interest simple_interest
(Cap,Rate,Fraction,NewCap):
```
        NewCap is Cap  + (Fraction * Cap * Rate / 100).
```

Suppose cpd is called with arguments: cpd(1000, 13, 5, R), i.e. what capital accrues over 5 years starting with 1000 and 13%. This top-level call results in a process with (1000, 13, 5, R) as its process arguments. This process is then reduced with the second clause of cpd; the second clause is used because Years is greater than 1. This spawns three processes, one to calculate Years1, one for simple-interest and one for cpd. The original cpd process has now completed. (In practice the process record is re-used.) The calculation of Years1 and simple-interest can proceed directly, but the new cpd will suspend until the value of Years1 is available, which will, of course, be 4. The result of simple-interest, NewCap, is passed into the new cpd and the next round of computation can begin. This is repeated until the value of Years is 1. This time the first clause of cpd is selected and the result variable, R, passed all the way through from the first call, is passed on to simple-interest and assigned the correct value.

Strand supports other programming clichés that space does not allow to be discussed here, the important clichés are: incomplete messages, short-circuit, bounded buffers, producer-consumer and blackboards.

19.7 INTEGRATION

Strand .supports the reuse or integration of existing sequential code in a parallel environment. This is supported by two languages features: user kernels and user data types. Users can add to the basic set of kernel guard tests and body procedures by linking in foreign language code. They can also define their own data types ; these appear to Strand processes as anonymous black boxes which can be included in Strand data structures, passed from machine to machine and manipulated by user kernels. These facilities allow existing sequential code to be interfaced to Strand, enabling it to be linked with other processes in a parallel environment.

Strand features that support integration can also be used to interface to specialized hardware. For example, to make use of a vector processor the user may define a data type vector, to contain a set of floating point numbers, and the following user kernels. These test the type of a user data item, convert between Strand data and user data and invoke the vector processor.

vector(X):	guard kernel fails unless X is a vector
list_to_vector(L,V):	body kernel to create a vector
vector_to_list(V,L):	body kernel to access a vector's contents
add_vector(X,Y,Z):	body kernel to sum vectors Z is (X + Y)
vector_prod(X,Y,Z):	body kernel to calculate cross products Z is (X * Y)
inner_prod(X,Y,Z):	body kernel to calculate dot products Z is (X . Y)

19.8 CONCLUSION

Extensive experience with implementation and application of concurrent logic programming languages, including the construction of large programming systems (Foster, 1989; Taylor, 1989), plus comparative studies of language implementations (Foster and Taylor, 1987), has shown that previous research languages are too complex for effective implementation and programming. Strand is a minimal language that makes the key concepts of concurrent logic programming accessible to parallel programmers in a simple framework. Practical experiences with Strand suggest that this quest for minimality has paid off: the language has been implemented on a wide range of machines and appears to be sufficiently expressive for a broad range of applications. Implementations exist for Intel iPSC/2, Sun workstations, 386/System V machines, transputer systems running Helios, and

Sequent as well as prototypes for Sun networks, Encore, BBN Butterfly, NeXT machine, and transputer systems which support 3L.

Compiled Strand programs can be, and are, moved between these systems without edits or even recompilation. This demonstrates that Strand provides a viable route for programming parallel architectures and allowing truly portable applications to be written.

REFERENCES

1.   Foster, I.T. and Taylor, S. (1989) *STRAND: New Concepts in Parallel Processing,* Prentice-Hall. To be published.

2.   Foster, I.T. (1989) *Systems Programming in Parallel Logic Languages,* Prentice-Hall, London.

3.   Taylor, S. (1989) *Parallel Logic Programming Techniques,* Prentice-Hall.

FURTHER READING

1.   Gregory, S. (1987) *Parallel Logic Programming in Parlog,* Addison-Wesley.

2.   Mierowsky, C., Taylor, S., Shapiro, E., Levy, J. and Safra, S. (1985) *The Design and Implementation of Flat Concurrent Prolog,* Dept. of Computer Science, Weizmann Institute of Science, Rehovot, Israel, Technical report CS85-09, July 1985.

20 Implementation of CS-Prolog and CSO-Prolog on transputers

P. Kacsuk, I. Futo and K. Wiederanders

Multilogic Computing Ltd., Hungary

20.1 INTRODUCTION

Transputer based parallel computers are successfully applied in the field of numerical computation. Another important application area would be artificial intelligence (AI). However, the use of multitransputers in this field is prevented by the lack of high-level AI programming languages which are able to exploit the parallelism of these computers.

Prolog and Lisp are the most popular high-level AI languages, however, the implementation of these languages on communicating process architectures raises many nontrivial questions:

1. how to recognise parallelism (explicit versus implicit);

2. how to map parallel processes to processors (statically versus dynamically);

3. how to distribute functions between the host and the multiprocessor space;

4. how to organize distributed backtracking in the case of Prolog.

The purpose of this paper is to show two parallel, high-level, Prolog-based languages and their implementation on multitransputer systems:

1. CS-Prolog (Communicating Sequential Prolog) is a parallel extension of Prolog for writing coarse-grain parallel Prolog programs in CSP style and for supporting distributed discrete events and continuous simulation.

2.   CSO-Prolog (CS-Object-Prolog) is an object-oriented extension of CS-Prolog to combine logic and object-oriented programming for multitransputer systems.

The structure of the paper is as follows. First an overview of CS-Prolog is given including the explanation of the extra built-in predicates and the exploitation of parallelism. Section 20.2 explains the main concepts of CSO-Prolog. Section 20.3 describes the distributed control mechanism of CS-Prolog while section 20.4 explains the distributed implementation techniques used for implementing CS-and CSO-Prolog on multitransputer systems.

20.2 THE LANGUAGE CONCEPT OF CS-PROLOG

CS-Prolog is a parallel extension of Prolog where the concept of processes are involved in the language. CS-Prolog shows many similar features with Occam 2 [1] and Parallel C[2]. All these three languages are based on the communication concept of Hoare's CSP [3] and are intended to be implemented on parallel, communicating process architectures like multitransputer systems. The basic notion of CS-Prolog is the same than in Occam:

1.   process

2.   communication

3.   time

In CS-Prolog each process represents a Prolog goal to be resolved. To each process an independent Prolog interpreter/compiler is assigned to execute the goal of the process in parallel with other processes. Conceptually CS-Prolog is a two-level language. On the higher level the notion of process is available to describe parallel activities. On the lower level the behaviour of each process is given by a Prolog program. The declarative semantics of Prolog is preserved within each process meanwhile the process is able to receive and send information from/to its environment (processes). Processes can be created and deleted during program execution. In case of failure backtracking ensures the selection of new alternatives.

The communication of synchronization of the parallel Prolog processes is done by messages. Unlike in other parallel logic programming languages [4], [5], [6] there is no way for the processes to communicate by means of a common shared database or logical variables. The processes can be suspended waiting for messages and they can send messages to activate other waiting processes. Unlike in Occam 2 the communication is asynchronous, the sender process can go on without waiting for the reception of the message. The concept of channels is missing in CS-Prolog but the original communication concept of CSP [13], namely the pattern matching and naming the communicating partner are involved in CS-Prolog.

The time concept of CS-Prolog is significantly different from the Occam concept. Instead of using the global real-time concept, CS-Prolog applies the local virtual-time concept. This means that all processes can have their own local times which might be different during the parallel progress of processes. This feature of CS-Prolog makes it a good candidate for distributed simulation applications too (either discrete event or continuous simulation) [11], [12], [14].

20.2.1 The extra built-in predicates of CS-Prolog

The process, communication and time concepts of CS-Prolog, are defined by means of a collection of built-in predicates which are described in details in [7]. Here only a short overview of the most important built-in predicates is given.

$$new(G,N,T,S,E)$$

A new process is created with goal G and name N on transputer T. The starting local time is S and the resolution of G should be finished by local time E. The N,T,S,E arguments are optional. If T is missing, then the process is allocated to the PE of the caller.

$$delete\_process\ (P)$$

Each processes whose name can be unified with P is deleted/

$$active\_process(AP,T)$$

Identifies the caller process AP and the transputer T where it is running.

$$send(M,PL)$$

The caller process sends message M to the process being in the process list PL. M should be a fully initiated terms by the moment of the call. It prevents the sender from receiving a binding value produced by the receiver process. This is the main difference between the communication concept of CS-Prolog and Delta Prolog [10].

$$wait\_for(M)$$

The caller waits for a message which is unifiable with M. During backtracking a new message can not be accepted (deterministic execution).

$$wait\_for\_dnd(M)$$

Delayed, nondeterministic version of wait_for. During backtracking a new message can be accepted. The implementation of wait_for_dnd assures that all possible solutions of a CS-Prolog program can be resolved by backtracking.

$$hold(T)$$

The local time of the caller process is increased by T.

$$run(G)$$

starts the multiprocess scheduler making it possible to run Prolog processes in parallel.

The new, delete_process, send, wait_for, wait_for_dnd and hold pocedures are backtrackable, i.e. after backtracking their side-effects are undone.

CS-Prolog is a superset of ordinary Prolog. Without using the built-in predicates enumerated above, CS-Prolog programs work just like any other Prolog programs.

20.2.2   Parallelism in CS-Prolog

The process level parallelism offered by CS-Prolog insures a new type of parallelism, called communicating parallelism (similar to Hoare's concept of communicating sequential processes [3]) which is not available in other Prolog languages. By means of communicating parallelism OR- and AND-parallelism can be achieved [7].

In case of partitioning of a CS-Prolog program into processes two main considerations should be under taken:

1. The granularity of parallelism should be tuned by the user for ensuring optimal correspondence to the physical processor.

2. Communication of processes should be relatively rare and the communicating processes should be placed on neighbour transputers as far as possible.

Relationship between ordinary Prolog and CS-Prolog programs can be investigated from two point of views:

1. transformation of existing Prolog into CS-Prolog ones;

2. reconsidering the Prolog solution of a problem by using the process concept of CS-Prolog.

1. By definition all standard Prolog programs are correct CS-Prolog programs. Exploitation of the simplest case of AND-parallelism can be done by a simple synctactical modification as shown below.

Standard Prolog program:

        a :- b, c.

Equivalent CS-Prolog program:

        a :- b & c.

where & is an operator defined as

        &(X,Y) :- new(X,_,T1), new(Y,_,T2).

where X and Y are ground terms. The transformation of ordinary Prolog programs into CS-Prolog programs exploiting full AND-parallelism is subject of a forthcoming paper.

2. The problem should be defined keeping in mind the process concept and this way other kinds of parallelisms can be achieved, for example OR-parallelism [7].

    In order to illustrate the parallel use of CS-Prolog let us consider the well known quicksort algorithm. Its realization is CS-Prolog for systems containing $2**N$ transputers is given in Appendix with 'N' as an input parameter. The program demonstrates how the programmer is able to allocate processes for transputers and control the granularism of processes.

    The main idea of the algorithm is that the list (L) to be sorted is divided into two sublists based on the first element (FE) of the list. The first sublist contains those elements of L which are smaller than FE. All the other elements of L are packed into the second sublist. In the next step the quicksort algorithm can be executed in parallel on the two sublists. When they are sorted the concatenation of their sorted lists will result in the sorted list of the original L list.

The parallel sorting of the two sublists is executed by two different processes. However, it is only worth creating these processes in the case when free transputers are available. The third argument of quicksort_p represents the number of free processors. When it is '1' the second alternative of quicksort_p is chosen (lines 23-27 in Appendix) and the sublist is sorted without generating new processes. Otherwise, the third alternative is chosen and the two sublists are sorted in parallel on different transputers by means of the solve_parallel predicate (lines 31-34 and 88-100). Notice, the method described here for starting parallel processes is a general one able to regulate the granularity of parallelism.

Notice that solve_parallel is a parallel program structure playing the same role as 'par' construct in Occam. The argument of solve_parallel is a list of subgoals to be executed in parallel by difference processes (line 89). The task of solve_parallel is to create a new process for each subgoal (lines 94-95). The goal solve_parallel is successfully terminated when all the processes created for its subgoals have successfully terminated (lines 96-97, 102-105). Therefore the goal after solve_parallel can only be started to execute when all subgoals of solve_parallel have solved.

In solve_parallel a free transputer is requested from the transputer manager process (lines 52-65) and in the 'new' built-in predicate this transputer is used in the third argument to specify the location of the newly created process (line 94). This technique of dynamic process allocation is proposed in any cases. By programming the transputer manager process the user is able to realize different allocation strategies.

In CS-Prolog remote unification is not permitted and as a consequence goals of 'new' processes could not contain output variables. However, in many cases the output variables would be necessary. To solve the problem the successfully terminating process explicitly sends back its resolved goal to the parent process (lines 102-103) where the incoming goal and the saved original goal are unified (lines 93,96-100). In order to identify the processes and their goals a process_id_manager process is used in the program (lines 71-82). For the request of solve_parallel (lines 92, 107-109) the process_id_manager sends unique process identifiers.

20.3 THE LANGUAGE CONCEPT OF CSO-PROLOG

CSO-Prolog is an object-oriented extension of CS-Prolog. In fact, it is a Prolog integrating three extra paradigms:

- object orientation (objects)

- parallel computation (processes)

- simulation   (model time)

With CSO_Prolog logic programming takes into account lessons learned in programming language development in recent years (encapsulation, reusability, extensibility).

Encapsulation is a programming technique for minimizing interdependencies among objects by defining strict external interfaces. Reusability is necessary for building up new software systems by ordering components from a catalogue of software modules and combining them, rather than to write everything from the scratch every time. Extensibility is the ease with which a software system may be changed to account for modifications of its requirements.

Beside these programming technology improvements the object-oriented paradigm offers new possibilities for representation of knowledge keeping the Prolog style declarative semantics (object structure, incomplete knowledge, open world assumption).

Objects break a program into pieces. Links between the difference objects (defined by relations) give it an object structure (hierarchy, tree or graph structure). It need not necessarily be a failure if in its database an object contains no definition for a predicate applicable for the goal to be proven or the provided predicate does not succeed. The goal might be proven successful within a related object, too. This is known as the open world assumption. The notion of incomplete knowledge extends the Standard Prolog inference mechanism: if there is no more choice for the proof of a goal no failure is raised automatically. Instead the knowledge is considered to be incomplete and an incomplete knowledge handler is invoked which performs the appropriate (system or user defined) actions.

CSO-Prolog is extremely influenced by CS-Prolog. So, the process concept of CSO-Prolog is perfectly the same as the CS-Prolog one. That is, explicitly specified communicating sequential processes prove their goals in parallel as described in chapter one.

Unlike other object-oriented languages, in CSO-Prolog messages passed between objects and messages sent between processes are conceptually different. Process messages are used for communication and synchronization of the parallel processes (see above). Object messages are responsible for the activation of object methods for goal proofs (see below).

20.3.1 Objects, methods and object message

In CSO-Prolog an object is a self contained entity which has an own, private database with Prolog style predicates (rules, facts). Rules and facts with the same functor (predicate name, arity) constitute the methods which characterize the objects behaviour. Passing a object message m(X,p) to an object o results in the invocation of the method m/2 out of the objects database. In Prolog terms that sentence reads like this: Passing a goal m(X,p) with all its matching rules and facts.

The methods of an object are applied only if the appropriate object messages are passed to the object and the object permits the application of this method via its external interface.

If the source and destination object of an object message are located on different processors system process messages are exchanged for managing the necessary communication.

20.3.2 Module, interface and permissions

Modularization (encapsulation, information hiding) requires strict external interfaces of the objects. In CSO-Prolog modules are implemented as objects which break the program into pieces. The external interface of these objects is strictly defined by permissions specifying the messages to be accepted and handled by methods of an object. Additionally, permissions fix the kind of transfer to be applied (inheritance, delegation). By means of permissions modules take full control of the usage of its methods from outside.

20.3.3   Superclass, subclasses, inheritance and relations

Object-oriented languages ensure reusability and extensibility by providing concepts to define new objects that are just like an old one except for a few minor differences. The new classes are the subclasses; the old one is the superclass. Objects are subclasses of the superclass. The subclasses have all the properties of the superclass. This is called inheritance. However, the subclasses can add new methods and instance variables (below) of their own.

In CSO-Prolog the superclass object gives inheritance permission for the methods which may be inherited by the subclasses. The subclasses, in turn, declare to be in relation to the superclass by self-defined relation specifications. Multiple relations may be defined with different taxonomies.

20.3.4   Class and instances

A system will often contain many similar objects. A description of the common object is provided in a class definition; individual objects are known as instances of the class. Some features of the individual objects differ from instance to instance and may change dynamically. These are called instance variables.

In CSO-Prolog classes and their instances are implemented as object, too. By means of instantiation permissions the class objects declares the instance variable predicates. On the other hand it provides the common rules (methods) for accessing them. The instance objects, however, provide static or dynamic definitions of the instance variable clauses. Inheritance of class methods enforces the correct usage of the appropriate individual instance variables.

20.3.5   Incomplete knowledge and open world assumption

The CSO-Prolog theorem prover implements the concepts of incomplete knowledge and open world by the following inference strategy: Suppose a goal (object message) g is passed to an object o for proving.

Before the proof of the goal is tired it is checked, if the object accepts g by giving a permission. If there is no such permission (and no-one can be inherited) the incomplete knowledge handler is invoked. Otherwise the following choices are exhausted in sequence until the proof succeeds (possibly during backtracking) or there is no more choice. In the latter case the incomplete knowledge handler is invoked too.

1. (instantiation) If the object specified instantiation permission the object message is schedule to the appropriate instance object of the class object a.

2. (local reasoning) If the object specified inheritance permission the goal is tried to be proven with the local, private database of object a.

3. (inheritance) If the object a is in relation with another object i.e. if it is a subclass of a superclass object, the object message is passed to the superclass.

Accepting an object message from a subclass as well as passing an object message to a superclass or instance implement the open world assumption. Incomplete knowledge leads to the invocation of the incomplete knowledge handler which simply raises a failure (that way initiating backtracking), or aborts with an error message, or follows some user defined strategy, respectively.

20.4 DISTRIBUTED CONTROL MECHANISM

The control mechanism of sequential Prolog systems are based on the LRDF control strategy that assures systematic travel through the whole Search Tree of Prolog programs. Similarly, we would like to define a distributed LRDF strategy assuring the systematic search for CS-Prolog programs.

20.4.1 Distributed forward execution

The basic control mechanism of CS-Prolog is identical with the LRDF strategy of sequential Prolog systems. The difference appears when the interpreter reaches a so-called communication point, which is a CS-Prolog built-in predicate effecting the execution of other Prolog processes. Two type of communication points are available in CS-Prolog:

- new: creating a new process

- send: sending a message to other processes

In both cases the execution of the caller process continues without delay and, as a result of these procedures, parallel processes can start or resume on other PEs.

20.4.2   Distributed backtracking

A major problem with the implementation of CS-Prolog (and of any distributed Prolog languages) is how to ensure the backtracking facility in a distributed environment. The main difference between the distributed foreward and the distributed backtracking is in their parallelism. While the former is parallel in nature, the latter is sequential. Distributed backtracking is done **sequentially,** controlled by one of the PEs until a new alternative ensuring the **parallel** reactivation of the other processes can be found by the process executing the distributed backtracking.

In CS-Prolog two kinds of backtracking are distinguished:

1. local backtracking

2. global backtracking

Backtracking between two communication points is called local and has no direct effect on the behaviour of other processes. Backtracking passing a communication point is called global since it can alter the behaviour of other processes. Similarly we can distinguish two kinds of choice points:

1. normal choice point

2. communication choice point

The normal choice point represents untried alternative clauses in a predicate. Communication choice points are created when wait_for_dnd procedures are executed.

According to the origin of the backtracking on a given PE again two kinds of backtracking can be distinguished:

1. failure backtracking

2. deadlock backtracking

Failure backtracking occurs when a process failed. Deadlock backtracking is needed when the system reaches a point where each Prolog process is either in a finished state or waiting for a message and there is no transient message in the multiPE network. This situation is called global deadlock. In global deadlock one process is chosen (called forced process) for executing deadlock backtracking while the others are waiting for reactivization by the forced process.

The main difference between the failure backtracking execution and the deadlock backtracking is in their parallelism. While the former is parallel in nature, the latter is sequential. Many processes can execute failure backtracking in parallel while others are going forward. Deadlock in parallel is done sequentially, controlled by one of the processes until it finds a new alternative ensuring the parallel reactivation of the other processes. Deadlock backtracking is sequential because it ensures systematic search of the possible combinations of messages.

Based on the introduced notions the algorithm of the distributed backtracking is as follows:

1. If during failure backtracking a process passes a communication point, an anti-message is sent to the receiver processes or to the created process causing forced backtracking for the processes. The backtracking of the original process continues to its last choice point.

2. If during failure backtracking a process arrives to a communication choice point then

    if

        there are further matching messages for the process
    then
        the next message is selected and the process goes
    into state
        running forward
    else
        the process becomes waiting on the communication choice
    point.

3. If during deadlock backtracking the forced process passes a communication point, forces the receiver or created process to become the new forced process and to execute the deadlock backtracking.

4. If during deadlock backtracking the forced process arrives to a communication choice point, then

if

there are further matching messages for the process
then

the next message is selected and the process goes
into state

running forward and reactivates the other processes
else

the process passes the communication choice point
and

continues the deadlock backtracking.

20.5 DISTRIBUTED IMPLEMENTATION OF CS-PROLOG

The distributed implementation of the CS-Prolog system is folded into 4 layers on each transputer:

- Communication Subsystem Layer (CSL)

- Communication Control Layer (CCL)

- Prolog Control Layer (PCL)

- Prolog Interpreter Layer (PIL)

The connection of the layers and their mapping on the transputers are shown in Fig. 20.1. Since the uniprocessor version of CS-Prolog was written in Parallel C. For describing the main activities on the PEs we use the task/thread concepts of Parallel C[2]. For each transputer the CCL, PCL and PIL layers are packed in one task while the CSL placed in a separate task. The Root transputer contains a special Host Interface Task consisting of CCL, PCL and an Host Interface Layer.

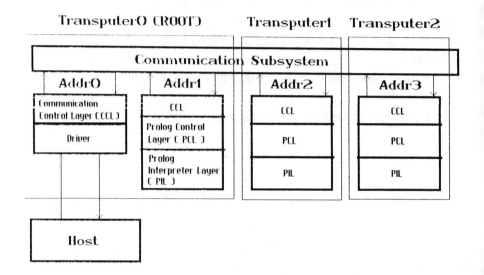

Figure 20.1 Overall system overview.

20.5.1 Communication Subsystem Layer (CSL)

CSL is the nearest layer to the physical hardware and responsible for hiding the physical topology of the transputer network. It realizes a logical network topology defined by the user and stored in the Topology Description Table.

CSL assures the following features of the intertransputer communication:

1. Messages can be of unlimited size but should be composed from packages with maximum size of 256 bytes.

2. The order of packages belonging to the same message does not change during the communication.

3. Packages are guaranteed to arrive to the target transputer except for the case of hardware error.

4. No communication deadlock can arise in the network.

20.5.2 Communication Control Layer (CCL)

The main tasks of CCL are as follows:

1. segmenting and reassembling of messages

2. broadcasting

3. Prolog level deadlock detection

The detailed description of these tasks are as follows:

1. CCL receives CS-Prolog messages from the Prolog Control Layer, disintegrates them into packages shorter than 256 bytes and sends them to the CSL. CCL receives messages from CSL and processes them based on their types. CCL generates and sends ACK (acknowledgment) messages for the CS-Prolog messages.

2. Broadcast messages are spread in the network via a broadcast tree starting at the Root transputer. The organization of the broadcast tree is done in CCL.

3. CCL receives and handles DEADLOCK TOKEN messages and detects global Prolog deadlock. For detecting deadlock the nodes are organized in a ring realized by CCL.

The work of CCL is as follows:

Outgoing CS-Prolog messages are taken from the Message Out Queue (MOQ) and passed to CSL by the Message Transmitter (MT) thread. Incoming messages from CSL are put into the Message In Queue (MIQ) by the Receiver (R) thread. The Receiver also generates and ACK message for the incoming messages and places them into Acknowledge Queue (AQ). The Acknowledge Transmitter (AT) thread takes the ACK messages from AQ and passes them to CSL. There are special broadcast type CS-Prolog messages. These are sent by the Broadcast Transmitter (BT) thread.

The ACK and DEADLOCK TOKEN messages are generated and processed in the CCL. The main reason for introducing the CCL was to detect the global Prolog deadlock as it is described in section 20.3. The Deadlock Detection (DD) thread is responsible for detecting local and global deadlock. In order to assist DD in determining the local deadlock state of the node the interpreter sets a Deadlock State Flag whenever it can not find any Prolog process to run.

The basic threads and data structures of CCL are shown in Fig. 20.2.

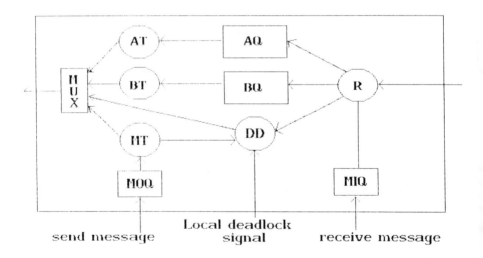

Figure 20.2 The structure of the Communication Control Layer.

20.5.3 Prolog Control Layer (PCL)

The task of PCL is to organize the work of the Prolog interpreters running on different processors into an integrated system resolving the initial goal statement of CS-Prolog. The simplified structure of PCL is shown in Fig. 20.3 where circles represent threads and rectangulars are the data structures.

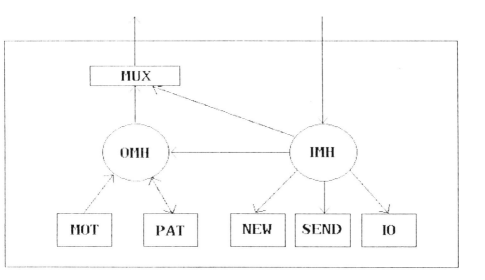

Figure 20.3 The structure of the Prolog Control Layer.

The main task of PCL are as follows:

- PCL has to administrate the process allocation on transputers. For this purpose the so-called Process Allocation Table (PAT) contains pairs of process names and their associated transputers where they were created. Whenever a message is sent to a Prolog process running on a different transputer it is the task of the Output Message Handler (OMH) to determine where to actually send the message.

- Based on the type of the incoming messages the Input Message Handler (IMH) thread places them in one of the Message Input Tables (MIT) or sets one of the State Vector Flags.

20.5.4   Prolog Interpreter Layer (PIL)

PIL realizes the distributed backtracking algorithm and contains the Prolog interpreter and the Prolog data structures. PIL also realizes the Process Level and Monoputer Level Scheduling [7]. The interpreter and scheduler basically work within the PIL, they call the underlying layers only in the following cases:

- creating a process by the new built-in predicate
- sending a message to a process running on another transputer
- executing IO built-in predicate
- detecting local deadlock

     PIL always generates CS-Prolog type messages and places them in the Message Out Table (MOT) of PCL.

20.6 CONCLUSION

CS-Prolog is a parallel extension of Prolog defined for implementing Prolog on transputers. CS-Prolog makes it possible to exploit coarse-grain parallelism in Prolog environment by defining processes for resolving different goals in a cooperative way. Furthermore the multi-window trace facility of CS-Prolog systems makes the developing process of parallel algorithms convenient and effective.

Besides other applications, CS-Prolog can be extended by objects and used as an object-oriented language called CSO-Prolog. This language gives the possibility to use object-oriented facilities for knowledge representation.

The distributed implementation of CS-Prolog is radically different from other proposed parallel implementations of logic programming languages. This is a parallel Prolog language which contains the distributed version of the original backtracking mechanism of Prolog. The distributed CS-Prolog interpreter is available since June 1989 and the compiled version is expected by the end of October 1989.

REFERENCES

1. INMOS Limited, *Occam 2 Reference Manual, Prentice Hall,* (1988).

2. 3L Parallel C User's Manual, (1988).

3. Hoare, C.A R., (1985) Communicating Sequential Processes, Prentice Hall.

4. Clark, K.L. and Gregory, S., (1984) *PARLOG Parallel Programming in Logic,* Research Report DOC84/4, Dept of Computing, Imperial College, University of London.

5. Shapiro, E.Y., (1983) *A Subset of Concurrent Prolog and its Interpreter,* Technical Report TR003, Inst. for New Generation Computer Technology, Tokyo.

6. Ueda, K., (1986) Guarded Horn Clauses, *Lecture Notes in Computer Science,* Springer-Verlag, Berlin, Heidelberg.

7. Futo, I. and Kacsuk, P., (1989) CS-Prolog on Multi-Transputer Systems. *Microprocessors and Microsystems,* Special Issue on Applying the Transputer 1, 13, 2, March 1989.

8. Periera, L.M. *et al.* (1986) Delta Prolog: A Distributed Backtracking Extension with Events, *Proc. of the 3rd Int. Conf. on Logic Prog.,* London.

9. Futo, I., (1988a) Some New Trends in PROLOG Developments and Applications in Hungary. *J. of New Generation Computing Syst.,* 1, 2.

10. Futo, I., (1988b) Distributed Simulation on Prolog Basis, *Proc. of the SCS Multiconf. on Distributed Simulation,* San Diego.

11. Hoare, C.A.R., (1978) Communicating sequential processes, *Comm. ACM,* 21, 8.

12. Futo, I., Kacsuk, P. and Wiederanders, (1988c) CS-PROLOG: A distributed simulation language for multi-transputers. *IFIP WG 10.1 Workshop on Concepts and Characteristics of Declarative Systems,* Budapest, Hungary.

FURTHER READING

1.   Clocksin, W.F. and Mellish, C.S., (1981) *Programming in Prolog,* Springer-Verlag, Berlin, Heidelberg.

2.   Special Issue on Open Systems Interconnection. *Proc. IEEE,* 71, 12, December 1983.

Appendix

```
 1:  %-------------------------------------------------%
 2:  %  Quicksort parallel version in CS-Prolog        %
 3:  %-------------------------------------------------%
 4:
 5:  problem( N ) :-
 6:     init_transputer_manager( N ),
 7:     init_id_manager,
 8:     get_list( List ),
 9:     quicksort_p( List, Sorted, N ),
10:     write( Sorted ), nl,
11:     send( id_mess( end, _ ), [id_manager] ).
12:
13:  %-------------------------!
14:  %  the list to be sorted   !
15:
16:  get_list( [ 11,5,12,2,14,9,13,4,15,7,6,3,8,1 ] ).
17:
18:  %-------------------------!
19:  %  the quicksort algorithm !
20:  %-------------------------!
21:
22:  quicksort_p( [], [], _ ).
23:  quicksort_p( [X | Tail], Sorted, 1 ) :-
24:     split( X, Tail, Small, Big),
25:     quicksort_p( Small, SortedSmall, 1 ),
26:     quicksort_p( Big, SortedBig, 1 ),
27:     conc( SortedSmall, [X | SortedBig], Sorted).
28:  quicksort_p( [X | Tail], Sorted, N ) :-
29:     split( X, Tail, Small, Big),
30:     M is N - 1,
31:     solve_parallel( [
32:        subgoal(quicksort_p( Small, SortedSmall, M),_,_,
33:        subgoal(quicksort_p( Big, SortedBig, M),_,_,_)
34:     ] ),
35:     conc( SortedSmall, [X | SortedBig], Sorted).
36:
37:  split( X, [], [], [] ).
38:  split( X, [Y | Tail], [Y | Small], Big) :-
39:     X > Y , !,
40:     split( X, Tail, Small, Big).
41:  split( X, [Y | Tail], Small, [Y | Big] ) :-
42:     split( X, Tail, Small, Big).
43:
44:  conc( [], L, L).
45:  conc( [X | L1], L2, [X | L3] ) :-
46:     conc( L1, L2, L3).
47:
48:  %---------------------------!
49:  %  transputer_manager process !
50:  %---------------------------!
51:
52:  init_transputer_manager( 1 ).
53:  init_transputer_manager( N ) :-
54:     get_free_transputers( N, TrList ),
55:     new( tr_manager( TrList ), tr_manager ).
56:
57:  tr_manager( [] ).
58:  tr_manager( [Tr | TrList] ) :-
```

```
59:     wait_for( mess(request, Sender) ),
60:     send( tr_id(Tr), [Sender]),
61:     tr_manager( TrList ).
62:
63: get_free_transputers( 2, [2,3] ).
64: get_free_transputers( 3, [2,3,4,5,6,7] ).
65: get_free_transputers( 4, [2,3,4,5,6,7,8,9,10,11,12,13,14,15] ).
66:
67: %----------------------------!
68: % process_id_manager process !
69: %----------------------------!
70:
71: init_id_manager :-
72:     new( id_manager( 0 ), id_manager ).
73:
74: id_manager( N ) :-
75:     wait_for( id_mess( Mess, Sender) ),
76:     id_response( Mess, Sender, N ).
77:
78: id_response( request, Sender, N ) :- !,
79:     send ( pr_id( N ), [Sender]),
80:     M is N + 1,
81:     id_manager( M ).
82: id_response( end, _, _ ).
83:
84: %-----------------------------------------------%
85: % Realization of AND-parallelism                %
86: %-----------------------------------------------%
87:
88: solve_parallel( [] ) :- !.
89: solve_parallel( [subgoal(Hgoal,Hname,Hstart_time,Hend_time) !
Tail] ) :-
90:     active_process( AP ),
91:     get_tr_id( Tr, AP ),
92:     get_pr_id( ID, AP ),
93:     assert_clause( saved( Hgoal, ID ) ),
94:     new( execute( Hgoal, AP, ID ), Hname, Tr, Hstart_time,
Hend_time ),
95:     solve_parallel( Tail ),
96:     wait_for( result( R, Rgoal, ID ) ),
97:     eq( R, succeeded ),
98:     find_clause( saved( Hgoal, ID ), N ),
99:     suppress_clause( saved, N ),
100:    eq( Hgoal, Rgoal ).
101:
102: execute( X, Parent, ID ) :-
103:     X, send( result( succeeded, X, ID ), [Parent] ).
104: execute( _, Parent, ID ) :-
105:     send( result( failed, _, ID ), [Parent] ).
106:
107: get_pr_id( ID, AP ) :-
108:     send( id_mess(request, AP), [id_manager] ),
109:     wait_for( pr_id( ID ) ).
110:
111: get_tr_id( Tr, AP ) :-
112:     send( mess(request, AP), [tr_manager] ),
113:     wait_for( tr_id( Tr ) ).
```

21 Writing parallel programs in non-parallel languages

M. Cole

Computing Science Department, Glasgow University

21.1 INTRODUCTION

Scalable MIMD computer architectures can be coarsely divided into two categories, according to the communications network structure. In a direct network there are point-to-point connections between certain system elements (processors, memories or processor-memory modules), with communications between elements which are not directly connected being forwarded by other intermediate elements. Typical examples include machines with processor-memory pairs located at the vertices of binary hypercubes or two dimensional meshes. With an indirect network, system elements take no part in the management of communication. Instead, messages are passed into some switching network (e.g. a butterfly) which handles all routing. Typically, communication time between any pair of elements is identical (but is an increasing function of machine size). We concern ourselves with the programming of direct network architectures, since these admit the possibility of describing algorithms in which total communication time can be kept independent of machine size, provided that a problem distribution can be devised which only requires communication between immediate neighbours.

21.2 PROGRAMMING DIRECT NETWORK ARCHITECTURES

At the lowest level, writing programs for direct network architectures requires the description of processes to be run at each node of the network together with an initial distribution of data across the memories. Any nontrivial application will require data to be transferred between adjacent nodes, and languages such as Occam are designed with this non-shared memory, message passing style in mind.

Other systems augment standard sequential languages with various message passing primitives. While this degree of control can lead to very fast programs, the responsibility for generating, distributing and controlling parallelism lies entirely with the programmer. Therefore, since the structure of a good solution may not be immediately apparent, there is considerable interest in the design and implementation of programming abstractions which allow programs to be written in a less architecture dependent way, while still achieving a reasonably localized exploitation of the underlying network.

Two closely related approaches tackle this problem by providing the programmer with the illusion of either a complete communications network (i.e. point-to-point communications between every pair of elements) or some form of globally shared memory. In the Occam world, instances of the former are often referred to as harnesses (e.g. the TINY communications harness [3] and the widely used task farm harness [7]). Communication of messages between processes that are not located on physically adjacent processors is handled invisibly by the harness code, with the task farm harness also handling task distribution for a simple class of programs. The simulation of shared memory has been the subject of extensive study both in theory [2] and in practice, where the Linda programming model [1], already implemented on a wide range of architectures, provides an interesting set of primitives on its globally shared tuple space. While abstracting away from details of the physical network, both styles of programming still require explicit indication of the sources of parallelism within a program.

At a much higher level of abstraction there is considerable interest in the use of declarative programming languages, in which there is no explicit flow of control, as sources of parallelism. For example, in a functional program implemented by graph reduction there may be many places in the graph at which computation may proceed at any point in time [13]. Functional language semantics allow these to be exploited safely and independently. The challenge to the implementor is to arrange for this work to be identified and distributed efficiently. Of course, in divorcing the programmer entirely from responsibility for the creation of parallelism, it becomes possible to write programs which, because of data dependencies, are inherently sequential.

In this paper, we introduce an approach which lies somewhere between the methods outlined above, in which we borrow the notion of harness from the lower level and the use of implicit parallelism from the declarative style. The result is a system in which the actual programming abstraction is devoid of explicit parallelism, but in which the program structures from which it will be derived are very close to the surface.

21.3 ALGORITHMIC SKELETONS

The term algorithmic skeleton was introduced [4] to describe an extension to the existing notion of harness in parallel software systems. Each skeleton describes the essential structure of a particular class of algorithms and can be represented at the programming level in one of two styles. A sequential imperative formulation describes the skeleton as a conventional program fragment with a small number of procedure bodies left undefined. Alternatively, a purely functional approach describes each skeleton as a higher order function, which can be applied as required to appropriate argument functions.

A widely used example of this approach is the divide and conquer paradigm in which the problem specific procedures or functions describe the test for a primitive problem, the partitioning method for non-primitive problems, the solution of primitive problems, and the combination of sub-solutions. Note that either imperatively or declaratively, the presentation is devoid of explicit parallelism (although in this instance its source is not hard to see). Instead, each skeleton has an associated parallel implementation, which handles parallel task creation and distribution invisibly. The implementation has only to guarantee to produce the same results as the sequential or functional specification. Each instance of the problem specific procedures or functions added by the programmer will be executed sequentially on some processor, with no attempt being made to detect and exploit any potential internal parallelism.

The divide and conquer approach has been extensively studied [8, 11, 12, 14]. In its loosest form, it requires considerable effort in dynamic scheduling to tackle unpredictable task tree evolution. A similar freedom is present in the use of algorithm motifs [6].

In the approach considered here, it is felt desirable to restrict the computational structure of each skeleton to the extent that a successful scheduling strategy can be statically pre-determined and built into the implementation harness. For example, our own formulation of divide and conquer [4] assumes that the partitioning process will produce a balanced, uniform degree task tree (with the degree being one of the problem specific parameters, supplied by the programmer).

This decision seems important if we are to successfully distribute across large sparsely connected direct networks (such as the two-dimensional grids considered in [4]). It represents a mid-point in the trade-off between ease of successful implementation and flexibility at the programming level. To give a flavour of the approach we now sketch the specification and implementation of another skeleton.

21.3.1   The iterative combination skeleton

The iterative combination skeleton captures the structural behaviour of algorithms which progressively coalesce an initially uncoordinated collection of data objects. An instance of such a problem is described by a set of homogeneous objects, including details of any relevant internal structure of each and of any relationships existing between them. Given a rule for combining or in some way relating two objects, and a measure of the value of such a combination, the algorithm iterates through a loop in which each object is combined with the most suitable remaining other object, if such exists. The loop is repeated until either all objects have been combined into one (i.e. the complete required structure has been imposed), or no further acceptable combinations exist. Imperatively, this behaviour may be informally expressed as illustrated in Fig. 21.1 (where S denotes the evolving set of objects).

> WHILE $|S| < > 1$ AND NOT failure to find any combinations DO BEGIN
>   FOR each s in S
>   find s' in S such that s' is the best partner for s
>   by considering all possible partners;
>   combine best partners to reduce $|S|$
> END

Figure 21.1 Sequential imperative formulation.

To produce a program for a specific problem, the programmer must provide details of the type of objects in S, the technique by which descriptions of two such objects may be combined and a measure of the value of such a combination to the overall solution (so that the best partner for each object can be identified). Sollin's minimum spanning tree algorithm [15] has this structure. The basic objects are spanning trees of portions of the graph (initially single vertices), two such trees are combined by including their shortest commonly adjacent edge, and the best partner for a tree (at some iteration) is that other tree to which it may be connected by the shortest such edge.

The parallel implementation proposed in [4] is for a mesh direct network architecture, but could be adapted (with greater or lesser efficiency) for any network which supports a variety of sizes of ring. Each iteration of the outer loop in the sequential specification is implemented by a sequence of parallel phases. Reorganization between iterations involves redistributing data to exploit the reduced problem size more effectively, with remaining objects being distributed one per processor in a ring of appropriate length.

The aim of the first phase of each iteration is to find the best partner for each object. Each processor becomes the home of one object for which it will determine the best partner. To do this, it must consider combinations of its own object with every other remaining object. We would like this work to proceed in parallel for all objects. Clearly the choice of best partner will be independent of of the order in which possible partners are considered. Therefore, if every processor considers the other objects in a different order, it should be possible to arrange that no two homes are considering the same possible partner simultaneously (in other words, at every parallel step the homes consider a different permutation of possible partners). This can be neatly achieved on the ring by introducing a second copy of each object, initialized by the home processor before each iteration. These copies are passed round the ring synchronously. Upon receiving a new visitor, each home must decide whether it is a better partner for its own object than the best seen so far. Thus, in one iteration (involving n objects on a ring of n processors) each processor executes the code shown in Fig. 21.2.

```
copy home.object into old.visitor;
for i := 1 to n-1 do
begin
        parallel begin
                pass old.visitor to next processor
                get new.visitor from previous processor
        parallel end;
        if new.visitor is the best possible partner so far
        then note its identifier and details;
        old.visitor := new.visitor
end
```

Figure 21.2 Code for first phase.

Since all communications are local, and since n tests for best partnership proceed simultaneously, we would expect to be able to perform an iteration in the time needed to perform only $O(n)$ tests sequentially, an $O(n)$ fold improvement on the obvious sequential implementation. For a real machine, with a fixed number of processors p, we can achieve an $O(p)$ fold improvement for $p < = n$ by distributing homes evenly between processors.

The second phase merges together the selected best partner groups. The algorithm presented in [4] achieves this with a further ring-based scheme, in which object copies visit all home processors, accumulating partners as they go.

Finally, since the second phase produces several copies of every new object, each residing in a different home processor, the implementation arranges that only one such copy is retained for the next iteration.

Returning to the programmer's level, the behaviour of the skeleton can be equally well presented as a higher order function in a functional language. Problem specific programs are generated by calling this with programmer defined functions as parameters. The program fragment in Fig. 21.3 gives the flavour of this approach (a full presentation can be found in [5]).

```
ic combine value accept xs
    = until finished iteration xs
        where iteration = unlabel.onestep.label
            onestep xs
                = (dropdoubles . mergepartners . findpartners) xs
    until p f x = x,        if p x
                = until p f (f x), otherwise
```

Figure 21.3 The functional formulation.

The first three lines define the top level ic (for iterative combination) higher order function. Its first three arguments are the functions which describe object combination, combination valuation, and comparison of valuations. These will be supplied by the programmer and used in the bodies of findpartners and mergepartners. The final parameter is the object set. The function until is a straightforward conditional loop control structure, while label and unlabel add and remove unique object identifiers (for internal use only). The real work of an iteration is done by onestep, where the sequence of three phases is clearly apparent.

Readers unfamiliar with the functional style may find it helpful to note that application of a function composition f.g to some argument x, means apply f to the result of applying g to x. Thus, in a sequence of compositions, the leftmost function is applied last.

21.4 COMBINING SKELETONS IN A FUNCTIONAL FRAMEWORK

As presented in the previous section, the technique of generating parallel programs by specialization of generic skeletons is a little disjointed. The implementation of each skeleton is considered in isolation and for any particular program, the skeleton chosen to provide top-level structure also describes all the parallelism which will actually be exploited. In a more integrated framework, it would seem desirable to be able to use various skeletons freely within the same program, thereby providing more scope for parallelism. Of course, the appropriate integration of corresponding implementations would then become a significant task.

With such flexibility in mind, it seems that functional style of presentation offers the more natural foundation. In a general context, the suitability of functional languages for the production of well-structured, modular software has been convincingly presented by Hughes [9]. We have already noted the natural correspondence between higher order functions and the generic behaviour of parallel phases. Kelly's language Caliban [10] has been designed to exploit this property, differing from our own approach in providing the programmer with the option of controlling parallel structure explicitly. Meanwhile, examination of explicitly parallel algorithms for directly connected architectures often reveals a problem solving style in which the whole computation is decomposed into a sequence of phases, each highly parallel but with different communication patterns (rather like a temporal sequence of spatially superimposed systolic algorithms). A similarly pleasing correspondence is apparent between the sequencing of such phases, with the implicit passage of data from one to the next, and the use of functional composition.

Our current work aims to exploit these features in a functional programming system in which higher order functions with underlying parallel implementations may be used freely in programs. It will be the compiler's duty to decide which should be exploited and which left to execute in the conventional sequential way. Such decisions will vary from program to program, depending upon the context in which the recognised functions appear and upon the source of expanding problem size in the raw data (which will be suggested by the programmer). While an optimal solution of this problem seems likely to prove intractable in general, we hope that reasonable results will be obtainable for many realistic programs. Thus, while using a pure functional language, the programmer will become aware of the programming style (use of certain higher order functions and their composition) which can be exploited by the underlying parallel system.

REFERENCES

1   Ahuja, S. Carriero, N.J. Gelernter, D.H. and Krishnaswamy, V. (1988) Matching Language and Hardware for Parallel Computation in the Linda Machine. *IEEE Trans. Comput.,* 37, 8, pp. 921-929.

2   Alt, H. Hagerup, T. Melhorn, K. and Preparata, F.P. (1987) Simulation of idealized parallel computers on more realistic ones. *SIAM J. of Computing,* 16, 5, pp.808-835.

3   Clarke, L. (1989) TINY: discussion and user guide. *Newsletter 7, Edinburgh Concurrent Supercomputer Project.*

4   Cole, M.I. (1989) *Algorithmic Skeletons: Structured Management of Parallel Computation.* Pitman and MIT Press.

5   Cole, M.I. (1990) *Towards Fully Local Multicomputer Implementations of Functional Programs.* Technical Report CSC 90/R7, Computing Science Dept, University of Glasgow.

6   Foster, I. and Stevens, R. (1990) *Parallel Programming with Algorithmic Motifs.* Preprint MCS-P124-0190, Argonne National Laboratory.

7   Hey, A.J.G. (1989) Experiments in MIMD Parallelism, in *Proc. of PARLE 89,* eds. E. Odijk, M. Rem and J.C. Syre, 2 LNCS 366, pp 28-42.

8   Horowitz, E. and Zorat, A. (1983) Divide-and-conquer for parallel processing. *IEEE Trans. on Comput.,* TC-32, 6, pp.582-585.

9   Hughes, R.J.M. (1989) Why Functional Programming Matters. *Computer J.* 32, 2, pp.98-107.

10   Kelly, P. (1989) *Functional Programming for Loosely Coupled Multiprocessors.* Pitman and MIT Press.

11   McBurney, D. L. and Sleep, M.R. (1987) Experiments with the ZAPP: Matrix Multiply on 32 Transputers, Heuristic Search on 12 Transputers. *School of Information Systems Internal Report SYS--C87--10,* University of East Anglia.

12   Peters, F.J. (1981) Tree Machines and Divide and Conquer Algorithms. *Proc. CONPAR 81, LNCS 111,* pp. 25-36. Springer Verlag.

13   Peyton-Jones, S.L. (1989) Parallel Implementations of Functional Programing Languages. *Computer J.* 32, 2, pp.175-186.

14   Rayward-Smith, V.J. and Clark, A.J. (1989) Scheduling Divide-and-Conquer Task Systems on Identical Parallel Machines. In *CONPAR 88,* (eds) C.R. Jesshope and K.D. Reinartz, pp.578-586. Cambridge University Press.

15   Sollin, M. (1977) An Algorithm attributed to Sollin. In *Introduction to the Design and Analysis of Algorithms.* (eds) S. Goodman and S. Hedetniemi,McGraw-Hill.

22 Programmer language compiler interactions

Oregon Graduate Institute of Science and Technology

Department of Computer Science and Engineering

22.1 THREE CAMPS

For many years users and researchers have discussed the best way to program parallel computers. Several different camps have emerged, each having large numbers of followers; here I divide the world into three such groups. Communication between the camps has often been at the level of challenges and insults, and few converts are made.

First is the *macho-compiler* camp. This camp believes that the best language for programming computers (any computer) is a sequential language, such as Fortran. Sequential languages have well-defined semantics, so they are deterministic, and are easy to learn. Programs can be debugged using a sequential machine without explicit support for simulating parallelism, and can generally be ported to a wide class of machines. Vectorizing compilers has been shown to be effective over the past 12 years, and compiler research over that time has found a large number of program transformations which can be applied automatically to optimize performance for a wide range of architectural features, such as multiple processors and memory hierarchies. In addition, there are many sequential programs already written, and sufficiently powerful compilers should be able to make these programs run in parallel without additional work by the user. Much of the research at Illinois, Rice and IBM Yorktown, USA is viewed as supporting this camp [AlK87,ABC88,KSC84].

Second and diametrically opposed is the *explicit parallelism* camp. This camp believes that parallel programs must be explicitly written with parallel syntax, or at least in a language that does not hide the parallelism. New languages with appropriate support for parallelism are required, and programs should be redesigned and rewritten with parallelism in mind. Each new language proposal is accompanied by an argument or testimonial stating it is easy and effective to learn and use. The parallel program can then be compiled and executed on appropriate parallel hardware without the need for implicit parallelism detection. This camp has been the hardest to support commercially, since those with the money to buy large parallel computers are loath to abandon their old programs, much as the US is loath to abandon the NTSC television standard in spite of its technical deficiencies. Many parallel computer companies start out touting their own special language, but the ones that survive usually end up supplying a parallel Fortran compiler. The eventual goal is to build a machine that will show once and for all the potential power of these languages, which will shut off the disbelievers. This camp includes work on functional or dataflow languages, such as SISAL and Id [ArE88,MSA85].

Third and perhaps in between the first two is the *CSP* (Communicating Sequential Processes) camp. This camp believes that parallel programs should be viewed as a set of processes or tasks, each of which is written in a sequential language. The tasks communicate using language extensions or subroutine libraries. Each task is written in a sequential language, so can be debugged using standard techniques. Moreover, this method matches software engineering practices of dividing a large program into smaller tasks, with the additional hook of letting the smaller tasks run in parallel. The language extensions are often prototyped using subroutine libraries or macro packages, making it easy to implement such a system; thus portability seems to be feasible. The work on Linda and LGDF fits into this camp [CaG88,DiB89].

22.2 CAMPFIRES

The arguments in favour of each camp are perhaps full of somewhat wishful thinking, but the arguments against are based more on experience. Many people argue that compilers, no matter how powerful, will never be sufficiently intelligent to detect all the parallelism in a program. Moreover, a sequential program often uses an algorithm that is inappropriate for parallel computation, and certainly wholesale algorithm replacement is out of reach of compilers. If this is true, then many programs will likely have to be rewritten anyway, so they should be rewritten in the most natural, portable, parallel fashion possible (my language, whoever I am). These arguments are hard to refute; there are many programs in which compilers fail to detect critical parallelism, no matter how powerful the compiler optimization algorithms.

Totally new languages are also hard for many people to swallow. They involve a whole new learning curve, including a long period when the programs are not very portable (due simply to lack of compilers). One early argument in favour of parallel languages was that they would obviate the need for fancy compilers, since the parallelism would be explicit. That argument is no longer generally held valid, since compilation of parallel or functional languages needs deep optimization, essentially equivalent in scope to automatic vectorization, to reduce the memory requirements of the running program.

CSP style programming also has problems in certain applications, if only because its style is inappropriate. When computing an array operation in parallel, the least natural thing to do is to write a program that will work on a single column of the computation. It is much easier to write and to understand a parallel loop construct, for instance. CSP also leaves the burden of managing the parallelism entirely on the programmer. For large scale data parallelism, CSP is the wrong formalism. In addition, the Linda and LGDF systems used today need global information in the compiler in order to generate code and schedule operations.

In summary, each camp has advocates and critics, but there is a great deal of similarity between the camps. In all three cases, programmers will have to rewrite (all or much) of their programs, either translating to a new language or changing code to allow the compiler to detect the parallelism. Also, in all three cases, a powerful compiler is needed to either detect, restrict or optimize the parallelism or communication. If we accept that rewriting programs is necessary (at least to some degree) and complex compilers are needed, the question is then what is the proper language and compiler on which to concentrate our efforts for future success in large scale parallel computation?

22.3 COMPILER CAPABILITIES

The requirements from the compiler depend critically on the language used and the target machine. Let us start by looking at how compilers can optimize code for parallelism, both where they have succeeded and failed in the past.

Automatic vectorization is certainly well-accepted as a method of writing programs to use vector instructions. In some sense, automatic vectorization is a success, since it does translate sequential code into vector code. Unfortunately, as has been pointed out so often, the compiler-generated code rarely achieves anything approaching peak rates. One reason is that the machines are sometimes limited by memory bandwidth (such as the Cray-1 and Cray-2), so even when running at vector speeds, the arithmetic units will not be busy if the operands are always fetched from memory. Thus the distinction between vector performance and supervector performance arose, where supervector performance is achieved when the program keeps the arithmetic units busy. Early compilers, which looked only at innermost loops, could not optimize for supervector performance; more recent compilers, which can vectorize outer loops, can take advantage of the vector register locality that can result in supervector performance [AlK84,Wol89c].

Many machines are now designed with memory hierarchies in the form of virtual memory, hardware managed cache memories, vector registers, and/or local memories. Programs with large data sets which are not optimized to take advantage of the memory hierarchy will run at the speed of the slowest level of the hierarchy. This is the architectural factor behind the design of the extended BLAS (BLAS-2 and BLAS-3). Many of the manual optimizations being used in the design of block algorithms can be automated [IrT88,Wol89b] (though compilers with these capabilities have not yet been developed).

The advent of standard parallel syntax will (perhaps surprisingly) *increase* the need for sophisticated compiler optimizations. For instance, the following loop:

$$\begin{aligned}
&\text{do 10 I = 1, N}\\
&\quad A(I) = B(I) + C(I)\\
&\quad D(I) = A(I) + 1\\
&10 \qquad \text{continue}
\end{aligned}$$

can (and would) be vectorized for a Cray-like machine; even a simple-minded compiler could generate the following pseudo-machine code:

```
do I = 1, N, 64
    VL = MIN(64,N-I+1)
    vload B(I),1,v1
    vload C(I),1,v2
    vadd v1,v2,v3
    vsto v3,A(I),1
    vadd v3,s1,v4
    vsto v4,D(I),1
enddo
```

The loop can also be expressed using Fortran-90 array assignments as:

$$A(1:N) = B(1:N) + C(1:N)$$
$$D(1:N) = A(1:N) + 1$$

Several compilers already accept this syntax; however, a simple-minded compiler would generate the machine code:

```
do I        = 1, N, 64
    VL      = MIN(64,N-I+1)
    vload   B(I),1,v1
    vload   C(I),1,v2
    vadd    v1,v2,v3
    vsto    v3,A(I),1
enddo
do I        = 1, N, 64
    VL      = MIN(64,N-I+1)
    vload   A(I),1,v1
    vadd    v1,s1,v2
    vsto    v2,D(I),1
enddo
```

Not only is there twice as much serial loop overhead, but the array A is reloaded for the second statement, making more demands on memory bandwidth. In addition, because of the semantics of the array assignment, a programmer can write a statement that requires a temporary array that is as long as the trip count of the implied loop, such as:

$$A(1:N) = A(IP(1:N))$$

where IP is an unknown index array. Detecting when this temporary is not required or when two adjacent array assignments can be strip-mined together requires exactly the same kind of analysis used by vectorizing compilers. Note that this analysis will be required for optimization even on sequential computers.

Program transformation techniques have been scaled up (theoretically) to optimize programs for large parallel systems, even those with distributed memories [CaK88,RoP89,Wol89a]. The potential for automatic compiler optimization seems large. Yet many advanced optimizations, while well-documented and possibly using current technology, are not currently implemented in today's compilers. It is hard to argue that compilers will automatically solve tomorrow's problems when they do not even solve today's. Remember that all three camps depend to some extent on intelligent compilers. Let us retrospectively consider the lessons we have learned from more than a decade of experience with automatic vectorization.

22.4 LESSONS FROM VECTORIZATION

When Cray Research, Inc., introduced its supercomputers fifteen or so years ago, the only method using high-level languages to access the vector hardware was through automatic vectorization of serial loops in the Fortran compiler. Cray had decided that rather than defining new language extensions (as had Control Data with semicolons and Q8 calls for the STAR-100 and Cyber 205), they would stick to existing languages and make the compiler discover vector operations. The advantages for Cray were that the language was already defined, and they would not be stuck supporting their own syntax after some committee defined a standard vector language; the advantages to their users were that their programs retained a certain degree of portability, they didn't need to learn any new obscure extensions, and old programs might automatically take advantage of the vector hardware. How often, in fact, did a dusty deck program run efficiently using the vector hardware? Judging from the comments in papers at the time, it seems that users were not very impressed with automatic vectorization (judging from papers written today, it seems that users are still not very impressed).

In spite of all this, Cray has many satisfied customers who now happily (or unhappily) write Fortran programs which vectorize well. Moreover, all vendors of vector computers now supply vectorizing Fortran compilers, and vectorization of loops is the primary source of vector code for these machines. How is it that people are dealing with compilers today? Are compilers that much better in 1990 than they were in 1976? The answer is yes and no. Compiler technology is certainly much stronger than it was 15 years ago; for instance, most vectorizing compilers today include the ability to interchange loops, which cannot only uncover additional parallelism in nested loops but can also improve the performance of the machine by changing vector lengths, memory strides, register locality and so on.

It is not clear, however, that a substantial fraction of dusty deck (or even fresh deck) programs can be automatically optimized for vector execution using even the best compilers today. What is clear is that users can (with a little bit of work) achieve good performance on many programs. How do they do this? First, they look at the compiler listing to see what could be done automatically. When the compiler can't automatically vectorize a loop, it can usually identify the variable or construct that prevents analysis. A reasonably intelligent user can decide whether that variable or construct really prevents parallel execution, and can respond by changing the program or adding directives or assertions, clearing the way for parallel code generation. Sometimes, the algorithm is simply inappropriate for execution on the machine, and must be abandoned; even here, the process begins by trying to vectorize the original program.

Thus, vectorizing compilers employ a special type of interaction with their users. By generating optimization tables or vector diagnostics, they tell the user how successful they were in optimizing the program (imagine a Vax compiler telling you how successful it was in optimizing a loop). Moreover, due to the large potential benefit to be gained from having a critical loop running in vector mode, users pay attention to these diagnostics and are willing to respond to them by rewriting loops or adding directives. In addition, users become trained to write code for the particular compiler to which they are accustomed. Because the early Cray compilers did not vectorize loops containing IF statements, programmers at some US government labs (which made heavy use of Cray machines) stopped writing loops containing IF statements. This practice, of course, skewed any benchmark results about compiler effectiveness, since the benchmarks themselves became tainted by their history. However, over the past decade, programmers have become trained how to write programs that compilers will vectorize.

22.5 APPLYING THE LESSONS

I state without proof that automatic vectorization is successful in its primary goal: convenient access to vector hardware without sacrificing portability. I claim that the path to its success has not been primarily due to the inherent power of vectorizing compilers, but due to the feedback and training effect of those compilers. Compilers can perform a wide array of sophisticated program transformations to optimize execution for many different system architectural features. The number of possible transformations precludes exhaustive search of all possible ways to execute a program, so compilers must either have less ambitious goals or accept hints from a knowledgeable user [Wol88].

The key point is that programs need to be optimized for parallel execution, regardless of the language or target machine. The optimization phase includes both identification of the parallelism in the algorithm, and mapping the parallel program optimally onto the machine. In the best of all worlds, the identification phase could be done by a compiler (à la vectorization) or by a user (with parallel languages or Fortran extensions), and the mapping phase could be left to the compiler. In the present (and foreseeable future), optimal mapping will include too many combinatorial aspects to be performed fully automatically. However, if the system can collect predicted and actual performance results, the programmer can use this information to recast the program into a different form or suggest specific compiler optimizations that allow more effective mapping onto the target machine. A current example of this type of interaction is exemplified by the EAVE system [Bos88]. EAVE advises the user (for instance) when loops might be interchanged so the compiler can take advantage of register locality by vectorizing outer loops. As compilers get more sophisticated, the types of interactions with the user will be at a higher algorithmic level. For distributed memory computers, for instance, the distribution of data around the ensemble of processors will likely be left to the user [KMV87].

With larger parallel systems, the relative performance penalty for sequential execution is so great as to be unacceptable. Vectorizing compilers will (when vectorization fails) always generate correct (albeit slow) scalar code. In a large parallel environment, failure to generate parallel code will be so detrimental to performance that the user must be willing and able to study the problem and change the program if necessary.

In summary, I see future programming environments for large parallel systems tending towards a closer collaboration between interactive compiler tools and the user, independent of the language used. The compiler will attempt to optimize the program automatically, using ever more sophisticated techniques, but the quest for reasonable response time and the inability of compilers to replace inappropriate algorithms will require that the user get into the loop, responding to compiler feedback about the performance of his program.

REFERENCES

1. Allen, J. R. and Kennedy, K. (1984) Rice University automatic loop interchange *Proc. of the SIG PLAN 84 Symposium on Compiler Construction*, Montreal, Canada, pp.233-246 New York.

2. Allen, J. R. and Kennedy, K (1987) Rice Univ. Automatic translation of fortran programs to vector form ACM Trans. on *Prog. Lang. and Systems* 9, 4, 1, pp.491-542.

3. Allen, F. Burke, M. Charles, P. Cytron R. and Ferrante J. (1988) IBM An overview of the PTRAN analysis system for multiprocessing. *J. Parallel and Distributed Computing* 5, 5, 1, pp.617-640 Academic Press, San Deigo (October 1988 update of ICS 87 paper).

4. Arvind, and Ekanadham, K. (1988) MIT future scientific programming on parallel machines. *J. Parallel and Distributed Computing* 5, 5, 1, pp.460-493 Academic Press, San Deigo (October 1988 Update of ICS 87 paper).

5. Bose, P.(1988)   IBM interactive program improvement via EAVE: an expert adviser for vectorization. *Proc. of the 1988 International Conference on Supercomputing* 1, pp.119-130 ACM 1988 St. Malo, July 4-8 1988.

6. Callahan, D. and Kennedy, K. (1988) Rice Univ. Compiling programs for distributed-memory multiprocessors *J. Supercomputing* 2, 2, 1, pp.151-169 Kluwer Academic Publishers.

7. Carriero, N. and Gelernter, D. (1988) Applications experience with Linda. *Proc. of the ACM SIG PLAN PPEALS 1988:* Parallel Programming: Experience with Applications, Languages and Systems, 1, pp.173-187.

8.   DiNucci, D. C.and Babb II, R. G, (1989) OGC Practical Support for Parallel Programming. *Proc. 21st Hawaii Int. Conf. on System Sciences*, B Shriver, 1, II, 1, pp.109-118 IEEE Computer Society Press.

9. Irigoin, F. and Triolet, R. (1988) Ecole Nationale Supérieure des Mines de Paris. *Supernode Partitioning Conf.* Record of the 15th Annual ACM Symp. on

Principles of Programming Languages, 1, pp.319-329 1988 ACM Press, New York.

10. Koelbel, C. Mehrotra, P. and Van Rosendale Purdue, J. (1987) ICASE Semi-automatic Process Partitioning for Parallel Computation. *Int J. Parallel Programming* 16, 5, 1, pp.365-382.

11. Kuck, D. J. Sameh, A. H. Cytron, R. Veidenbaum, A. V. *ex al.* (1984) Univ. Illinois The effects of program restructuring, algorithm change, and architecture choice on program performance. *Proc. of the 1984 Int. Conf. on Parallel Processing* (ed) R M Keller 1, 1, pp.129-138 IEEE Computer Society Press.

12. McGraw, J. Skedzielewski, S. Allan, S. Oldehoeft, R. *ex al.* (1985) *LLNL and others SISAL: Streams and Iterations in a Single Assignment Language,* version 1.2 (R Tech. Rpt. M-146) Lawrence Livermore National Laboratory.

13. Rogers, A. and Pingali, K. (1989) Cornell Univ. Process Decomposition Through Locality of Reference. *Proc. SIG PLAN 89 Conf. on Programming Language Design and Implementation*, 1, pp.69-80.

14. Wolfe, M. Kuck and Associates, Inc. Vector optimization vs. vectorization, *J. Parallel and Distributed Computing*, 5, 5, 1, pp.551-567 Academic Press, San Deigo (Update of ICS 87 paper).

15. Wolfe, M. (1989a) *Oregon Graduate Center Loop Rotation*, Tech. Rpt. CS/E 89-004 Oregon Graduate Center.

16. Wolfe, M. (1989b) KAI iteration space tiling for memory hierarchies. *Parallel Processing for Scientific Computing*, (ed G Rodrigue) 1, 1, pp.357-361 Society for Industrial and Applied Mathematics, Philadelphia, PA.

17. Wolfe, M. (1989c) Oregon Graduate Center optimizing supercompilers for supercomputers research monographs, in *Parallel and Distributed Computing* Pitman Publishing, London.

23 Linda coordination language; subsystem kernel architecture (on transputers)*

S. Zenith

Yale University Department of Computer Science

23.1 INTRODUCTION

Linda provides a simple model for the expression of parallel programs using conventional languages. It's implementation in its C-Linda form is now in wide use in research establishments and industry. One of the key attractions of Linda is that it enables architecture independent, portable, parallel programs to be written.

Linda uses inputs and outputs which interact with a distributed global space (tuple space). Inputs provide a template against which the data available in the space is compared, and terminates when a match can be found (excepting predicate variants which are discussed later).

Analysis of Linda programs shows that it is very often not necessary to perform complex matching operations at runtime. This may come as a surprise to many who intuitively felt that tuple space was an expensive utility.

The transputer provides a uniquely simple component for the construction of parallel machines, and has proven to be a flexible and interesting system for research into the behaviour of distributed memory MIMD machines.

---

* The author retains copyright, this paper also appears as a Yale Research Report RR794. Funding for this work was provided in part by NSF grants CCR-8657615.

The transputer's flexibility also suits experimentation with machine systems architecture.

This paper presents a preliminary report of an effort underway at Yale University. The paper presents a novel approach to the architecture for a machine suited to the implementation of Linda.

23.2 THE SIMPLICITY OF LINDA

Linda is a simple paradigm for parallel processing based on the concept of generative communication , which unifies the concepts of process creation and communication. Linda was first described by David Gelernter Gel85 , and the first implementation is described by Nick Carriero Car87 .

The Linda language combines with some associate language (typically a conventional sequential language such as C, Ada, or Fortran) to form a language for the expression of parallel algorithms. The associate language provides the semantics of computation whilst Linda provides the semantics for concurrency and communication.

Linda is elegant and easy to understand, so the following is a concise, but complete description of the language.

23.2.1 Tuple space

Linda utilizes a concept known as tuple space. Tuple space is a global associative memory, which stores objects called tuples. A tuple consists of a sequence of typed fields, for example

$$(foo, 6, 23.5)$$

is a tuple which is a sequence of values; a string foo, an integer value 6, and a floating point value 23.5. It is distinct from the following tuples

$$(foo, 6, 23.5, 32.5)$$
$$(6, 23.5, foo)$$
$$(4, 5)$$

These are passive tuples i.e. passive data objects.

A tuple may also contain fields which are processes evaluated subsequent to entering tuple space. These are known as active tuples.

23.2.2 The Linda primitives

It may be easier at this stage to simply think of tuple space as a bag of objects. Linda provides four basic primitive operations which act upon tuple space:

out(t)   to put tuple t into tuple space
(i.e. to put an object into the bag).

in(t)   to get tuple t from tuple space
(i.e. to pick an object from the bag).

rd(t)   to read tuple t in tuple space
(i.e. to look at an object without removing it from the bag).

eval(t)   to evaluate tuple t
(i.e. put an object into the bag for evaluation).

out(t) and eval(t) place a tuple (t) into tuple space and then terminate.

in(t) removes some tuple t from tuple space and then terminates.

rd(t) reads the value of some tuple t and then terminates.

This definition naturally implies that if there is no tuple which initially matches t present in tuple space then the primitive **in** or **rd** will not terminate until it acquires a tuple t subsequently added to tuple space.

eval(t) acts like **out(t)** , except that t is evaluated subsequent to its entry to tuple space and will typically transform into a passive data tuple, for example

$$\text{eval } (P(), Q())$$

creates processes P() and Q() which are placed in tuple space and are evaluated concurrently. P() and Q() may themselves interact with tuple space, and leave results (as tuples) in tuple space. If P() and Q() are functions which return the integer values 6 and 7 respectively, then the active tuple (P(), Q()) will transform into the passive tuple (6, 7) . Thus is born the term generative communication .

Note that the current definition says nothing of the process model and the scoping of free variables (nor pointers) in evaled processes. In the current C-Linda implementation (developed jointly by Yale and Scientific Computing Associates) eval(P) amounts to a specialized fork of P.

23.2.3 Selecting tuples

Tuples have no physical or virtual address in tuple space. A tuple is selected by **in** or **rd** by associative matching .

Each field of a tuple may contain an actual or formal, for example, if N is a variable of integer type

$$(6, ?N)$$

contains a formal N and will match with any of the following tuples

$$(6, 7)$$
$$(6, 8)$$
$$(6, 1024)$$

The input in(6, ?N) will select a matching tuple from tuple space, and perform the actual to formal assignment. If several matching tuples exist in tuple space then an arbitrary selection is made.

Similarly, the output out(6, ?N) will place a tuple in tuple space, and may be selected by an input which has an actual of integer type in the place of the formal, e.g. in(?I, 11) or in(6, 23).

23.2.4 Predicate primitives

More recently Linda has acquired two variant forms of **in** and **rd**. These are the primitives **inp** and **rdp**, which are predicate functions which test for presence, for example

$$\text{if (inp(t)) found} = \text{true}$$

inp(t) attempts to remove some tuple t from tuple space and then terminates. **rdp(t)** attempts to read the value of some tuple t and then terminates. In both cases the predicate is true if the function succeeds in its attempt and is false otherwise.

In addition, the predicate functions have a side effect. That is, they will behave like their non-predicate equivalents if their result is true.

23.3 IS LINDA EFFICIENT?

The single most significant criticism levelled at Linda generally takes the form

> Yes, that's all very nice and elegant, but surely, it cannot possibly be implemented efficiently!

False intuition leads many to make this statement. But there is little evidence to support this intuition, in fact there is now much evidence available to support the counter contention that, indeed, not only can Linda be implemented efficiently, but that the paradigm itself allows the development of efficient algorithms GC88 . This is due in part to effective data distribution provided by tuple space, which reduces multiple copying of the same data, and in part to optimizations which can be performed on Linda operations.

Data distribution is a pre-occupation for the programmer in simple message passing models (such as Occam Occam), where the programmer is forced to consider, in some detail, multiplexing and routing issues when distributing data among groups of processes.

23.4 OPTIMIZING LINDA OPERATIONS

23.4.1 Division of tuple space into distinct subsets

A Linda program is analysed by the compiler and the tuple space operations are transformed into simpler operations which require little or no run-time matching.

Tuples can immediately be divided into sets based on their structure, that is, the number, type and order of their fields. We know that tuples of one type structure can never match a tuple of a differing structure. Therefore, inputs and outputs can be distinguished as operations on one of these sets. Further, these distinct sets can themselves be divided, by usage of formal and actual data.

Consider the tuple set of type

(STRING, INT, INT)

it's common in Linda programs to find that one or more of the fields in a tuple of this type structure is a common constant (a constant used in both inputs and outputs of the tuple). In which case, operations on the set of tuples of this structural type can be further divided. Let us assume that the analyser discovers that in all operations on tuples of this type structure the first field is some common constant. For example, assume these constants are the strings, foo and bar, the tuple set described can be further divided into the subsets

(foo, INT, INT)
(bar, INT, INT)

tuples of the first type structure distinguished by common constants. Again, since operations on one subset can never match a tuple effected by an operation on a tuple of the other subset we can focus tuple space operations on the relevant sets.

23.4.2 Implementation of distinct subsets

Let us further assume, for the purposes of illustration, that the types discussed in the previous section are the only types of tuples which appear in a Linda program. The inputs and outputs in the program can now be divided into operations upon these distinguished sets. Such that we now have two distinct sets of type

(INT, INT)

the constant fields can be discarded since their value is now represented by selection of one subset or the other.

Once analysis of the constants in a tuple is discerned, inspection of the usage of tuples on input and output enables a decision to be made about the method of implementation for each set.

In addition to position and type, each field in a tuple has a further characteristic we have yet to discuss. That is whether the field is an actual or formal (known as the polarity of the field). When matching the respective fields of an input with existent tuples there are four possible polarity combinations to consider

? both fields are actual
× both fields are formal
√ input field is actual and the respective field is formal
√ input field is formal and the respective field is actual

where ? indicates a comparison of the fields value must be made for equality, × indicates that a comparison of the fields always yields the value false, and √ indicates that a comparison of the fields always yields the value true.

To summarize, in the first case, where both fields are actual values, the fields match if their values are equal. In the second case, where both fields are formal, no match can be made. In the third case, where the input field is actual and the corresponding field is formal, a match is always made. In the final case, where the input field is a formal and the corresponding field is an actual, a match is always made, and provided all the component fields of the tuple match, an actual to formal assignment is required.

There are three possible usage patterns for our given example subset of tuple space, (INT, INT)

- the remaining two fields are formal;

- the remaining two fields are actual data;

- one field is formal, the other is actual.

Here we are not concerned with the values of the particular fields, since we have already established that there is no commonality (by constant).

If, by analysis of the inputs and outputs of tuples in the distinguished set, it can be seen that inputs of the set are always formal and outputs of the set are always actual, then it is clear that no run-time matching is required to satisfy an input, since corresponding fields will always match. We can implement such a set as a simple queue. In our example case, an output adds two integer values to a queue, an input removes or reads two integer values from a queue, and subsequently performs an actual to formal assignment.

If, however, analysis shows we are not so fortunate, but that one of the fields in the tuple is always actual, then that field provides a criteria which can be used to select a match at run-time, that is, a key which can be used to locate a matching tuple. In such cases, where a key is always provided, the set can be implemented as a hash table, which may be distributed. In fact, for efficiency, the implementation provides a single common hash table for such cases.

In our example case, let us say the first field is always actual on input and output, we can always use this field to select the correct hash slot for matching tuples. This leaves the last field to match, if this is a formal, the first value we find will do, and we can return this value for assignment.

More complex cases, may arise in analysis. Where every field is actual in every output tuple, but not so for every input tuple, a key is not always available. In such cases, it will be necessary at times to perform an exhaustive search of the set. To optimize such cases, such a set is implemented as a private hash table, that is, a single hash table for the distinct set. Distributing a hash table which may require exhaustive searching, raises coordination and consistency issues which in this implementation we choose to avoid by not distributing the table.

When no key is available we are compelled to perform an exhaustive search of the set. We could choose to implement a list and to exhaustively search the list for each input. However, in fact, such instances are rare, and occur only in some cases where formals appear in outputs. This usage of tuples is so idiosyncratic, and we have so rarely seen it, that no compiler has implemented the case.

There remain some special cases to consider. Conversely, to the first case considered, although bizarre, if it can be seen that outputs of the type structure are always formal and inputs of the type are always actual, then again it is clear that no run-time matching is required to satisfy an input, since corresponding fields will always match. Further, because no actual to formal assignment is required we simply need to keep track of the instances of each input or output, we can implement such a set as a counting semaphore.

But a simpler and more realistic case exists. That is the case where all the fields are constant. We might expect tuples which have a single string structure to be such a case. Consider, a program whose tuple space operations are all on a single tuple

(STOP)

no value requires storage, we only need to keep a count of the number of instances of this tuple in tuple space. Typically, such tuples are used to perform coordination between processes. Operations on such a set can be modelled by a single counting semaphore. An output increments the count, an input either decrements the count or tests for a value greater than zero.

23.5 DISTRIBUTED MEMORY IMPLEMENTATION

Clearly, the above model can be effectively implemented on a shared memory architecture machine.

In approaching the problem of implementation on distributed memory architectures, a single burning issue exists; that is, how to provide effective access to the data structures implementing each set.

On shared memory machines we can expect access time to a tuple set to be some narrowly bounded range of values, since all sets reside in a single address space and are equally accessible to all processors. The access time, however, on conventional distributed memory architectures is less predictable, and placement decisions (i.e. on which node in the network a set is placed) will have a profound effect on access performance.

23.5.1 Intel iPSC/2 implementation

An implementation of the system exists on the Intel iPSC/2 (Bjornson, 1989). In this implementation the sets are distributed among the available processors. In addition, for the large common hash table previously described, where some key always exists, tuples can be hashed to particular nodes.

Tuples are thus guaranteed to be sent to the same node. This strategy was chosen since it provided tuples with a single location. Alternatives require some form of multicasting and consistency management. In addition, such multicasting approaches lead to data duplication, and commensurate memory consumption.

In addition, some work has been done on detailed rehashing of tuple keys, which allows discernable locality to be exploited.

23.5.2 A Linda subsystem

The transputer version adopts a similar strategy to that used in the iPSC/2 implementation, except for one important distinction; tuple space is implemented as a separate subsystem.

Here we adopt a general philosophy that processors are cheap, and where possible we will use one to implement some subsystem component. Thus, provided the processor can meet a given demand, we are unconcerned by the degree of utilization such processors receive, since they serve to provide a specific system service. We do not consider the processor present on a disk, video or network controller in the calculation of the computational power of our machine. In the same way, we exclude the processors that implement the Linda subsystem from the calculations to equate the power of our machine.

This can be justified by noting that the prime cost in the Linda subsystem is in fact the memory component, and that cheap transputers (around 30 a piece in volume) can be used where the current prototype uses more expensive devices.

23.5.3 Machine architecture

The Linda subsystem is implemented as a simple ring of processors. Two additional transputers are attached to each node in the ring and act as computation nodes. It is these devices which perform the computation in a program.

The ring provides a well understood and scalable architecture up to interesting sizes. As the size of the ring escalates, short circuit nodes can be added, with minimum cost, to keep the mean distance messages travel to some constant. The prototype machine has 16 nodes in all, 10 are used as computational nodes, 5 are used as the Linda subsystem and 1 is used as a system monitor. By our calculation therefore, if we generously allow each node to be equivalent to 5 Vax MIPS, for Linda programs, the machine is capable of 50 Vax MIPS, or a peak 200 Risc MIPS, and a sustained 22.5 Mflops.

Like the iPSC/2 implementation, the sets are distributed (in our case, evenly) across the Linda subsystem.

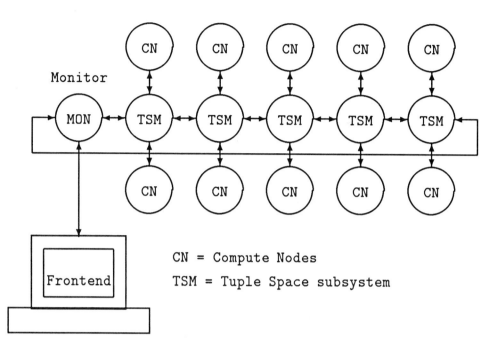

Figure 23.1 Machine architecture.

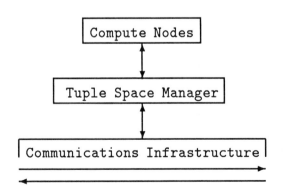

Figure 23.2 Node components.

23.6   PROCESS AND COMMUNICATION INFRASTRUCTURE

The original C-Linda system was found to be heavily dependent on underlying operating system support, principally in the form of process creation (fork), and communications infrastructure. The transputer provides simple support for process creation and point-to-point communication between neighbours.

It was therefore necessary to confront two major problems

1. provide a communications infrastructure;

2. consider the implementation of eval.

23.6.1   Routing messages

The ring is configured as two unidirectional rings, one travelling clockwise, the other anti-clockwise. The routing system is a modified version of a deadlock free ring architecture based on the published work of Bill Roscoe (1988). This provides the main communications infrastructure on the machine.

23.6.2   Transforming eval

The Linda subsystem, communications infrastructure, and compute node managers are all Occam routines. In the final analysis, a C-Linda program in this implementation, is some number of C routines connected into a harness of these Occam routines.

The process model in current Linda is ambiguously defined, and existing C-Linda implementations have simply utilized the fork primitive, provided by the Unix operating system.

The C-Linda system on transputers requires a more disciplined approach to process creation. Functions which appear in eval may not assign or input to a free variable. The value of a free variable which appears in an expression in the function is undefined. Pointers are not allowed as parameters to functions which appear as a field in an eval . Functions which calculate the value of a parameter yield that value before the eval is performed. In addition, an eval may not appear in a recursively defined function.

To implement eval the Linda program is decomposed into its component processes, that is, each function which appears in an eval is extracted so that it may later be separately compiled and included in the Occam harness.

Single, isolated evals, are simply transformed, each function present in the eval is replaced by an out. For example

> eval (P(a), Q(b))

becomes

> out (P, a)
> out (Q, b)

and a new process is constructed to perform each function. Q becomes a sequence

> in (Q, b)
> out(Q, result, Q(b))

where b is a declared local variable. One of the new processes is made responsible for constructing the final passive tuple. So that P becomes a sequence

> in ("P", a)
> r1 = P(a)
> in ("Q", "result", r2)
> out(r1, r2)

where a , r1 , and r2 are locally defined variables. The transformation is complete.

Very often evals appear in loops. In such cases it is difficult to determine at compile time the number of processes that will be generated by such a loop. Occam forbids the creation of replicated parallel processes without a constant bound.

However, a slight modification to our approach for isolated evals will solve the problem. Again, the eval is replaced by an out . However, now the eval transformation creates some number of the processes, placed in loops. So a repetition

> for (i = 0; 1 < n; i + +) {
>   eval(i, P(i));
> }

becomes

```
for (i = 0; 1 < n; i + +) {
    out (i, P, i);
}
```

and some optimal number of the following process, dependent on the number of processors available on the machine, are created. These take the form

```
int n, m;
for (;;) {
        in (n, P, m);
        out(n, P(m));
}
```

Initial implementation only allows a single function to appear in evals which are included in loops this way.

This approach to process distribution and scheduling is suited to the static nature of the transputer's process and communication model. All the processes which implement the program are known at runtime. Processes are coordinated (scheduled) via tuple space interactions; processes wait in a non-busy fashion on a channel and are scheduled by the machine when required.

All the eval transformations take place before the program is analysed by the C-Linda analyser. This enables the complete program to be analysed as one part, without modification to the existing analyser. After analysis, the program is fed to another filter which decomposes and separately compiles the programs components and ties them together with a suitable Occam harness. This Occam program can then be loaded into the network in a conventional fashion.

23.6.3 Building machines the Lego way

The unique building block approach provided by the transputer TRAM architecture, allows the flexibility to build a machine suited to a wide range of needs.

The Inmos TRAM architecture (Inmos, 1989) provides the system designer with compact boards (as small as 1.05in by 3.66in) which hold a processor and some amount of memory. Inmos make a range of these boards each with a different configuration. This enables a true Lego approach to combining some number of processors. These compact boards can be simply combined on a variety of motherboards, available for several bus architectures. Thus differing topologies are constructed as easily as a child constructs a new toy with Lego. This is a very flexible system which allows processors to be mixed and matched.

The prototype Linda system uses a total of 16 TRAMS, all T800 transputers (transputers with on board floating point unit) with 2MByte of DRAM memory and 128k of fast static RAM. In a machine specifically targeted at the Linda system, the nodes which implement the Linda subsystem do not require floating point support, and so cheap integer units can be used (T425s). In addition, the distribution of memory in the machine would be radically different and may be configured for a particular application set.

Further, since the power of the transputer is somewhat diminished in comparison to more recent developments in microprocessors, extra computational resource can be added at the compute nodes. For example, several vendors now build TRAMS which include an Intel i860, and Inmos itself has a TRAM with a combined Zoran vector processor.

Given a relevant C compiler (or compiler support for the Zoran) for these additional components, extending the scope of the Linda system to cope with a hetrogenous architecture is entirely feasible.

23.7 IMPROVING THE ARCHITECTURE

One concern in the architecture presented is the communications latency in the machine. Much of this latency is involved in routing the appropriate tuples to their particular nodes for storage.

The development, in several quarters, of communications routing devices, which allow the interconnection of any two nodes in a network, with some bounded (low) latency is anticipated. Given such communications infrastructure, the general approach presented here has added power.

Also, there may be some benefit if the three components which constitute a node in the ring shared the same address space, this too would have the effect of reducing communication latency. This is easier to do and can be achieved using existing technology.

23.8 CONCLUSION

A full and proper conclusion on the effectiveness and efficiency of the architecture detailed here cannot be made without detailed characterization of the machine's performance. These results are not available currently. Details of the performance characteristics of this machine will be presented subsequently.

REFERENCES

1. Gelernter, D. (1985) Generative communication in Linda. *ACM Trans..*

2. Carriero, Jr. N.J. (1987) *Implementation of Tuple Space Machines,* PhD Thesis.

3. Occam Inmos Ltd (1988) (S. E. Zenith and D. May), *Occam 2 Reference Manual,* Prentice Hall.

4. Gelernter, D. and Carriero, Jr. N.J. (1989) How to write Parallel programs: a guide to the perplexed , *ACM Computing Surveys.*

5. Roscoe, W. Routing messages through networks: an exercise in deadlock avoidance, in *Parallel Programming of Transputer Based Machines,* (ed T. Muntean).

6. Bjornson, R. (1989) *Experience with Linda on the iPSC/2,* Yale Research Report DCS/RR-698.

7. Inmos Ltd, (1989) *Transputer Technical Notes,* Prentice Hall.